JOURNAL FOR THE STUDY OF THE OLD TESTAMENT
SUPPLEMENT SERIES
134

JSOT Press
Sheffield

Together in the Land

A Reading of the Book of Joshua

Gordon Mitchell

Journal for the Study of the Old Testament
Supplement Series 134

Copyright © 1993 Sheffield Academic Press

Published by JSOT Press
JSOT Press is an imprint of
Sheffield Academic Press Ltd
343 Fulwood Road
Sheffield S10 3BP
England

Typeset by Sheffield Academic Press
and
Printed on acid-free paper in Great Britain
by Biddles Ltd
Guildford

British Library Cataloguing in Publication Data

Mitchell, Gordon
    Together in the Land: A Reading of the
    Book of Joshua. - (JSOT Supplement Series,
    ISSN 0309-0787; No. 134)
    I. Title II. Series

ISBN 1-85075-409-8

CONTENTS

PREFACE

The present work had its origins in a doctoral thesis completed in 1990 under the supervision of Professor Rolf Rendtorff and submitted at the Ruprecht-Karls-Universität in Heidelberg. A number of people have played a part in its production. To begin with, for the choice of the topic, thanks are due to the Chaplain's Services of the South African Defence Force, whose appeal during the seventies and eighties to the concept of holy war was disgusting enough to overcome my lethargy. For advice and encouragement my gratitude to the following persons should be recorded: Professors Jasper Burden, Norman Gottwald, Magnus Ottosson, Manfred Weippert, and of course Rolf Rendtorff for his most perceptive guidance. Dr Christa Schäfer-Lichtenberger has been a fine critic and adviser. Tribute must also be paid to Frank England for his editorial work in making the text read more fluently, and to Jill Martin for her painstaking work in correcting the manuscript. And finally, *omistettu vaimolleni Tiinalle.*

Gordon Mitchell
Department of Religious Studies
University of Cape Town

ABBREVIATIONS

AGSU	Arbeiten zur Geschichte des Spätjudentums und Urchristentums
ANET	J.B. Pritchard (ed.), *Ancient Near Easter Texts Relating to the Old Testament* (Princeton: Princeton University Press, 3rd edn, 1969)
ATANT	Abhandlungen zur Theologie des Alten und Neuen Testaments
AzTh	Arbeiten zur Theologie
BASOR	*Bulletin of the American Schools of Oriental Research*
BBB	Bonner biblische Beiträge
BDB	Brown–Driver–Briggs, *A Hebrew and English Lexicon of the Old Testament*
BETL	Bibliotheca ephemeridum theologicarum lovaniensium
Bib	*Biblica*
BibOr	Biblica et Orientalia
BJRL	*Bulletin of the John Rylands Library*
BN	*Biblische Notizen: Beiträge zur exegetischen Diskussion*
BWANT	Beiträge zue Wissenschaft vom Alten und Neuen Testament
BZ NF	*Biblische Zeitschrift, Neue Folge*
BZAW	Beihefte zur ZAW
CBQ	*Catholic Biblical Quarterly*
CRB	Cahiers de la Revue Biblique
DBAT	*Dielheimer Blätter zum Alten Testament*
EHS.T	Europäische Hochschulschriften. Reihe 23: Theologie
EncJud	*Encyclopaedia Judaica*
ErIs	*Eretz-Israel*
EvT	*Evangelische Theologie*
FRLANT	Forschungen zur Religion und Literatur des Alten und Neuen Testaments
HAT	Handbuch zum Alten Testament
HO	Handbuch der Orientalistik
HUCA	*Hebrew Union College Annual*
IB	*The Interpreter's Bible*
IDB	*Interpreter's Dictionary of the Bible*
IEJ	*Israel Exploration Journal*
IOSOT	International Organization for the Study of the Old Testament
JBL	*Journal of Biblical Literature*
JSOT	*Journal for the Study of the Old Testament*

JSOTSup	*JSOT* Supplement Series
JSS	*Journal of Semitic Studies*
Or	*Orientalia*
OTL	Old Testament Library
OTS	*Oudtestamentische Studien*
PJ	*Palästinajahrbuch des deutschen evangelischen Instituts*
RB	*Revue biblique*
SBS	Stuttgarter Bibelstudien
Schol	*Scholastik*
SEÅ	*Svensk exegitsk årsbok*
SJOT	*Scandinavian Journal of the Old Testament*
ST	*Studia Theologica cura ordinum theologorum Scandinavicorum edita*
StAns	Studia Anselmiana
StANT	Studien zum Alten und Neuen Testament
StC	Studia Catholica
StudOr	Studia Orientalia
TBü	Theologische Bücherei
THAT	*Theologisches Handwörterbuch zum Alten Testament*
ThLZ	*Theologische Literaturzeitung*
ThR	*Theologische Rundschau*
ThWAT	*Theologisches Wörterbuch zum Alten Testament*
TynBul	*Tyndale Bulletin*
UF	*Ugarit-Forschungen*
VT	*Vetus Testamentum*
VTSup	*VT* Supplement Series
WBTh	Wiener Beiträge zur Theologie
WMANT	Wissenschaftliche Monographien zum Alten und Neuen Testament
ZAW	*Zeitschrift für die Alttestamentliche Wissenschaft*
ZDPV	*Zeitschrift des deutschen Palästina-Vereins*
ZZ	*Die Zeichen der Zeit*

INTRODUCTION

1. *The Problem*

The text of Joshua presents the reader with a puzzling contradiction. One the one hand, there are commands to slaughter all of the enemy, descriptions of complete destruction and statements recording the success of the conquest, and on the other hand, Rahab's family, the Gibeonites and others continue to live in the land. To this puzzling contradiction, several explanations have been offered.

2. *A History of Research*

Martin Noth
According to Noth,[1] the stories in chs. 2–11 are originally regional narratives, most of them having been developed as aetiological explanation, and later gathered at the Benjaminite tribal sanctuary of Gilgal. During the period of the monarchy, the stories are presented as the history of all the tribes by 'der Sammler'. During the exile, 'the Deuteronomists' insert the lists of tribal boundaries and localities (in chs. 13–21), and add chs. 1, 12 and 23. At the 'deuteronomistic' stage the idea of חרם and the complete destruction of the original population are introduced into the narrative.

This theory offers a way of explaining the puzzling contradiction in the text. For Noth, the Rahab and Gibeonite stories are developed as a means of explaining the presence of foreign enclaves in Israel's midst.

However, Noth has difficulty in explaining the format of the notes about the unconquered nations in 13.13; 15.63; 16.10; 17.12-13. His solution is to assign these accounts to a post-deuteronomistic stage. A further difficulty remains: 23.1-16 refers to an incomplete conquest and the presence of foreigners in the land. Noth regards this as

1. M. Noth, *Josua* (HAT, 7; Tübingen: Mohr, 2nd edn, 1953).

deuteronomistic, which seems to contradict the deuteronomistic view
of complete destruction.

Rudolf Smend

Smend also realizes that the ideas of the annihilation of the nations and
their continued existence in the land are incompatible, and therefore
belong to different redactional strata.[1] He designates 13.1b-6 and
23.1b-16, together with 1.7-9, as part of a later deuteronomistic
redaction which he calls DtrN. Both 13.1b-6, which refers to the
'remnant of the land', and 23.1-16, which refers to the 'remnant of
the nations', contradict the dominant emphasis on complete conquest.
The call for further conquest and the call for absolute obedience are
linked to the call to obedience in 1.7-9.

The work of this 'nomistic' successor to the Deuteronomistic
Historian dates from the period of the end of the exile, and thus the
DtrH is reworked so as to emphasize Torah, the presence of
foreigners and the danger of syncretism.

There are, however, other references to foreigners in Joshua which
are not discussed by Smend. Graeme Auld attempts to extend Smend's
hypothesis.

Graeme Auld

Auld points out that 13.13, 15.63, 16.10, 17.11-13 and 19.47 LXX
show that a particular group of foreigners remained in the land. This,
he states, reveals a 'harmony in spirit, method and language' with the
other DtrN passages in Joshua.[2]

Unfortunately, neither Smend nor Auld explains the prominence
given to Rahab and the Gibeonites in the Joshua narrative. It is these

1. R. Smend, 'Das Gesetz und die Völker. Ein Beitrag zur Deuteronomistischen
Redaktionsgeschte', in H.W. Wolff (ed.), *Probleme biblischer Theologie. G. von
Rad zum. 70. Geburtstag* (Munich: Kaiser, 1971), pp. 494-509; and R. Smend,
'Das uneroberte Land', in G. Strecker (ed.), *Das Land Israel in biblischer Zeit*
(Göttinger Theologische Arbeiten, 25; Göttingen: Vandenhoeck & Ruprecht, 1983),
pp. 91-102.

2. A.G. Auld, *Joshua, Moses and the Land: Tetrateuch–Pentateuch–Hexateuch
in a Generation since 1938* (Edinburgh: T. & T. Clark, 1980), pp. 64-65, 67. His
linguistic argument is that these statements all begin with reference to חיה, a word
also found in 13.6 and 23.5, 9, 13 and the first three include חיה which is also found
in 23.8, 9. Unfortunately for his argument, these phrases also appear outside the
'nomistic' passages, as will be shown in subsequent chapters.

stories that constitute one of the major contradictions to the idea of the complete destruction of the occupants of the land.

Adam Welch

The lacuna in the above explanations is the thorough research that has been done on the concept of חרם. Christianus Brekelmans,[1] A. Dekkers[2] and Götz Schmitt[3] come to the conclusion that the concepts of complete destruction and the continued presence of foreigners in Israel's midst are not necessarily incompatible. This is because חרם is not meant to be taken literally, but is to be understood in a dramatic way. It tells the Israelites not to have anything to do with foreigners, particularly with regard to their religion.[4] These scholars refer with approval to Adam Welch's interpretation of Deut. 7.1-5, in which a command to destroy the occupants of the land is immediately followed by a command not to make covenants with them or to intermarry. The first command concerns religious theory, the second religious practice.[5] In other words, the reports of foreigners are a technical necessity in order to make clear the meaning of חרם. Thus, Schmitt is of the opinion that ch. 23, which presents Israel living together with the remnant of the nations, a situation which constitutes a religious threat, is in fact the *Sitz im Leben* of Joshua as a whole.[6]

1.   C.H.W. Brekelmans, *De Herem in het Oude Testament* (Nijmegen: Centrale Drukkerij N.V., 1959).

2.   A. Dekkers, 'Der Kriegsherem und das Naturrecht mit einem Religionswissenschaftlichen Vergleich' (unpublished dissertation; Vienna, 1964).

3.   G. Schmitt, *Du sollst keinen Frieden schliessen mit den Bewohnern des Landes: Die Weisungen gegen die Kanaanäer in Israels Geschichte und Geschichtsschreibung* (BWANT, 91; Stuttgart: Kohlhammer, 1970).

4.   On the issue of the rejection of a foreign cult in the DtrH, cf. M. Rose, *Der Ausschliesslichkeitsanspruch Jahwes* (BWANT, 106; Stuttgart: Kohlhammer, 1975), who discovers a variety of expressions at several redactional levels.

5.   A.C. Welch, *The Code of Deuteronomy: A New Theory of its Origin* (London: James Clark, 1924), pp. 189-206; *Deuteronomy: The Framework of the Code* (London: James Clark, 1932), pp. 69-80. These classic works are cited by Brekelmans, *De Herem*, pp. 83-84; Dekkers, 'Der Kriegsherem', pp. 64-66; Schmitt, *Du sollst keinen Frieden schliessen*, p. 9.

6.   Schmitt, *Du sollst keinen Frieden schliessen*, p. 148. At this stage, Schmitt is only considering the final stages in the development of the text, and recognizes that חרם has had other functions at an earlier stage.

While this explanation does have plausibility, a more thorough examination of the text is required in order to substantiate it. The fact is that foreigners play a far more important role in the narrative than merely that of a device to give the notion of חרם logical consistency. The Rahab and Gibeonite stories, along with the references to nations who remained in the land (13.13; 15.63; 16.10),[1] are united by their common conclusion which utilizes the formula, 'and they dwelt in the midst of Israel unto this day'. A more adequate explanation needs to be sought.

Robert Polzin

A novel attempt to explain contradictions of this kind is contained in the work of Robert Polzin.[2] He perceives a dialogue running through the DtrH, and suggests that there is a 'voice' of Authoritarian Dogmatism continually being undermined by the 'voice' of Critical Traditionalism. Thus, amongst other things, the continued presence of foreigners in Joshua is understood as a way of undermining חרם which is identified with Authoritarian Dogmatism.

It is interesting to note that Robert Gordis anticipated Polzin's approach.[3] He has proposed that a fundamental key to understanding the problems in Ecclesiastes and Job lies in the recognition that a message could be communicated by initially quoting a position that is an extreme, and subsequently expressing a contradictory point of view that is closer to the truth.

It is possible to overextend this method by understanding every contradiction as a message about the undermining of authority. More rigorous protocols seem to be required. Again, it needs to be asked whether 'undermining' is the most accurate way of describing the relationship between opposing points of view, or whether it is more

1. To this list may be added 17.11-13. While not utilizing the formula 'and they dwelt in the midst of Israel unto this day', it is linked to 13.13; 15.63; 16.10 by a formula noting Israel's failure to conquer.

2. R. Polzin, *Moses and the Deuteronomist: A Literary Study of the Deuteronomic History* (New York: Seabury, 1980). His work is supplemented by R.D. Nelson, 'The Anatomy of the Book of Kings', *JSOT* 40 (1988), pp. 39-48.

3. Cf. particularly, R. Gordis, 'Quotations as a Literary Usage in Biblical, Rabbinic and Oriental Literature', *HUCA* 22 (1949), pp. 157-219. There is a similarity of technical language: he speaks of the development of 'dialogue' (p. 173) and the 'undermining' (p. 205) of an earlier proposition.

appropriate to speak of 'unresolved tension'.[1] An answer to these questions will only be possible after a thorough study of the narrative techniques in Joshua, which, in turn, raises the question of an appropriate method to be used in approaching the text.

3. *Method*

The brief survey of research demonstrates that the methodology must be able to relate the mutually contradictory texts concerning foreigners to each other in the context of the whole book, while, at the same time, accounting for the history behind the text. An approach that meets these requirements is evident in the more recent work of Rolf Rendtorff.[2] He demonstrates that the synchronic and diachronic are not mutually exclusive, and that it is really a matter of where the emphasis is placed. He concentrates his attention on a synchronic analysis of the compositional structures of a literary work.[3]

Two recent studies view the narrative of Joshua as an essential unity, although they employ different approaches. M. Ottosson concentrates his attention on the unifying themes of the work and applies the term 'holistic approach',[4] and J. van Seters maintains that the bulk of Joshua 1–12 is the work of a post-exilic *author* who makes use of the scribal convention found in the campaign reports of the Assyrian annals.[5]

Nevertheless, account must be taken of the diachronic dimension of the text. There can be little doubt that the book of Joshua is made up

1. Cf. M. Sternberg, *The Poetics of Biblical Narrative: Ideological Literature and the Drama of Reading* (Indiana Literary Biblical Series; Bloomington: Indiana University Press, 1985), who points out the important role of 'ambiguity' in biblical narrative, a feature which can be developed by juxtaposing opposing points of view.

2. Cf. R. Rendtorff, *Das überlieferungsgeschichtliche Problem des Pentateuchs* (BZAW, 147; Berlin: de Gruyter, 1977) and *Das Alte Testament: Eine Einführung* (Neukirchen–Vluyn: Neukirchener, 1983).

3. On the spectrum of methods, his approach called 'Kompositionsgeschichte' lies somewhere between Redaction Criticism and Structural Analysis, or, more precisely, it is Redaction Criticism that has incorporated the advances in the field of Structural Analysis.

4. M. Ottosson, *Erövring och fördelning av Land: Studier i Josuaboken* (to be published).

5. J. van Seters, 'Joshua's Campaign of Canaan and Near Eastern Historiography', *SJOT* 4 (1990), pp. 1-12.

of a variety of material. While this provides for a diversity of approaches, the study undertaken here focuses on the manner in which the narrative is developed within the compositional framework. Each story will be interpreted within its own perimeters, and only subsequently related to the overall narrative in Joshua. I will be sensitive to the differences which emerge within the narrative, and to the differences which are explained as being due to the variety of source material.

The same caution needs to be observed when relating Joshua to the DtrH as a whole. This point is well illustrated by the two directions in which studies have proceeded since the publication of Martin Noth's *Überlieferungsgeschichtliche Studien* in 1943.[1] On the one hand, there have been theologies that have concentrated on unifying theological themes,[2] while, on the other hand, there have been a number of studies of individual sections that reach the conclusion that there are important differences in the manner in which each book, and even individual sections, are redacted by the 'Deuteronomistic Historians'.[3] The caveat must be heeded: there is continuity as well as discontinuity.

Continuity and discontinuity are also evident in studies on the role of foreigners in the Hebrew Bible. In his classic work, *Die Stellung der Israeliten und der Juden zu den Fremden*, Alfred Bertholet illustrates that there is a great deal of variety in the understanding of foreigners in the various books of the Hebrew Bible, and in the different periods of Israel's history.[4] The exilic and post-exilic periods, the most likely time of the formation of Joshua, reveal equivocal attitudes amongst the Israelites towards foreigners.

1. M. Noth, *Überlieferungsgeschichtliche Studien* (Tübingen: Max Niemeyer Verlag, 2nd edn, 1957).

2. Notably, H.W. Wolff, 'Das Kerygma des Deuteronomistichen Geschichtswerks', *ZAW* 73 (1961), pp. 171-86; N. Lohfink, 'Bilanz nach der Katastrophe. Das deuteronomistische Geschichtswerk', in J. Schreiner (ed.), *Wort und Botschaft: Eine theologische und kritische Einführung in die Probleme des Alten Testaments* (Würzburg: Echter, 1967), pp. 196-208.

3. For discussion and bibliography, cf. A.N. Radjawane, 'Das deuteronomistische Geschichtswerk', *ThR* 38 (1974), pp. 177-216; and, more recently, H. Weippert, 'Das deuteronomistische Geschichtswerk. Sein Ziel und Ende in der neueren Forschung', *ThR* 50 (1985), pp. 213-49 (224-35).

4. A. Bertholet, *Die Stellung der Israeliten und der Juden zu den Fremden* (Freiburg: Mohr, 1896).

In the book of Joshua, two statements are made concerning foreigners:

1. They occupy the land and all of them are to be killed.
2. Some survive.

The first statement will be discussed in Part I and the second statement in Part II. The latter section will also include a discussion about the formulae that have been employed in recording the presence of the nations. When the same story is discussed for a second time it will be subjected to a different set of questions. The Conclusion will deal with the important fact that a single story may say something about the complete destruction of the nations, and the survival of some of the people.

PART I
THE NARRATIVE OF CONQUEST

Chapter 1

'TAKE POSSESSION OF THE LAND WHICH THE LORD GIVES YOU TO POSSESS' (1.1–5.15)

In the opening chapters of Joshua, little attention is focused on the theme of the nations, apart from the occasional reference to them as occupying the land which Israel is to possess. However, there is the gradual introduction of warlike themes into the narrative. These themes attract this author's attention because they express Israel's attitude to the foreign enclaves in their midst: the nations are to be engaged in battle and removed from the land. The evaluation of these warfare texts is the subject of considerable methodological dispute: the texts are themselves a battleground.

1. *Method in Studying Warfare Texts*

The book of Joshua contains other equally prominent themes. This allows J. Wijngaards to argue that there are two traditions relating to the gift of land in the book of Joshua:[1]

1. a Schechemite tradition in which the gift of land is a juridical act, similar to the ancient Near Eastern royal land grants; and
2. a Gilgalite tradition of the gift of land by military conquest.

While aspects of this hypothesis are difficult to verify, it is undoubtedly true that there is variety within the text. Evidence suggests, however, that it is more accurate to speak of the gradual introduction of a military mood into the narrative.[2] Before turning to

---

1. J.N.M. Wijngaards, *The Dramatization of Salvific History in the Deuteronomic Schools* (OTS, 16; Leiden: Brill, 1969).
2. Cf. G.W. Coats, 'An Exposition for the Conquest Theme', *CBQ* 47 (1985), pp. 47-54. He views chs. 1–5 as a transition from wilderness to conquest, and a military mood is introduced gradually into the text. This is achieved by the references

the central argument of this chapter, it is necessary to set up some conceptual beacons to guide us on our path.

Excursus on the 'Battle Report' [1]
The starting point of any discussion of warfare in ancient Israel is always Gerhard von Rad's *Der Heilige Krieg im alten Israel* (1951).[2] Focusing on the manner in which the accounts of warfare are presented as theological statements, von Rad argues that the ideology of 'holy war' originates in the Israelite cult. He proposes that these accounts are ideological, and ultimately literary, constructions and should not be understood literally.

This thesis has been contested by M. Weippert who demonstrates that all the elements of Israelite cultic practice and divine intervention are to be found in the ideologies and practices of other ancient Near Eastern peoples.[3] While this observation is undoubtedly true, the precise nature of the similarities and differences of the Hebrew Bible narrative to other bodies of literature requires further analysis.

Whereas von Rad has emphasized the religious character of the Hebrew Bible battle reports, several other scholars have isolated some of the more purely military aspects, and discovered a pattern. W. Richter outlines the main elements as follows:[4]

a. Verbs of movement (בוא, הלך, יצא).
b. Verbs of military activity (נלחם, חנה, אסף).
c. Verbs indicating the outcome of the battle depending on the object (city: לכד, לקח; persons: נגף, נכה; often extended to include flight: רדף, נוס).

---

to 'fear' in 2.24 and 5.1 and, more particularly, by the introduction of the 'Divine Warrior' in 5.13-15.

1. In German scholarship, the 'battle report' is known as a 'Schlachtbericht' (Richter), or a 'Kampfbericht' (Plöger).

2. G. von Rad, *Der Heilige Krieg im alten Israel* (Göttingen: Vandenhoeck & Ruprecht, 5th edn, 1969).

3. M. Weippert, '"Heiliger Krieg" in Israel und Assyrien. Kritische Anmerkungen zu Gerhard von Rads Konzept des "Heiligen Krieges im alten Israel" ', *ZAW* 84 (1972), pp. 460-93.

4. W. Richter, *Traditionsgeschichtliche Untersuchungen zum Richterbuch* (BBB, 18; Bonn: Peter Hanstein, 1963), pp. 262-66. The translation is from J. van Seters, 'The Conquest of Sihon's Kingdom: A Literary Examination', *JBL* 91 (1992), pp. 182-97 (187).

d. A concluding element indicating the extent of the war (מן +
place name, עד + place name) and the description of the
defeat (מכה גדולה, מגפה גדולה).

This schema can sometimes be introduced by the formula 'I have
given them into your hand', thus incorporating it into the category of
holy war. Similarly, the instances of ישב, לקח, ירש particularly appear
in relation to the conquest of the land. Richter points out that the
schema is not rigid and that it is shaped by each unique context. He
adds that the brevity of the battle report is usually due to its
subordinate role in the literary context.

J.G. Plöger's analysis of the battle reports in Deuteronomy and
Joshua produces a schema not unlike Richter's:[1]

a. A situation report detailing the name of the enemy and the
place of battle.
b. A statement that victory is assured as YHWH has 'given the
enemy into your hand'.
c. A victory report, the destruction of the enemy and the
capture of booty.

The patterns outlined by Richter and Plöger bear a strong
resemblance to those found in the Assyrian annals. In the analysis of
the campaign report of the period 934–722 BCE, W. Schramm lists the
features that recur.[2] In general, these are:

a. A statement that the operation takes place at the command of
Assur, who is directly involved and thus guarantees victory.
b. An account of how cities rebel, which usually includes a
refusal to pay tribute and the formation of enemy coalitions
to do battle against the Assyrians.
c. A description of the journey, often beginning with the
crossing of the Euphrates.
d. An account of the fear inspired by the glory of Assur and the
Emperor.

---

1. J.G. Plöger, *Literarkritische, formgeschichtliche und stilkritische
Untersuchungen zum Deuteronomium* (BBB, 26; Bonn: Peter Hanstein, 1967),
pp. 16-17.
2. W. Schramm, *Einleitung in die Assyrischen Königsinschriften II (934–722
V. Chr.)* (HO, 1; Leiden: Brill, 1973).

e.   An account of how cities are spared when they bring the tribute. The tribute is then listed in detail and at length.

f.   An account of an easy but devastating victory: the enemy is slaughtered (sometimes including the women and children), particular attention being given to the fate of the rebel king and his family; the cities are razed to the ground, thereby being reduced to a pile of rubble (variations can include an account of a terrified remnant fleeing the scene of the battle, or of captives who are not slaughtered but enslaved or deported).[1]

g.   A detailed list of the booty taken.

h.   An account of the booty and captured gods being offered to Assur.

i.   A statement that the whole land belongs to the victor who installs his representative governor and sets the amount of the annual tribute.

Reflecting on these similarities, J. van Seters concludes that many of the battle accounts in the Hebrew Bible employ Assyrian scribal conventions when recording military campaigns.[2] He points out that, wherever the Assyrians are conquerors, they display their royal inscriptions, a practice which would have had a cultural impact upon Israel. However, the nature and significance of these similarities require closer examination.

D.M. Gunn contests van Seters' argument and claims that van Seters' approach overlooks the unique literary presentation of individual passages.[3] Gunn's argument is upheld if one compares the battle reports in Joshua to those in Deuteronomy 1–3 and Judges, in

1.   A defeat is never mentioned but is either ignored, described as a great victory, or conflated with another account of victory; cf. A.K. Grayson, 'Assyria and Babylonia', *Or* 49 (1980), pp. 140-94 (171).

2.   Van Seters, 'Sihon's Kingdom', pp. 182-97; 'Oral Patterns or Literary Conventions in Biblical Narrative?', *Semeia* 5 (1976), pp. 139-54. Cf. also M.C. Astour, 'Political and Cosmic Symbolism in Genesis 14 and in its Babylonian Sources', in A. Altmann (ed.) *Biblical Motifs: Origins and Tranformations* (Cambridge, MA: Harvard University Press, 1966), pp. 65-112.

3.   D.M. Gunn, 'The "Battle Report": Oral or Scribal Convention?', *JBL* 93 (1974), pp. 513-18; 'Narrative Patterns and Oral Tradition in Judges and Samuel', *VT* 24 (1974), pp. 286-317; 'On Oral Tradition: A Response to John van Seters', *Semeia* 5 (1976), pp. 155-63

which the basic account is utilized in a unique way in each context.[1] It seems reasonable to conclude that the comparisons with the campaign reports of the annals can often serve a valuable heuristic function, but that the narrative of Joshua has a dynamic of its own and offers a unique literary presentation.

Returning to the question of whether the idea of 'holy war' is unique to Israel, several difficulties have emerged with regard to von Rad's use of the term. The major problem is that, in arriving at the concept, material from a variety of literary contexts has been gathered and insufficient account has been taken of differing literary presentations of the concept. As has been noted, many of the features of the holy war form are to be found in the literature of Israel's neighbours, and the thesis of an Israelite cultic origin for the concept is difficult to sustain. Nevertheless, in spite of these modifications to the theory of the uniqueness of the notion of holy war in Israel, it is still possible to use the term as a working concept when speaking of Israel's wars, particularly in the conquest of the land. For convenience, the cluster of theological ideas surrounding the conquest are designated 'holy war',[2] and this complex of ideas is in the foreground of the early chapters of Joshua, while the concept of warfare itself remains in the background.

2. *The Development of the Theme of Warfare in the Narrative of Joshua 1–5*

a. *An Introduction (1.1-18)*
Chapter 1 is generally regarded as part of the redactional framework of the book of Joshua because it introduces the major themes in the text.[3] This makes it all the more striking that the central theme—the complete destruction of the enemy in chs. 6–12—should be mentioned only indirectly. Instead, the opening chapters are dominated by other interests.

---

1. In the case of Deut. 1–3, W.A. Sumner, 'Israel's Encounters with Edom, Moab, Ammon, Sihon, and Og According to the Deuteronomist', *VT* 18 (1968) pp. 215-28 (215-16).

2. Cf. particularly, W.L. Moran, 'The End of the Unholy War and the Anti-Exodus', *Bib* 44 (1963), pp. 333-42.

3. Cf. for example, J.A. Soggin, *Joshua* (OTL; London: SCM Press, 1972), pp. 25-34.

i. *The gift of land.* The major theme in ch. 1 concerns the land which the Lord is giving to the people of Israel.[1] It is part of a theological framework in which YHWH, land and people are interrelated. Here נתן is in all eight instances related to ארץ.[2] In 1.1-11, ארץ is the land Cisjordan on the other side of the Jordan, whereas in 1.12-18 it is used of Transjordan.[3] Another difference is that when נתן is used of Cisjordan, YHWH is the subject; and when it is used of Transjordan,[4] Moses is the subject. This difference arises because Transjordan has already been conquered under Moses, and נתן is then used in the sense of 'apportion'. Consistent with the above is the appearance of Joshua as the subject of the verb in the land allocation account of chs. 13–21.[5]

When YHWH is the subject, נתן functions as part of a confession. It is noteworthy that all references to the Lord's gift of land occur in speeches and not in battle reports (2.9, 14, 24; 5.6; 8.1; 9.24; 18.3; 22.4; 23.13, 15, 16; 24.13).[6] These passages have nothing to say about the enemy. The exception is 8.1 which uses ארץ in the sense of territory surrounding a particular city.

Thus the gift of land has a confessional character and does not appear in battle reports. From 6.2 onward, the expression נתן ביד occurs more frequently as part of the battle reports.[7] Invariably, the name of the city, the king, or the people, is mentioned. Chapter 1,

---

1. On the central role of the idea of land in Israel's faith, cf. particularly G. von Rad, 'Verheissenes Land und Jahwehs Land im Hexateuch', *ZDPV* 66 (1943), pp. 191-204 (= *Gesammelte Studien zum Alten Testament I* [TBü, 8; Munich: Kaiser, 1958], pp. 87-100); H. Wildberger, 'Israel und sein Land', *EvT* 16 (1956), pp. 404-22; R. Rendtorff, 'Das Land Israel im Wandel der Alttestamentlichen Geschichte', in W.P. Eckert and N.P. Levinson (eds.), *Jüdisches Volk—gelobtes Land: Die biblische Landverheisung als Problem des jüdischen Selbstverständnisses und die christlichen Theologie* (Munich: Kaiser, 1970), pp. 153-68; W. Brueggemann, *The Land: Place as Gift, Promise, and Challenge in Biblical Faith* (Philadelphia: Fortress Press, 1977).

2. In 1.3, נתן is used with מקום; however מקום is here parallel to ארץ in 1.2.

3. The exception to this neat division is 1.15a which refers to the Lord's gift of Cisjordan.

4. 1.14 and 1.15. Manuscripts of LXX do not have Moses as the subject in 1.14 and the MT reading is probably an attempt to harmonize it with the next verse.

5. The transition begins in 11.23; then, in 19.49, the people of Israel give Joshua an inheritance.

6. Plöger has noticed the same pattern in Deuteronomy, cf. *Untersuchungen*, pp. 21-22.

7. 6.2, 16; 7.7; 8.1, 7, 18; 10.8, 19, 30, 32; 11.8; 21.44; 24.8, 11.

with its juridical concept of the gift of land, is in a world far from the
ugliness of war, even though the logical consequence of its themes is
conquest. The closest one gets to an idea that the land is occupied by
others is in the territorial description which is merely geographical.

ii. *Territorial description.* An interesting feature of the territorial
descriptions of the 'land' in Joshua is that all have as their main
interest the listing of the nations who have been destroyed, or who
still need to be destroyed (9.1; 11.17; 12.7; 13.5). The exception is
1.4. It could be argued that the parallel description in 1.3, 'every
place that the sole of your foot will tread upon', suggests military and
political domination of an enemy people.[1] However, this meaning is
unlikely here because the same phrase is used later of Caleb in an
obviously juridical sense (Josh. 14.9; cf. Deut. 1.36). It is also
significant that verbs suggesting movement appear in contexts dealing
with the transfer of land ownership, such as עבר, עלה, בוא את.[2] This is
why in Deut. 2.5 Moses is at pains to point out that, even though the
Israelites are passing through the land of Esau, they will not receive
any of its land: 'not so much as for the sole of the foot to tread on'.

It can be concluded that, unlike territorial descriptions found later
in the narrative, the primary concern of ch. 1 is that the land is a
divine gift, and this establishes Israel's right to it. The unmilitaristic
character of the chapter is also noticeable in the way the notion of
'rest' is employed.

iii. *A place of rest.* The notion of YHWH giving the land as a place of
rest emphasizes the quality of life associated with ארץ.[3] Life in the
land is the opposite to life in the wilderness.[4] In 1.13 YHWH gives a

---

1.   Cf. particularly 1 Kgs 5.3-5, where 'the Lord put them (the enemy round
about) under the soles of his feet' is parallel to 'the Lord has given me rest'. Both
serve to mark an epoch change from war to peace; the epoch of temple construction.

2.   Cf. Plöger, *Untersuchungen*, p. 84.

3.   Cf. G. von Rad, 'Es ist noch eine Ruhe vorhanden dem Volke Gottes. Eine
biblische Begriffsuntersuchung', *ZZ* 11 (1933), pp. 104-11 (= *Gesammelte Studien
zum Alten Testament I* [TBü, 8; Munich: Kaiser, 1958], pp. 101-108); and, more
recently, G. Braulik, 'Zur deuteronomistichen Konzeption von Freiheit und
Frieden', in J.A. Emerton (ed.), *Congress Volume Salamanca 1983* (VTS, 36;
Leiden: Brill, 1985), pp. 28-39, and p. 30 n. 5 for further bibliographical
information.

4.   In a series of highly innovative studies, W. Brueggemann draws attention to

place of rest to the Transjordan tribes in Transjordania, and in 1.15 YHWH promises to do the same for the remaining tribes. While land can be given by Moses, only YHWH gives rest.[1] Of the remaining instances of נוח, most are in the mundane sense of 'deposit'.[2] Chapter 22.4 is part of a speech to the Transjordanian tribes and is very similar to 1.15, while the remaining two, 21.44 and 23.1, speak of very concrete rest from real enemies surrounding them.[3]

Undeniably, there is also an element of warfare in the understanding of rest. While this is suggested by the men of valour who would pass over armed for war in 1.14, ch. 1 is still some distance from the enemy and the clamour of battle.

iv. *Courage and the Torah*. The repeated exhortations to be courageous (1.6, 7, 9, 18) are made to fit into the overall structure of command and obedience by 1.7:

> Only be strong and very courageous, being careful to do according to all the law which Moses my servant commanded you; turn not from it to the right hand or to the left, that you may have good success wherever you go.

The double imperative, introduced by רק and strengthened by מאד, makes it the strongest statement in the chapter. The emphasis on Torah is continued in the next verse. In contrast, all the other exhortations to be courageous in Joshua (8.1; 10.8, 25; 11.6) are in the context of warfare.[4] This has occasioned the view that the references to Torah in ch. 1 are a later insertion into the text, introducing an element of conditionality and providing an explanation

---

a contrast between, on the one hand, the chaos of exile associated with 'wilderness'; and, on the other hand, the ordered life in the land understood as 'rest'; cf. W. Brueggemann, 'Kingship and Chaos (A Study in Tenth Century Theology)', *CBQ* 33 (1971), pp. 317-32; 'Weariness, Exile and Chaos', *CBQ* 34 (1972), pp. 19-38.

1. In 1.13-15 and 22.4 Moses gives land, but on both occasions it is only the Lord who gives rest.

2. 3.13; 4.3, 8; 6.23. The last, which describes depositing Rahab outside the camp, could have ideological significance.

3. Braulik, 'Freiheit und Frieden', pp. 36-39.

4. On the 'fear not' formula as a feature of holy war terminology, cf. von Rad, *Der Heilige Krieg im alten Israel*, pp. 9-10.

for the exile.[1] However, from several points of view, the reference to
Torah makes better sense if viewed as an integral part of its context.

Firstly, a great deal of scholarship has been devoted to a study of
the 'installation' genre in the chapter.[2] This genre consists of:

   a.   encouragement
   b.   description
   c.   promise of assistance

It has been argued that the ideological background to this chapter is
the transmission of the royal office from one king to another. It is a
thesis difficult both to prove or to disprove.

Nevertheless, for our purposes, it is important to note the role of
divine law in the 'description of task'.[3] It is also indisputable that an
important theme of the chapter is the succession from Moses to
Joshua.[4] Furthermore, the 'fear not' formula is not necessarily connected to warfare.[5] Therefore, on form critical grounds, the argument
is unconvincing that the emphasis on Torah in Josh. 1.7 is a later
insertion.

Secondly, it has been convincingly demonstrated that there is an
integral connection between the themes of law and land in Hebrew
literature,[6] a relationship which is particularly noticeable in Josh.
23.15-16. Therefore, in a chapter that gives so much attention to the

---

1.   Cf. particularly Smend, 'Das Gesetz und die Völker', pp. 494-509. He
views it as the work of DtrN.

2.   Cf. N. Lohfink, 'Die deuteronomistischen Darstellung des Übergangs der
Führung Israels von Moses auf Josue', *Schol* 37 (1962), pp. 32-44; J.R. Porter,
'The Succession of Joshua', in J.I Durham and J.R. Porter (eds.), *Proclamation and
Presence: Old Testament Essays in Honour of Gwynne Henton Davies* (London:
SCM Press, 1970), pp. 102-32; R.D. Nelson, 'Josiah in the Book of Joshua', *JBL*
100 (1981), pp. 531-40; but cf. D. McCarthy, 'An Installation Genre?', *JBL* 90
(1971), pp. 31-41.

3.   Cf. for example, 1 Kgs 2.1 ff.; 1 Chron. 22 & 28.

4.   Joshua's installation by Moses in Deut. 31.7 ff., and by YHWH in Deut.
31.23 ff., are in the same genre. In both texts a warning about keeping the law and
directions for reading it, are found immediately after the appointment.

5.   Cf. P.-E. Dion, 'The "Fear Not" Formula and Holy War', *CBQ* 32 (1970),
pp. 565-70.

6.   For thorough studies of the relationship in Deuteronomy, cf. P. Diepold,
Israel's Land (BWANT, 95; Stuttgart: Kohlhammer, 1972), pp. 90-96; Plöger,
Untersuchungen, pp. 91-100. For a more general study, cf. Brueggemann, *The
Land*, pp. 59-67.

question of land, one would expect an emphasis on law as well. Indeed, the chapter is structured around the issue of obedience!

a. YHWH speaks to Joshua (1.2-9; cf. 1.13).
b. Joshua speaks to the leaders (1.11).
c. Joshua speaks to the Transjordanian tribes (1.13-15).
d. The people respond with a pledge of obedience(1.16-18).

Thus it can be concluded that the exhortations to be courageous in this chapter have been put to other uses than war, giving them a unique meaning in this book. Although this juridical emphasis dominates in ch. 1, elements of the forthcoming battle also appear.

v. *Joshua as conqueror and divider.* There are two main sections in the book of Joshua:

1–12   the conquest of Cisjordan.
13–21   the division of Cisjordan.

In 1.2-9, Joshua receives the dual role of conqueror and divider.[1] His role as conqueror comes to the fore in the instructions he gives to the officers in 1.10-11, and in his reminder to the Transjordanian tribes about their military responsibilities in 1.13-15. In this context עבר and ירש relate to conquest. The division of the land is briefly introduced by הנחיל in 1.6,[2] a word which has no intrinsic connection to war.[3] However, this is certainly not the case with ירש.

vi. *Possessing the land.* N. Lohfink has demonstrated that there is a difference in meaning between the *qal* and *hiph'il* forms of ירש in the Hebrew Bible.[4] The *qal* form, which can usually be translated 'conquer', has land as its object 128 times, and people 25 times. He suggests that the latter could be intended as ironic metaphor.[5] The main emphasis on the *qal* form is on the juridical right to land by

---

1. Lohfink, 'Moses auf Josue', pp. 32-44.
2. The distinction between these terms should not be overdrawn because there is considerable overlapping, cf. E. Blum, *Studien zur Komposition des Pentateuch* (dissertation, Heidelberg, 1988), pp. 68-69.
3. McCarthy, 'An Installation Genre', p. 38.
4. Cf. N. Lohfink, ירש, *ThWAT*, III, pp. 953-85; 'Die Bedeutungen von hebr. jrš qal und hif', *BZ NF* 27 (1983), pp. 14-33.
5. Lohfink, 'Die Bedeutungen', p. 18.

virtue of conquest.[1] The *hiph'il* form is almost always employed in the
sense of destroying someone so that his property can be taken over.[2] It
can be used in parallel with such words as נכה, חרם, שמד.[3]

In Joshua, most usages of the *qal* form are in relation to the gift of
land (1.11 [× 2], 15; 13.1; 18.3; 23.5; 24.4, 8). Only three relate to
the destruction of people as well as the taking of land (12.1; 21.43;
19.47), In contrast, the instances of ירש (*hiph*) are always related to
the destruction of people (3.10; 8.7; 13.6, 12, 13; 14.12; 15.14, 63;
16.10; 17.12, 13, 18; 23.5, 9, 13). They form part of the battle
reports or battle promises, and are frequently parallel with words for
destruction like נכה. The difference between the two forms is clearly
illustrated in 23.5, where the *qal* is in relation to the land, and the
hiph'il to the nations.

The understanding common to both is that the right to land is
grounded in the authority resulting from victory, and which is legit-
imized by divine intervention. The meaning of the noun ירשה (1.15;
12.6, 7) is also based on this understanding. Yet even here there is a
subtle difference between ch. 1 and the remainder of the book. While
12.6, 7 contain descriptions of particular enemies that have been
defeated, 1.15, like all the other instances of ירש in the first chapter,
does not mention an enemy and concentrates on the conquest of the
land. Something similar can be seen in the function of עבר.

vii. *The River Jordan*. There are, undoubtedly, military connotations
associated with עבר. An advance by an invading army,[4] and an invasion which sometimes involves an armed crossing of the Jordan,[5]
could be so characterized. Crossing territory also means encroach-
ment on someone else's property and implies a claim to its ownership.[6] Furthermore, international treaties expressly prohibit crossing
into another's territory. This is perceived as a belligerent act.[7]
Therefore, on the one hand, the crossing of the Jordan may be

---

1. Cf. Deut. 2.9-12, 19-23, where the right to possession by non-Israelite
nations is clearly stated.
2. Lohfink, 'ירש', p. 961.
3. For example, Deut. 7.1 ff.; cf. Lohfink, 'Die Bedeutungen', p. 21.
4. Josh. 6.7; 2 Sam. 29; 1 Kgs 8.21; Isa. 10.28-29; Hab. 1.11; Ps. 48.5, etc.
5. Judg. 6.33; 12.1, etc.
6. Gen. 31.52; Judg. 11.18-20; 2 Sam. 19.41-43, etc.
7. *ANET* 202, verse 23 f., etc.

understood as a juridical act that marks the beginning of holy war, and on the other hand, when considered in relation to Joshua 3–4, in which the military connotations are completely dominated by an emphasis on the crossing seen as a major miracle, the crossing is much more than a military act.

In preparation for the crossing, the Israelites are instructed to gather provisions which, on the surface at least, is the sort of practical preparation one would expect to find being made on the eve of an invasion.

viii. *Preparing provisions.* The command to prepare provisions to take with them on the expedition to conquer the land is somewhat puzzling.[1] In many holy war passages there are similar commands, but these are about sanctification, as in 11.6. Furthermore, the reference in 1.11 is also in tension with 5.11-12. The latter marks the beginning of the life in the land epoch which is characterized by the cessation of manna and Israel beginning to live on the fruit of the land.[2] It is possible that this is another example of the narrative trying to say something both about the uniqueness of Cisjordan and about Transjordan, thus getting into a logical tangle.[3] In ch. 1, the Transjordanians play a particularly important role and dominate the final verses.

ix. *Armed for war.* The clearest indication of the forthcoming battle is that the mighty men of the Transjordanian tribes are to 'pass over armed before your brethren and help them' (1.14). As the following table will demonstrate, Reuben, Gad and the half-tribe of Manasseh are prominent participants in the conquest, even though they already have their own land.

Deut. 3.18-22   Moses commands
Josh. 1.12-15   Joshua reminds
         4.12-13   Narrator records[4]

---

1.   The word used, צידה, normally means the food one takes to survive a partic-ular journey, cf. Gen. 42, 25; 45.21; Exod. 12.39; Josh. 9.11, etc.
2.   Soggin, *Joshua*, pp. 75-76.
3.   For a fuller discussion cf. below in Chapter 4.
4.   On the relationship to a parallel passage in Num. 32.21, cf. N. Lohfink, 'Die Schichten des Pentateuch und der Krieg', *Gewalt und Gewaltlosigkeit im Alten Testament* (Questiones disputatae, 96; Freiburg: Herder, 1983), p. 100 n. 101.

> 12.1-6   have a place in the summary of conquests
> 22.1-6   their return is recorded.

Just as their presence marks the beginning of the war, so their departure marks the end of the conquest.[1] Their participation in holy war emphasizes their unity with Israel. That this question is a concern is evident in ch. 22 where the most extreme objection is mentioned: their land is 'unclean' and they are guilty of malpractice. This objection is dismissed convincingly.

Another indication of the interest in Transjordan is evident in the details of the territorial description found in 1.4.[2]

> From the wilderness and this Lebanon as far as the great river, the river Euphrates, all the land of the Hittites to the Great Sea toward the going down of the sun shall be your territory.

Most scholarly discussion has concentrated on the question of the Euphrates as a northern boundary. Opinions have ranged from it being a historical possibility during the reign of David[3] to one of it as 'a dreamlike idealization'.[4] However, what makes the description unique is the inclusion of the Lebanon as a northern boundary.[5] The interesting fact is that the other territorial descriptions in Joshua (9.1; 11.17; 12.7; 13.5; cf. Judg. 3.3) all regard the Lebanon as a northern boundary. The question then returns to why there is the need to mention the Euphrates. An explanation could be that the Euphrates is sometimes considered to be an eastern boundary.[6] Its inclusion in the

1. The significance of their departure will be discussed below in Chapter 4.

2. Similar descriptions which include the Euphrates as a boundary are Deut. 1.7; 11.24; cf. Gen 15.18.

3. Cf. for example N. Lohfink, *Die Landverheissung als Eid: Eine Studie zu Gn 15* (SBS, 28; Stuttgart: Verlag Katholisches Bibelwerk, 1967), p. 74. He says that under the rule of David Israel controlled the area as far as the middle Euphrates.

4. M. Ottosson, 'Tradition and History, with Emphasis on the Composition of the Book of Joshua', in K. Jeppesen and B. Otzen (eds.), *The Productions of Time: Tradition History in Old Testament Scholarship* (Sheffield: Almond Press, 1984), pp. 81-143 (98). Cf. Diepold, *Israels Land*, pp. 178-79, who sees it as a Josianic ideal.

5. Cf. Deut. 11.24.

6. Cf. Wijngaards, *The Dramatization of Salvific History*, pp. 94-100. David established his power at the Euphrates in the war in Transjordan (2 Sam. 8.3), and Solomon ruled over the whole region west of the Euphrates, from Tipshah to Gaza (1 Kgs 4.24).

chapter relates to the interest in Transjordan. The paradox between the promised land understood as Cisjordan and understood as including Transjordan is never finally resolved in this chapter, or in the remainder of the book.[1] The symmetry between the two serves as a means of relieving the tension.

Excursus on the symmetry between Transjordan and Cisjordan. The symmetry between the two regions is expressed primarily through the symmetry between Moses and Joshua. Although ch. 1 makes it clear that Joshua has replaced Moses, the reader is never allowed to forget the predecessor. The Lord reminds Joshua of what he said to Moses,[2] and of what Moses commanded and did.[3] Joshua reminds the people of what Moses said and did.[4] The people remind Joshua of the Lord speaking to Moses[5] as well as of the words and deeds of Moses.[6] At regular intervals, the narrator refers to what Moses said,[7] as well as to the fact that the Lord spoke to him.[8] When referring to the deeds of Moses, as is frequently done, the narrator describes his role in the occupation of Transjordan.[9]

There is no doubt that Joshua is the Lord's new spokesperson. His status as successor and equal is emphasized by a series of analogies. As the Lord has been with Moses, so he is with Joshua (1.5, 17; 3.7); as the people have been in awe of Moses, so they are in awe of Joshua (4.14); the Transjordanian tribes promise to obey Joshua as they have

---

1. Cf. M. Weinfeld, 'The Extent of the Promised Land—the Status of Transjordan', in G.S. Strecker (ed.), *Das Land Israel in biblischer Zeit* (Göttinger Theologische Arbeiten, 25; Göttingen: Vandenhoeck & Ruprecht, 1983), pp. 59-75; D. Jobling, 'The Jordan a Boundary: Transjordan in Israel's Ideological Geography', in *idem, The Sense of Biblical Narrative: Structural Analyses in the Hebrew Bible II* (JSOTSup, 39; Sheffield: JSOT Press, 1986), pp. 88-134.

2. 1.3; 20.2.

3. 1.7, 13; 1.14

4. 8.33-35; 20.2; 22.5 and 18.7.

5. Interestingly, the first to do so are the Gibeonites in 9.24; then Caleb in 14.10; and the daughters of Zelophehad in 17.4.

6. Caleb appeals on the basis of what Moses said (14.6, 9, 10) and did (14.7, 11).

7. 4.10, 12; 8.31-35; 11.12, 15, 20, 23; 13.33.

8. Regarding the allotment of land in 14.2, 5; and the Levites in 21.8.

9. 12.6; 13.8, 12, 15, 21, 32; 14.3; 22.7. The word used consistently for the destruction of these pre-Israelite inhabitants is נכה.

obeyed Moses (1.16-18; 22.2); and as Moses has caused Reuben, Gad
and the half-tribe of Manasseh to inherit Transjordan, so Joshua will
cause the remaining tribes to inherit Canaan (22.7).

The summary of the conquest in ch. 12 is presented in two sections,
each introduced by 'now these are the kings of the land'. The first
offers the territory in Transjordan which matches the kingdoms of
Sihon and Og (12.1-6), while the second refers to the territory in
Cisjordan (12.7-24). The symmetry serves as something of a rebuke
in ch. 13 in which an account of the unconquered territory in
Cisjordan (13.2-6) is followed by an account of the complete conquest
of Transjordan (13.18-33). The unfavourable comparison is made
particularly obvious by the fact that the Geshurites and the
Maacathites, who remain unconquered in Cisjordan (13.13), have been
conquered in Transjordan (13.11).

The fact that the same enemies, the Amorites, the Anakim, together
with the Geshurites and Maacathites are defeated on both sides of the
Jordan is another means of expressing the unity of the two territories.
In the interests of this unity, the role of Transjordanian tribes in the
conquest is given particular prominence, a prominence which is
noticeable in the introduction to the narrative in ch. 1 where the
Transjordanians are singled out for special attention (1.12 ff.).

x. *A preliminary conclusion.* In the first chapter, interest is centred on
matters other than war; particularly on the themes concerning the land
as a gracious gift, and the issue of obedience.[1] Words that are
normally associated with warfare later in the book are here adapted
for other purposes.[2] The story of Rahab in the next chapter serves as a
gradual transition to the theme of conquest.

b. *The Story of Rahab and the Spies (2.1-24)*
It is generally argued that ch. 2 is derived from an earlier story that
has been incorporated into the book. In the process, the figure of
Joshua has been added, as well as the location at Jericho. The
characteristic theology of the DtrH appears in Rahab's confession.[3]

1.   Lohfink, 'Die Schichten des Pentateuch und der Krieg', p. 67, maintains that
the themes of 'DtrL' (Deut. 1–Josh. 22) are those of conquest and law.
2.   Cf. Nelson, 'Josiah', p. 537: 'The whole chapter is strangely unmilitaristic,
given that it introduces a book full of war and bloodshed'.
3.   Cf. for example, Noth, *Josua*, pp. 9-11.

While agreeing that the story probably has an earlier independent history, I shall argue that it fits very comfortably into the overall narrative. The main reason for this opinion is that the 'spy story' has distinctive literary and theological functions in the Hebrew Bible, which favours viewing the story of Rahab as part of the wider context.

The spy stories in the Hebrew Bible are not merely exciting features of war accounts, but are part of theological reflection. All occur in narratives of the conquest and holy war, and with remarkably similar wording and structure;[1] and all are a means of emphasizing the Lord's gift of land, and mark a stage in the process of conquest. In addition, they provide a dramatic focal point for establishing faith.

Both Joshua 2 and Judges 18 emphasize the gift of land,[2] while Numbers 13–14 and Deuteronomy 1 also highlight the contrast between faith and doubt. Lohfink's study of the story in Deuteronomy 1 shows how it functions to illustrate Israel's disobedience as the first act in a long dark history.[3] The act is highlighted by a series of polarities. Usually, in accounts of holy war, it is the enemy's heart that melts, but here it is Israel's (Deut. 1.28); and, usually, a description of the enemy's strength is contrasted to Israel's smallness as part of a confession of faith, but here it is used in a confession of doubt. Similarly, the exodus, which is normally confessed to be a mighty act of God, is seen as a journey to death.

In contrast to Deuteronomy 1, the response to the report of the spies in Joshua 2 is calm and positive. Rahab does not in any way disclose any practical information that might enable the Israelites to capture the city. She merely expresses the terror and dismay of the Canaanites, who are confronted by the awesome power of Israel's

1. S. Wagner, 'Die Kundschaftergeschichten im Alten Testament', *ZAW* 76 (1964), pp. 255-69. He concludes that it is possible to speak of a *Gattung*. Cf. also F. Stolz, *Jahwes und Israels Kriege: Kriegstheorien und Kriegserfahrungen im Glauben des alten Israel* (ATANT, 60; Zürich: Theologischer Verlag Zürich, 1972), p. 81, who suggests that the spy stories are a stylistic feature of the DtrH.

2. On the similarities between the two accounts, cf. M. Rose, *Deuteronomist und Jahwist: Untersuchungen zu den Berührungspunkten beider Literaturwerke* (ATANT, 67; Zürich: Theologischer Verlag Zürich, 1981, pp. 147-48; F. Langlamet, 'Josué, II, et les traditions de l'Hexateuch', *RB* 78 (1971), pp. 5-12, 161-83, 321-54 (334-37).

3. N. Lohfink, 'Darstellungskunst und Theologie in Dtn 1.6–3.29', *Bib* 41 (1960), pp. 105-34 (110-20).

God. The use of the words אימה, מסס and מוג suggest the human terror associated with the appearance of the Divine Warrior.[1] The intention of the story is not to show the cunning or military skill of Joshua's army. Rather, it serves as a typical story of holy war. While many stories of holy war recognize no tension between human and divine action,[2] there is sometimes an emphasis that it is YHWH alone who works.[3] The latter is true of ch. 2. The concern is to show that the conquest did not begin until the will of the Lord had been determined.[4] Rahab's confession is thus the focal point of the story,[5] emphasizing, as it does, the themes of holy war and the gift of land. It becomes clear that, when the Lord does lead his people into battle, there are only two possible responses from the enemy: terror or the obedient submission of faith.[6] Furthermore, when the function of 'fear' in the book of Joshua is discussed, it will be demonstrated that it has an all-important literary and theological function in the work as a whole.

Although the spies only approach Jericho, their intention is to reconnoitre the entire land (2.1, 2, 3, 18, cf. 6.22). This ambiguity is also present in the other two spy stories in the book.[7] In 14.7, the spies who go to Ai are described as reconnoitring all the land. In 14.7, Caleb is said to have surveyed the whole land. However, the extent of his inheritance indicates that he examined only a very limited area (cf. 14.9).

The land takes on universal significance when YHWH is given the title of the God of heaven and earth (2.11). His gift of land is mentioned in Rahab's confession (2.9), the spies' speech to Rahab (2.14)

1. D.J. McCarthy, 'Some Holy War Vocabulary in Joshua 2', *CBQ* 33 (1971), pp. 228-30.

2. Lohfink, 'Darstellungskunst und Theologie', p. 112 n. 5.

3. Cf. von Rad, *Heilige Krieg*, pp. 44-50.

4. Cf. G.M. Tucker, 'The Rahab Saga (Joshua 2): Some Form-Critical and Traditio-Historical Observations', in J.M. Efird (ed.), *The Use of the Old Testament in the New and Other Essays* (Durham, NC: Duke University Press, 1972), pp. 66-86.

5. The significance of her confession will be discussed below in the final chapter.

6. D.J. McCarthy, 'The Theology of Leadership in Joshua 1–9', *Bib* 52 (1971), pp. 165-75.

7. The connection between spying and ארץ appears to be a stereotyped expression in the Hebrew Bible, for example, Gen. 42.9, 11, 14, 16, 30, 31, 34; 1 Sam. 26.4; 2 Sam. 15.10.

and in their report to Joshua (2.24). The one speech follows the other and together they form the structure of the story. The remaining references to land in ch. 2 are part of the introduction of the trembling enemy described as כל־ישבי הארץ. Rahab's confession clearly focuses the interest on the land. What is remarkable is that Rahab, a notable exception to the significant חרם legislation, is the first to introduce it into the narrative. Equally striking is the covenant made with an occupant of the land. In Joshua, it is never explicitly stated that the prohibition against covenants and the command to destroy the occupants of the land are two sides of the same coin, as in Deut. 7.1-5.[1] Nevertheless, the essential feature of the covenant with Rahab and the later covenant with the Gibeonites is that their lives are to be spared. In passages dealing with the conquest, notably Exodus 23; 34; Deut. 7.1-5, the command against making covenants is in relation to the occupants of the land, and is part of a complex of ideas relating to the conquest and life in the land. Therefore, there is much more to the prohibition than the suggestion that covenants are forbidden because they involve calling upon the gods of foreigners.[2] When viewed in relation to the subsequent development of the idea of חרם and the complete destruction of Jericho, it is evident that the covenant with Rahab is no incidental feature.

In the story, Rahab is on Israel's side. The enemies of Israel, whom she persists in tricking, are represented by the king of Jericho and his messengers. While the fear on the part of the occupants of the land and the aggression of the king of Jericho serve as an adumbration of the forthcoming battle, prominence is given to Rahab the foreigner who is not to be killed. Instead of directly proceeding to the battle, as might have been expected, the pace of the narrative now slows down to that of a liturgical ritual for the description of the crossing of the Jordan.

---

1.   The extent to which it is possible to assume the understanding in Deuteronomy is debatable, nevertheless, cf. A.C. Tunyogi, 'The Book of the Conquest', *JBL* 84 (1965), pp. 374-80). This contains the argument that the continuity of the חרם supports a claim that the 'primitive form' of Deuteronomy and Josh. 1–11 are originally one work.

2.   J. Halbe, *Das Privilegrecht Jahwes Ex. 34:10-26: Gestalt und Wesen, Herkunft und Wirken in vordeuteronomistischer Zeit* (FRLANT, 114; Göttingen: Vandenhoeck & Ruprecht, 1975), p. 126 f. For a further criticism of Halbe's explanation, cf. Blum, *Studien zur Komposition des Pentateuch*.

c. The River Crossing (3.1–5.1)

i. *The significance of the crossing.* The river crossing is a lengthy and slow-moving account which dominates the early chapters. Whereas, in Joshua 1, the conquest is symbolized by the projected river crossing, which is seen as a means of entry, here the emphasis is on the crossing itself. What is confusing for the reader is that there is more than one report of the crossing, and that these reports differ in detail from one another. Several explanations have been offered for this puzzle. The most widely accepted explanation is that the present text is the result of a combination of earlier sources.

A representative example of an historical-critical approach is that of E. Otto. He proposes two accounts:[1]

1.   Twelve representatives are chosen while on the east bank (3.12) to carry the stones into the Jordan (4.5) where they are laid down by Joshua (4.9).
2.   Twelve representatives in the Jordan are chosen to collect stones in the river and to carry them to the west bank (4.2, 3, 8) where Joshua sets them up (4.20).

Another explanation is offered by J. Wilcoxen. He points out that the repetitions and inconsistencies are confined to the ceremonial aspects of the narrative.[2] These are then explained as typical features of liturgical texts.

Finally, B. Peckham has shown that the material in chs. 2–3 is arranged in a structure of command and obedience.[3] He argues that the tangle in the narrative is due to this logical arrangement dominating the narrative sequence.

While the above explanations have plausibility, there is a further possibility. For convenience, I shall refer to Otto's two sources. In 1, the 12 representatives come from the east bank and the stones are set in the Jordan. In 2, the 12 representatives are already at the west bank (4.1). They remove the stones from the centre of the river and set

---

1.   E. Otto, *Das Bundes-Mazzotfest von Gilgal: Ein Beitrag zur Kultgeschichte Israels und Überlieferungsgeschichte des Hexateuch* (dissertation, Hamburg, 1973).

2.   J.A. Wilcoxen, 'Narrative Structure and Cult Legend: A Study of Joshua 1–6', in J.C. Rylaarsdam (ed.), *Transitions in Biblical Scholarship* (Chicago/London: University of Chicago Press, 1968), pp. 43-70 (53-54).

3.   B. Peckham, 'The Composition of Joshua 3-4', *CBQ* 46 (1984), pp. 413-31.

them up on the west bank. This could be another example of the symmetrical relationship between Cisjordan and Transjordan that occurs throughout the book of Joshua.

Whatever the solution, by means of repetition the emphasis is placed on the river crossing.[1] The story reads like an account of a religious festival.[2] The details are carefully recited: procession order, the participation of priests, the ark and the collecting, carrying and placing of the stones. The climax is the dry-shod crossing which is predicted, described and later reflected upon.

At first, this emphasis on the miraculous is surprising. The Jordan is not a major geographical obstacle.[3] There are several fords,[4] and many passages in the Hebrew Bible deal with the crossing in a nonchalant manner.[5] An explanation has been sought in the ancient Near Eastern mythology of a 'Chaoskampf', which has been utilized in Israelite religious thought.[6] Several psalms describe YHWH subduing the waters, for example, Pss. 74; 89; 24; 65. In Psalm 114, the Red Sea and the Jordan are parted, showing the manner in which mighty cosmic and historical acts can be juxtaposed. The defeat of the primaeval waters is also an element in accounts of creation, and the appearance of dry land marks the first act of creation (Gen. 1.9; Pss. 33.7; 74.15; 104.8, 9; Isa. 51.10; etc.). Therefore, the crossing marks a transition, an entrance into an ordered world while leaving behind the wasteland of chaos.[7] Doubts have been expressed about whether all

---

1. It could be argued, for example, that a strong interest in a certain subject would cause a redactor for emphasis to keep both versions of a story, cf. Otto, *Das Bundes-Mazzotfest von Gilgal*, p. 52.

2. Cf. Soggin, *Joshua*, pp. 50-67, for the argument that the narrative is the result of the historization of an ancient liturgy used in an annual procession between the Jordan and Gilgal. Cf. also Ottosson, *Erövring och fördelning av Land*, who says that the account is based on a P narrative.

3. Cf. M. Noth, 'Der Jordan in der alten Geschichte Palästinas', *ZDPV* 72 (1956), pp. 123-48.

4. Cf. T. Fast, 'Verkehrswege zwischen dem südlichen West- und Ostjordanland', *ZDPV* 72 (1956), pp. 149-51. These fords are even mentioned in Josh. 2.7.

5. Gen. 32.11; 2 Sam. 17.22; 1 Kgs 22.2-40, etc.

6. Cf. A. Curtis, 'The "Subjugation of the Waters" Motif in the Psalms; Imagery or Polemic?', *JSS* 23 (1978), pp. 245-56.

7. Cf. T.L. Thompson, 'The Jordan Crossing: *SIDQOT YAHWEH* and World Building', *JBL* 100 (1981), pp. 345-58.

the details about a cosmic battle are part of the thought world of this narrative.[1] Nevertheless, it is likely that the language retains the power and depth of the myth. W. Brueggemann is correct when he says that 'Jordan' is laden with symbolic power. He writes: 'It is the boundary between the precariousness of the wilderness and the confidence of at-home-ness.'[2] The crossing marks the transition from a time of promise to a time of fulfilment.

The miraculous character of the crossing is emphasized by the note in 3.15 that this is the season when the Jordan overflows its banks. The slow-moving and unconcerned account of the crossing reveals a trust in the Lord's absolute control over the river. Although the meticulous obedience to the commands of the Lord is emphasized, there is no doubt that it is the Lord alone who is the effective cause of events. This understanding is supported by the parallel drawn with the Red Sea crossing in 4.21-24. Both are described in creation language as יבשה and הוביש.[3] Similarly, Ps. 66.6, which also refers to the dry-shod crossings, יברו ברגל הפך ים ליבשה בנהר, makes no mention of the destruction of any Egyptians.[4] In Psalm 114, both crossings are placed in the context of the Chaoskampf.[5] One of the differences between the Red Sea miracle and other accounts of holy war is precisely this: in the first, it is the Lord alone who works; while, in the others, human

---

1. Cf. O. Kaiser, *Die Mythische Bedeutung des Meeres in Ägypten, Ugarit und Israel* (BZAW, 78; Berlin: Töpelmann, 1959), pp. 135-40; D.J. McCarthy, ' "Creation" Motifs in Ancient Hebrew Poetry', *CBQ* 29 (1967), pp. 393-406.

2. Brueggemann, *The Land*, p. 45.

3. The exodus theme is further emphasized by the narrative immediately proceeding to an account of two rituals associated with the exodus story, circumcision and passover. The relationship is particularly obvious in 5.2-9, where יצא מצרים, or simply יצא, occurs in 5.4 (× 2), 5 (× 2), 6; and in 5.9 circumcision symbolizes a rolling away of the reproach of Egypt. The appearance of the Divine Warrior in 5.13-15 also resembles the theophany of the burning bush in Exod. 3.5. It is therefore hardly surprising that R. de Vaux, *The Early History of Israel* (Philadelphia: Westminster, 1978), p. 606, can argue that 'the entry into the Promised Land was presented as the antithesis of the exodus from Egypt'.

4. On this comparison, cf. G. Kühnert, *Das Gilgalpassah: Literarische, überlieferungsgeschtliche und geschichtliche Untersuchungen zu Josua 3–6* (Steinen–Endenburg, 1982), pp. 37-38.

5. M. Weiss, *The Bible from Within* (Jerusalem: Magnes Press, 1984), pp. 352-78, on the relationship of the parallel crossings to the theme of creation and Chaoskampf in Ps. 114.

involvement also plays a part.[1] Thus, the link to the Red Sea crossing serves to highlight the miraculous character of the Jordan crossing in which 'miracle' is understood in its liturgical and mythological dimensions.[2] The miracle occurs at the entrance of the ark into the river, and in 4.13 the armed men are recorded as passing before the Lord.

It has been argued that there is a tradition of the ark as a war palladium which underlies the liturgical narrative.[3] However, the use of 3.13 to support this claim is dubious because the verse is devoid of any military emphasis. The only unambiguous indications that the ark could be used as a war palladium are 1 Samuel 4–7 and 2 Samuel 6.[4] References to the ark in Josh. 7.6 and 8.33 occur in a military context but it has no military function. Although the ark has a definite role in the description of the battle in 6.1 ff., I shall argue that the military is dominated by the liturgical. The mere fact that the ark is carried in procession cannot weigh upon the argument because this can occur in both contexts. While there is a very strong cultic emphasis in the ideology and practice of warfare in the ancient Near East,[5] the reverse is also true. However, before any conclusions can be reached on the relationship between the cultic and the military in the river crossing, the significance of the Transjordanians being 'armed for war' has to be discussed.

ii. *Transjordanian tribes lead.* The only warlike material in chs. 3 and 4 is found in 4.13, in which the Transjordanians pass over armed and ready for battle. It is almost as though they are there to protect the rest of the people. The prominence given them corresponds to the emphasis on unity suggested by the 12 stones and the 12 representatives, as well as the statements about 'all Israel' crossing the river.[6] The curious thing is that it is the tribes who already possess the land who have a military bearing.

1. Von Rad, *Heilige Krieg*, pp. 45-47.

2. On the way in which both elements appear in the narrative of the crossing, cf. J.R. Porter, 'The Background of Joshua III–V', *SEÅ* 36 (1971), pp. 5-23.

3. E. Vogt, 'Die Erzählung vom Jordanübergang. Josua 3–4', *Bib.* 46 (1965), pp. 125-48.

4. Cf. Stolz, *Jahwes und Israels Kriege*, pp. 29-68.

5. Weippert, '"Heiliger Krieg" in Israel', pp. 460-93.

6. כל־ישראל in 3.7, 17; 4.14. The interest in Israel as a comprehensive entity is maintained throughout the book.

The atmosphere is that of a religious ceremony. While it is unlikely that the cultic descriptions merely refer to the cultic dimension of holy war, such an explanation is possible. Indeed, J. van Seters has attempted to explain the Jordan crossing in terms of the campaign reports in the Assyrian annals in which a river crossing at the flood stage occurs at the outset.[1] However, the brief notes concerning the crossing can hardly be compared to the long and involved ritual found in the opening chapters of Joshua. The crossing itself is the centre of activity, and the enemy remains very much in the background.

iii. *The nations.* So much attention is given to the river crossing that there is hardly any sense of an impending battle. The enemy is briefly focused upon in 3.10:

> Hereby you shall know that the living God is among you, and he will not fail to possess before you the Canaanites, the Hittites, the Hivites, the Perizzites, the Girgashites, the Amorites and the Jebusites.

In what appears to be a confession,[2] the Lord is introduced as אל־חי, a title used only three times in the rest of the Hebrew Bible. This is followed by אדון כל־הארץ in 3.11, 13 (cf. 2.11), which serve to emphasize divine presence and activity.[3] It is significant that the title 'Lord of all the earth' is also found in Psalm 114. I have noted that Psalm 114 places both the Red Sea and Jordan crossings in the setting of a mythological battle. In its present context, 3.10 establishes a connection between the successful river crossing and the Lord's forthcoming successful defeat of the occupants of the land. The substantial focus on the river crossing gives way to the ensuing battle.

The river crossing receives brief attention in 5.1 when the kings hear of the miracle of the crossing and are filled with terror. Later in the narrative the kings hear of a previous battle and are terrified (cf. 2.10-11; 9.1, 3, 9, 10; 10.1-2; 11.1-2). These mighty acts serve the same literary function and may be regarded as being part of the compositional structure.[4] In the previous verse, 4.24, the focus is possibly broader than the occupants of the land, and the river miracle will cause all peoples of the earth (כל־עמי הארץ) to know that the Lord

---

1. J. van Seters, 'Joshua's Campaign of Canaan', pp. 1-12.
2. Stolz, *Jahwes und Israels Kriege*, p. 67.
3. On the cosmic and creational sense of these ascriptions and parallels in Ugaritic material, cf. Porter, 'The Background of Joshua', pp. 18-23.
4. Cf. below, Chapter 7.

is mighty.[1] The references to the fear on the part of the occupants of the land in 5.1 further serve to introduce a military mood into the narrative.

The sense in which the crossing is characterized as a battle is also suggested in 3.5, in which, prior to the crossing, the Israelites are told to sanctify themselves. This act is often a preliminary feature of holy war.[2] Indeed, the amount of attention devoted to the crossing itself suggests that it cannot simply be likened to the first of the battles or understood as the first stage of conquest, but is a description of the conquest as a whole. The highly abstract nature of the enemy would explain why the nations only need appear at the end of the story. Even then, the attention moves rapidly from them and returns to the cultic and the miraculous.

d. A New Epoch (5.2-15)

The positioning of the circumcision and passover directly after the river crossing and immediately before the first conquest serves to emphasize Israel's distinctiveness from the local population,[3] and to make Israel 'cultically correct for conquest'.[4] It will become evident that these ceremonies serve to signal a transition in Israel's destiny.

i. *The circumcision (5.2-9)*. This event marks a new epoch in the story of Israel. The change is emphasized by a series of contrasts:

Wilderness generation	New generation
Disobedience	Obedience
No circumcision	Circumcision
In the desert	In the land
Death	On the brink of new life
Promise not to see land	Promise to give land

It is evident that the contrast is to be noted. On the one hand, there is the three-fold repetition of מדבר. On the other hand, there is the description of the land as a place flowing with milk and honey, an expression often employed in situations of doubt and faith preceding

---

1. Cf. below, Part II.
2. Von Rad, *Heilige Krieg*, p. 7.
3. Ottosson, 'Tradition and History', p. 90.
4. T.C. Butler, *Joshua* (Word Biblical Commentary, 7; Waco, TX: Word Books, 1982), p. 53.

conquest.[1] The circumcision is said to have rolled away חרפת מצרים. Perhaps it is also significant that חרפה is often linked to Israel's landlessness under heathen lords.[2] The function of גוי in 5.6 serves to accentuate Israel's role as the one who takes possession of the land, although it is possibly used perjoratively of Israel.[3] A. Cody points out that גוי is the word chosen when a people is recognized as those who take possession of the land.[4] The death of the wilderness generation is an important signal to the reader that the conquest of the land is about to begin.[5] Just as all the men have died in the desert, so all are now circumcised. The word used to stress this completeness is תמם which plays a significant role in the river crossing.[6] The Lord is in complete control. The sinners are punished and the obedient need have no doubt about their reward.

The meaning of the rite itself could be connected to similar mythology as the river crossing and suggest purification if Transjordan is considered unclean, as implied in 22.19.[7] The pace is remarkably

---

1. On the importance of the phrase in the spy stories, cf. G.W. Coats, *Rebellion in the Wilderness: The Murmuring Motif in the Wilderness Traditions of the Old Testament* (Nashville: Abingdon, 1968), pp. 140 ff.

2. Otto, *Das Bundes-Mazzotfest von Gilgal*, p. 165.

3. It is used on occasions to depict Israel's unworthiness to be distinguished from the nations (Deut. 32.28; Judg. 2.20; Jer. 5.29; 7.38; 9.8; 12.12; 31.36; 33.34; etc.). An argument could be made for saying that all the instances of Israel as גוי (Josh. 3.17; 4.1; 5.6, 8) occur before the circumcision and that the remaining one in 10.13 is an exception because it is part of a poetic song that has been included in the narrative. However this is too narrow a textual base for the claim, particularly when the multiple functions of the term are considered.

4. A. Cody, 'When Is the Chosen People Called a Gôy?', *VT* 14 (1964), pp. 1-6. He refers to Isa. 26.2, 15; Ezek. 37.22; 35.10; and all the instances in Joshua. One cannot be certain that this pattern is more than coincidental as it could be argued that עם has a similar meaning in Joshua, simply because virtually every context in the book is in some way related to the conquest.

5. Cf. Deut. 2.14-16, and the comment of Moran in 'The End of Unholy War and Anti-Exodus'.

6. 3.16 all the water is cut off;
   3.17; 4.1, 11 all the people cross over;
   4.10 all the words of YHWH are completed.

7. Porter, 'The Background of Joshua', pp. 17-18. If viewed against an exilic or post-exilic background, circumcision takes on a confessional character and the call to circumcision is a call to a recovery of an identity as the people of the Lord, cf. K.A. Deurloo, 'Om Pesach te kunnen Vieren in het Land (Joz. 5.2-9)' in

leisurely considering the close proximity of the enemy in Jericho. The people remain in the camp until the circumcised are healed. It is recorded that the next ceremony, the passover, takes place in Gilgal which is in צרבות יריחו (5.10), a location that has decidedly military connotations (4.13).[1] They are at a notable religious shrine which is in the middle of a battleground! This is a further illustration of the dominance of the cultic over the military at this stage in the narrative.

ii. *The Passover (5.10-12)*. The celebration of the Passover also marks a point of transition from the time in the wilderness to the time in the land.[2] This is expressed by the cessation of manna, a food having been associated with the wilderness period.[3] It is a reminder of the Lord's provision, but, at the same time, there is another dimension. In the Pentateuchal accounts of manna, the gift is always associated with Israel's murmuring and rebellion against the Lord over the issue of food and water, and is linked to a desire to return to Egypt. It symbolizes an anti-exodus.[4] The complaints are about the wilderness being a place of starvation and death. The message is clear: life in the land means a life of obedience to YHWH.

Perhaps it is significant that the verb used in relation to פסח is עשה. While this link is fairly rare (Exod. 12.47, 48; Num. 9.25; 2 Chron. 35.17; Ezra 6.9), it is not surprising in this case. Here it emphasizes obedience, which is an important structural element in the book. It expresses the obedient response to the Lord's commands and occurs at all the significant turning points in the narrative (1.7, 8, 16; 4.8; 5.3, 10, 15; 6.14; etc.). Absolute obedience is a feature of life in the land.

Food plays a particularly important role in the story. The occurrence of קלוי along with מצות in the context of Passover is

M. Boertien (ed.), *Verkenningen in een Stroomgebied. Proeven van Oudtestamentisch Onderzoek. Ter gelegenheid van het afschied von Prof. Dr. M.A. Beek van de Universiteit van Amsterdam* (Amsterdam, 1974), pp. 41-50 (42).

1. Cf. Kühnert, *Das Gilgalpassah*, pp. 139-43. He views 4.13 and 24.11 as reflecting a battle on the plains of Jericho.

2. Rose, *Deuteronomist und Jahwist*, p. 43, argues that it is the first passover and not the first battle that demarcates the beginning of a new epoch.

3. Cf. Exod. 16.35.

4. B. Malina, *The Palestinian Manna Tradition: The Manna Tradition in the Palestinian Targums and its Relationship to the New Testament Writings* (AGSU, 7; Leiden: Brill, 1968), p. 24. Cf. Coats, *Rebellion in the Wilderness*, p. 250, on the exilic background to the murmuring tradition.

unique. However, קלוי does occur as a first fruit offering (Lev. 2.14; 23.14) and, as is illustrated by Exod. 23.15-16, the two rites are not incompatible.[1] The use of תבואת ארץ כנען underlines the understanding of the Passover as a harvest rite.

While תבואה usually means the harvest or total crop yield, it can also be found in a liturgical context (Deut. 14.28; 16.15; 22.9; etc.). The fifth term for food in the space of these two verses is עבור הארץ, and it occurs twice. Although it is only found here, it is usually translated as 'fruit of the land'. Its similarity to עבר, which is a key word in the crossing, and possibly to ערבות, the place of the forthcoming battle, must be more than a coincidence.[2] אכל occurs three times, which ensures that there is no doubt about the emphasis on food as well as on eating. This focuses attention on the land and on the Lord's provision. The Israelites eat grain that they have not planted in a land they have not yet conquered. They are enjoying a foretaste of life in the land.

The focus on the land is maintained throughout the fifth chapter. In the circumcision story, the land is emphasized by a series of contrasts with the wilderness. It is lauded as a land flowing with milk and honey. The theme concerning the goodness of the land is developed in the Passover story. The Divine Warrior story enforces the point that it is also a holy land. These factors ensure that ch. 5 is the strongest statement of the land promise in the book. What is surprising is that sharp contrast that appears in the next chapter, which contains the story of the destruction of Jericho. But before this happens, an awe-inspiring event occurs.

iii. *The appearance of the Divine Warrior (5.13-15)*. The dramatic appearance of the main actor in the story makes a vivid impression on the reader.[3] YHWH is himself the war hero, and he is the only one in

---

1. It is evident that קלוי can be used in the sense of provisions for a military expedition (1 Sam. 17.17; 25.18; 2 Sam. 17.28). However, the immediate context makes it unlikely here, cf. Kühnert, *Das Gilgalpassah*, p. 74 n. 4.

2. This word-play unites the various themes surrounding the entry into the land, cf. Rose, *Deuteronomist und Jahwist*, p. 44.

3. It is often assumed that the story is based on a very old cultic tradition, cf. Noth, *Josua*, pp. 23-24. However, van Seters, 'Joshua's Campaign of Canaan', pp. 1-12, demonstrates that such a divine visitation could feature in the campaign reports of the annals.

the story whose military bearing is so emphasized. The position of this text immediately before the battle at Jericho shows that the human effort is only a faint shadow of the divine.

He is described as bearing a drawn sword, and he identifies himself as leader of the army of the Lord, שר-צבא-יהוה,[1] The fact that Joshua prostrates himself demonstrates that he has encountered the Lord. Joshua asks: Are you for us, or for our adversaries? His response makes most sense in the context if הלנו is read as an affirmative.[2] This would make it clear that the army of Israel can be considered as a part of the heavenly army.[3] In antiquity, the wars on earth have been understood as reflections of war between the gods in heaven. This has blurred the lines between the human and the cosmic.[4] Studies by F.M. Cross and P.D. Miller argue that, although the Lord's kingship is not established by the mythological battles of the gods but by historical victories of his earthly and heavenly armies over the enemies of Israel, the conflict is cosmic in scope in the Israelite literature.[5]

In a dramatic way, Joshua's commission is re-confirmed. The command to remove his shoes, the symbols of power, dignity and ownership,[6] highlights the role of YHWH as master and Joshua as the obedient servant.[7] The story emphasizes that the action is performed because of the holiness of the ground. It is probable that ארץ means the whole land, as it does in most instances in the book.

1.   Elsewhere only in Dan. 8.11, שר-הצבא.

2.   Cf. J.A. Soggin, 'The Negation in Joshua 5.14 (Emphatic *Lamed*)', in *idem* (ed.), *Old Testament and Oriental Studies* (BibOr, 29; Rome: Biblical Institute Press, 1975), pp. 219-20.

3.   On צבא and צבאות for both human and heavenly armies, cf. P.D. Miller, *The Divine Warrior in Early Israel* (Cambridge, MA: Harvard University Press, 1975), pp. 152-55.

4.   Before a battle the gods were consulted and the soldiers were understood as being in the battle simply to support the gods, cf. Weippert, '"Heiliger Krieg" in Israel', pp. 481-83.

5.   F.M. Cross and G.E. Wright, 'The Divine Warrior in Israel's Early Cult', in A. Altmann (ed.), *Biblical Motifs: Origins and Transformations* (Cambridge, MA: Harvard University Press, 1966), pp. 11-30; Miller, *The Divine Warrior in Early Israel*.

6.   Cf. H.C. Brichto, 'Taking-off of the Shoe(s) in the Bible', in P. Peli (ed.), *Proceedings of the Fifth World Congress of Jewish Studies Vol. I* (Jerusalem: World Union of Jewish Studies, 1969), pp. 225-26.

7.   At this point the story is particularly reminiscent of Exod. 3.5.

As the attention turns to Jericho, the focus on the land is not lost. There is a sense in which Jericho is a cipher for the whole land. In ch. 2 the spies who come to Jericho reconnoitre the whole land and report that the whole land is in their hands. In 24.11-13, there is the idea that the whole conquest has been physically accomplished at Jericho.[1]

The events of chs. 3–5 indicate the transition from life in the wilderness to life in the land. Now Israel is in a position to begin taking possession of the land. Little has been said about war and the fate of the nations, but all this is about to change.

3. *Conclusion*

The narrative begins with Israel on the far bank of the Jordan, a river which separates it not only from the land of promise, but also from the occupants of that land. There follows the account of the crossing which dominates the early chapters and encapsulates the *whole* conquest in its symbolism. In the midst of the narrative is the enigmatic appearance of Rahab who serves to draw attention to the fate of the nations. At the same time she constitutes an exception. The duality of her role is brought to its climax in the story of Jericho.

---

1. McCarthy, 'Leadership in Joshua 1–9', pp. 165-75 (174).

Chapter 2

'THE CITY AND ALL THAT IS WITHIN IT SHALL BE DEVOTED TO
DESTRUCTION' (6.1–8.29)

1. *A Cultic Miracle at Jericho (6.1-27)*

At last, after the slow-moving preparation, Israel is at the walls of
Jericho and ready to do battle. Yet there is still no immediate
conquest. The principal player in the drama is the Lord, who makes a
speech detailing exactly what the Israelites are to do. Obedience, and
not military ability, is all that is important. Victory will be achieved
by the miracle of the walls falling down. The information brought
back by the spies is irrelevant, and the suggestion that the seven days'
procession around the city has been a ruse to lower the enemy's guard
is foreign to the story.[1]

The instructions concern a procession around the city for a period
of seven days and contain precise information concerning logistics and
strategy.[2] The priests and the ark are included in the procession. The
trumpet blasts and the shout mark the climactic moment when the
walls collapse. Then the people enter the city. Joshua repeats the
instructions to the people. They obey without hesitation.

Undoubtedly, the whole episode is overtly cultic, with its compli-
cated ritual and climactic theophany.[3] The story is dominated by cultic
detail: the procession with the ark, the presence of priests, the trumpet

---

1. For this suggestion, cf. A. Malamat, 'Israelite Conduct of War in the
Conquest of Canaan According to the Biblical Tradition', in F.M. Cross (ed.),
*Symposia Celebrating the Seventy-Fifth Anniversary of the Founding of the
American Schools of Oriental Research (1900–1975)* (Cambridge, MA: American
Schools of Oriental Research, 1979), pp. 35-55.

2. The confusing nature of this account which is sometimes evident is usually
explained as the result of conflating more than one source; cf. Butler, *Joshua*, p. 67.

3. Cf. H.-P. Müller, 'Die Kultische Darstellung der Theophanie', *VT* 14
(1964), pp. 183-91; also cf. von Rad, *Heilige Krieg*.

blasts and the shout, are all features that could appear in a purely cultic context as easily as in a military one.[1] While we need to recognize that the ancient Near Eastern peoples have regarded religion as being integral to warfare, as to every aspect of life, in this instance the emphasis is obviously on cultic miracle. The great symbolic value of the first victory is emphasized by the elaborate ceremonial, and the detailed account of the thorough destruction.

While a return to von Rad's thesis of cultic origins of holy war is no longer tenable, the question of the relationship between cultic description and battle report remains highly significant to this study. Most of the discussion surrounding this relationship has been concentrated on the book of Deuteronomy, in which the destruction of the enemy is synonymous with the destruction of a dangerous cult.[2] The issue of cultic purity as a motive for destroying the nations is not specifically stated in Joshua. However, the close relationship between war and cult (particularly in ch. 6) makes it an interpretive possibility that must be considered. The unusually single-minded emphasis on destruction in the narrative might shed some light on the issue.

2. A Tale of Slaughter and Destruction

Joshua gives the command that the entire city is to be destroyed. The exceptions are the goods destined for the temple treasury and the family of Rahab. A key word in the argumentation is חרם, which appears on six occasions, twice as a verb (6.18, 21) and four times as a noun (6.17, 18 × 3).[3] The act of destroying the city is expressed

---

1. Cf. Butler, *Joshua*, p. 70.

2. M. Noth, in a review of von Rad's *Deuteronomium-Studien* in *ThLZ* 73 (1948), pp. 536-37, says that the priestly-cultic influence is overemphasized. Thus he calls into question the thesis of the origins in the circles of country Levites. In a careful study of the role of the nations in Deuteronomy, O. Bächli, *Israel und die Völker: Eine Studie zum Deuteronomium* (ATANT, 41; Zürich/Stuttgart: Zwingli, 1962), comes to the conclusion that the call to exterminate the nations is indeed a call to cultic purity; Cf. further H.-J. Kraus, 'Vom Kampf des Glaubens', in H. Donner and R. Hanhart (eds.), *Beiträge zur Alttestamentlichen Theologie: Festschrift für Walther Zimmerli* (Göttingen: Vandenhoeck & Ruprecht, 1977), pp. 239-56.

3. Brekelmans, *De Herem*, pp. 43-47, has argued that in Lev. 27–21; Deut. 7.26; Josh. 6.17; 1 Kgs 20.42; Isa. 34.5; Mal. 3.24, it is in the sense of a *nomen qualitatis*, whereas normally it is a *nomen concretum*. His argument rests principally

both as a verb וחרימו (6.21), and as a noun simply by stating that the city is חרם (6.17, 18). Similarly, Israel is warned that she will be destroyed תחרימו and the camp becoming חרם should she take from what is חרם (6.18). The play on the word can be seen clearly in the full text of 6.18:

ורק־אתם שמרו מן־החרם פן־תחרימו ולקחתם מן־החרם
ושמתם את־מחנה ישראל לחרם ועצרתם אותו

Various attempts have been made to explain the emphasis on complete destruction, some historical and some literary. The historical explanations are notoriously difficult to demonstrate.[1] This study will confine itself to comparisons with other bodies of literature.

a. A Comparison with the Accounts of Destruction in the Assyrian Annals[2]

The record of the complete destruction of the enemy is also evident in the annals.[3] Arguably, the brutality recorded there is for propaganda

on the parallel between Josh. 6.17 and 6.19:

חרם היא . . . ליהוה
קדש הוא ליהוה

N. Lohfink, חרם, *ThWAT*, III, pp. 191-213 (198), however points out that each of these references can just as well be understood as *nomen concretum* or as *nomen actionis*.

1. Various historical explanations have been offered for the origin of the story of the destruction of Jericho, ranging from the notion of an aetiology designed to explain deserted ruins (A. Alt, 'Erwägungen über die Landnahme der Israeliten', *PJ* 35 [1939], pp. 8-63 [= A. Alt, *Kleine Schriften zur Geschichte des Volkes Israel I* (Munich: C.H. Beck, 1953), pp. 126-75]) to the thesis that the interest in gruesome destruction was to counter the horror propaganda of the Assyrians (Lohfink, *Gewalt und Gewaltlosigkeit im Alten Testament*, p. 74).

2. The most striking similarity outside the annals is to be found in the Mesha inscription:

And Chemosh said to me, 'Go, take Nebo from Israel!' So I went by night and fought against them from the break of dawn until noon, taking it and slaying all, seven thousand men, boys, women, girls, and maid-servants, for I had devoted them to destruction for (the god) Ashtar-Chemosh. And I took from there the...of Yahweh, dragging them before Chemosh. (*ANET*, pp. 320-21, trans. W.F. Albright).

This is the only known instance outside the Hebrew Bible of חרם in a battle report. However, no mention is made of destroying booty.

3. Cf. W.E. Müller, *Die Vorstellung vom Rest im Alten Israel* (Borsdorf–Leipzig: Wilhelm Hoppl, 1939), pp. 8-18.

purposes,[1] as the aim of Assyrian warfare is to subjugate and not destroy.[2] Complete annihilation is usually associated with punishment for rebellion,[3] and the enemy is sometimes described as an oath-breaker.[4] The offence is not only against his suzerain, but also against his suzerain's gods.[5] The language used to describe his destruction is very like the curses found in treaty texts.[6] Indeed, it is in the rhetoric of destruction that the annals are at their most repetitive and stylized, with similar language being used in many accounts.[7] While an historical basis for the narrative of the annals in the practice of war exists, the evidence shows that the primary concern is literary. Nevertheless, there is variety: sometimes all are killed, sometimes a remnant escapes and sometimes the victors show mercy on a defeated enemy. The *differences* in the treatment meted out to an enemy are not at issue as they are in Joshua 6–7. Although there are parallels between חרם and the language of destruction in the annals, there is nothing that quite matches the function that חרם has in the narrative of Joshua.[8]

H.W.F. Saggs presents a convincing argument that the battle reports in the Hebrew Bible, particularly those associated with the idea of חרם, depict brutality that is difficult to parallel in the literature of

---

1. Cf. H.W.F. Saggs, 'Assyrian Warfare in the Sargonid Period', *Iraq* 25 (1963), pp. 145-154.

2. G.F. Hasel, *The Remnant: The History and Theology of the Remnant Idea from Genesis to Isaiah* (Berrien Springs: Andrews University Press, 2nd edn, 1974), pp. 89-100; cf. W.J. Martin, *Tribut und Tributleistungen bei den Assyrern* (StudOr, 8, 1; Helsinki: Finnish Literary Society, 1936); and, more recently, M. Elat, 'The Impact of Tribute and Booty on Countries and People within the Assyrian Empire', *28. Recontre Assyriologique Internationale, Wien 6–10 Juli 1981* (Horn, Austria, 1982), pp. 244-51.

3. H.W.F. Saggs, 'Assyrian Prisoners of War and the Right to Live', *28. Recontre Assyriologique Internationale, Wien 6–10 Juli 1981* (Horn, Austria, 1982), pp. 85-93.

4. E.g. *ANET*, pp. 285, 295, 298, 300.

5. T. Fish, 'War and Religion in Ancient Mesopotamia', *BJRL* 23 (1939), pp. 387-402 (392).

6. D.C.T. Sheriffs, 'Empire and the Gods: Mesopotamian Treaty Theology and the Sword in the First Millenium BC' (dissertation, Stellenbosch, 1976).

7. Schramm, *Einleitung*, pp. 66, 100.

8. Dekkers, 'Der Kriegsherem', pp. 138-62; cf. Brekelmans, *De Herem*, pp. 17-36.

surrounding nations.[1] This is a further reason to pause and begin a brief enquiry into the specific function of חרם in the Hebrew Bible.

b. *A Comparison with the Functions of* חרם *in the Hebrew Bible*
The word occurs some 80 times in the Hebrew Bible, 51 times as a verb, and 29 times as a noun. It can convey various shades of meaning, depending on the context:

a. *As a gift to the Lord.* Num 18.14; Ezek. 44.29; Lev. 27.21, 28 × 3, 29; Mic. 4.13.

b. *As a juridical decision.* The *hophal* form of the verb appears in Exod. 22.19 as the punishment for sacrificing to other gods. In Lev. 27.29, it refers to someone condemned to death, and in Ezra 10.8, it is employed to exclude someone from the community.

c. *As an act of warfare and destruction.* It is used in this sense in all instances in Deuteronomy to 2 Kings, as well as in Num. 21.2, 3; Isa. 11.15; 34.2, 5; 37.11; 43.28; Jer. 25.9; 50.21, 26; 51.3; Mic. 4.13; Zech. 14.11; Mal. 3.24; Dan. 11.44; 1 Chron. 2.7; 4.41; 2 Chron. 20.23; 32.14, thus accounting for some 85 per cent of the usage.

In the DtrH, this last understanding is employed in a special way. Some statistical information will give an idea of the restricted use of the expression:

Deuteronomy	9 times	(2.34; 3.6 × 2; 7.2, 26 × 2; 13.16, 18; 20.17)
Joshua	27 times	(2.10; 6.17, 18 × 4, 21; 7.1 × 2, 11, 12 × 2, 13 × 2, 15; 8.26; 10.1, 28, 35, 37, 39, 40; 11.11, 12, 20, 21; 22.20)
Judges	twice	(1.17; 21.11)
1 Samuel	8 times	(15.3, 8, 9 × 2, 15, 18, 20, 21)
1 Kings	twice	(9.21; 20.42)
2 Kings	once	(19.11)

The fact that it appears in clusters does not seem to be insignificant. Particularly noticeable is the concentration in chs. 6–11 of Joshua, and in 1 Samuel 15. In Deuteronomy, it is associated with the key texts dealing with the conquest. In Judges, it is evident in the introduction and conclusion of the work. After the cluster in 1 Samuel 15, there

1. Saggs, 'Assyrian Prisoners of War', pp. 85-93.

are only three scattered references to חרם, the significance of which will be discussed later. At this stage it is clear that the term is used primarily in relation to the pre-Israelite occupants of the land.

In the Hebrew Bible generally, several words are used for the total destruction of an enemy, often clustered together in order to emphasize its completeness. Joshua is no exception.[1] While חרם can be used simply to describe the destruction of an enemy, it is also used in a more restricted and specialized manner.

Some scholars believe that the emphasis on חרם is part of a later deuteronomistic redaction.[2] On the one hand, it can be removed without unduly disturbing the flow of the narrative. Furthermore, this explains the contradiction between all the inhabitants being destroyed and their ongoing existence. On the other hand, the word appears at key places, and normally is crucial to the context.[3] The discussion demands more precision. Particular attention needs to be given to how it functions in the DtrH.

c. *A Comparison with* חרם *in Deuteronomy*

In the legislative sections of Deuteronomy, חרם appears as a technical term for the destruction of the inhabitants of the land in contrast to nations far away (20.15; cf. 17). It is always used on the grounds that their continued existence presents a religious threat (Deut. 7.2, 26; 20.17-18). Similarly, an apostate Israelite city is subject to חרם (13.16).[4] It is always applied to a community as a whole, and distinguished from the individual ban which is denoted by בער (*pi*) (13.6; 17.7, 12; etc.).[5] The references to חרם in 7.2, 26 are accompanied by descriptions of the destruction of pagan cult objects. In the case of the apostate city (13.13-19), all the booty is to be burned and the city destroyed. The common factor in all these accounts is that the enemy in no sense is considered a military threat. However, it is considered to be a major religious threat. Therefore, the enemy is to be destroyed along with its cult.[6]

---

1. Cf. below, the discussion of the battle reports, particularly in Josh. 10–11.
2. E.g. Noth, *Überlieferungsgeschichtliche Studien*, p. 36.
3. Cf. Dekkers, 'Der Kriegsherem', pp. 69-96.
4. This act of punishment has the character of a military expedition.
5. When the Achan incident is covered the formula בערת הרע מקרבך will be discussed.
6. Cf. Exod. 22.19 where חרם is used as a punishment for religious apostasy.

The remaining two instances occur in battle reports of the conquest (2.34; 3.6). These serve to situate the conquest of Transjordan on the same level as that of Cisjordan.[1] Whereas the destruction of the inhabitants appears as an absolute command in the legislative passages, in the battle reports the decision to destroy is perceived to be a consequence of the refusal of peace after an aggressive attack launched against Israel.

A key to understanding the concept חרם in Deuteronomy is presented in 7.1-5. Here the command to destroy the inhabitants is followed by the command not to make covenants with them or to intermarry.[2]

A. Welch says that the first is religious theory, while the second is religious practice.[3] During the Second Temple period (cf. Ezra 10.8), and in later Judaism, חרם has been used of social ostracism.[4] This raises the possibility of linking the two understandings. At the same time, however, it must be recognized that חרם has a variety of functions and possibly numerous levels of meaning.

Many of the sacral features often associated with war are lacking in Deuteronomy: ark, priests, trumpets and spoil dedicated to the temple. Yet Deuteronomy regards חרם as a means of destroying the dangerous religious practices of the inhabitants of the land. In the remainder of DtrH it is never stated that חרם is a means of safeguarding religious purity. From the time of the monarchy, the religious threat is seen to come from apostate Israelites and, occasionally, through pagan wives who come from nations *outside* the land. Cultic reform appears in a cyclic pattern, and usually involves the destruction of forbidden cult objects,[5] but חרם does not appear at all in these texts.

A striking contrast to Deuteronomy occurs in Joshua 6 in which the enemy is not said to constitute a religious threat and thus merit extermination. In Joshua the practice of חרם is never directly associated

1.   U. Köppel, *Das deuteronomistische Geschichtswerk und seine Quellen: Die Absicht der deuteronomistischen Geschichtsdarstellung aufgrund des Vergleichs zwischen Nu 21, 21-35 und Dtn 2, 26-3* (EHS.T, 122; Bern, 1970), p. 96.

2.   Deut. 7.1-5 is made up of five prohibitions. Each is introduced by לא.

3.   Welch, *The Code of Deuteronomy*, pp. 189-206.

4.   M. Greenberg, 'Herem', *EncJud* 8 (Jerusalem, 1971), pp. 344-50.

5.   H.-D. Hoffman, *Reform und Reformen: Untersuchungen zu einem Grundthema der deuteronomistischer Geschichtsschreibung* (ATANT, 66 Zürich: Theologischer Verlag Zürich, 1980).

with the destruction of cult objects. There is no hint of the equally well attested practice of capturing the enemy's gods and presenting them as captured booty to one's own gods.

Although in Joshua חרם is not associated with destroying a foreign cult, it is associated in Joshua 6 with a tremendous amount of cultic language. Therefore, Welch's thesis of חרם as a literary device for the rejection of a foreign cult must be considered. However, before it is possible to discuss this question adequately, it is necessary to analyse the literary function of the 'nations' which are destroyed, as well as the function of חרם in the remainder of Joshua and the DtrH.

d. A Comparison with the Use of חרם Elsewhere in Joshua

The primary use of חרם in Joshua concerns the complete destruction of pre-Israelite occupants of the land. In ch. 22, and for the first time in Joshua, חרם is brought into relationship with the worship of other gods. This occurs because Achan's crime is placed in parallel to the forbidden altar and the apostasy at Peor.

The accounts of Israel's military defeat and the destruction of Achan make it clear that the legislation in ch. 6 functions as a test of obedience. In 1 Samuel 15 Saul is faced with a similar test that will decide his fate.

e. A Comparison with חרם in 1 Samuel 15

חרם is a key word in the story recorded in 1 Samuel 15, and is employed eight times. In this context it means the total destruction of the Amalekites together with the booty. The initial command from Samuel creates what D. Gunn calls an 'obedience situation'.[1] Saul is severely punished for his failure to obey to the last detail.

The Lord's treatment of Saul is contrasted to that of David who is allowed to capture spoil during his Amalekite campaigns (1 Sam. 30.20-31; cf. 2 Sam. 8.12).[2]

The fact that the Amalekites are singled out as the victims of חרם is hardly surprising. There is a curse against them in several major traditions. YHWH himself is their enemy (Exod. 17.8-16; Num. 24.20; Deut. 25.17-19). A persistent enemy of Israel, they are distributed over a large territory and appear during the exodus, conquest and life

---

1. D.M. Gunn, *The Fate of King Saul: An Interpretation of a Biblical Story* (JSOTSup, 14; Sheffield: JSOT Press, 1980), p. 70.
2. Cf. Gunn's interpretation of Saul as a tragic figure, a plaything of fate.

in the land.[1] They have a reputation for inhumanity, are called 'sinners' (1 Sam. 15.18) and the 'plunderers of Israel' (1 Sam. 14.48; 2 Sam. 8.12). They are included in the lists of pre-Israelite nations that are to be destroyed (Num. 13.29; 14.25, 43, 45; 1 Sam. 27.8).[2] They are among the kings who do battle with Abraham (Gen. 14.7) as well as among those against whom the Psalmist appeals in Psalm 83, suggesting that 'Amalek' is primarily a symbolic category. Thus the Amalekites come to be seen as Israel's primaeval enemy.[3] It is not surprising that the name of their king in 1 Samuel 15, Agag, should reappear again as the villain in the book of Esther, Haman the Agagite.

The destruction of the Amalekites takes place during a particular epoch in Israel's history. They are to be destroyed when Israel is no longer harassed by the surrounding nations (Deut. 25.17-19; cf. 1 Sam. 14.47-48). This issue marks the transition from the reign of Saul to the reign of David.

The possibly superficial associations of the Amalekites with Joshua 6 are contained in the following references: their part in repossessing Jericho (Judg. 3.12-13); Joshua is linked to the exodus battle against them (Exod. 17.8-16);[4] the ark is used against them (Num. 14.44), and the evidence that both stories are associated with Gilgal. The Amalekites never appear as a religious threat to Israel. Perhaps this is significant for any comparison to the nations represented in Joshua 6. The major similarity between Joshua 6 and 1 Samuel 15 is that in both accounts חרם is used as a test of obedience. In both instances the test is failed and followed by disaster.

f. *Preliminary Conclusions on the Function of* חרם *in the DtrH*

Although the meaning of חרם in the DtrH varies from context to context, there is a certain uniformity in meaning as well. With only

1. For a discussion of their role in the various traditions, cf. J.H. Grønbaek, 'Juda und Amalek: Überlieferungsgeschichtliche Erwägungen zu Exodus 17, 8-16', *ST* 18 (1964), pp. 26-45. The ambiguities in the Saul story are discussed in Sternberg, *The Poetics of Biblical Narrative*, pp. 482-515.

2. Note that in Num. 14.45 they are linked to Hormah, as are the Canaanites.

3. J. van Seters, 'The Terms "Amorite" and "Hittite" in the Old Testament', *VT* 22 (1972), pp. 64-81 (76).

4. Cf. K. Möhlenbrink, 'Josua im Pentateuch. Die Josuaüberlieferungen ausserhalb des Josuabuchs', *ZAW* 59 (1942–43), pp. 14-58.

one exception (2 Kgs 19.11, the kings of Assyria against the nations),[1] the subject of חרם is always Israel,[2] and with one other exception (1 Kgs 20.42, Ben-hadad of Syria) the object is always the pre-Israelite occupants of the land, the Amalekites and the wicked Israelites (Deut. 13; Josh. 7; Judg. 21.11). Together they are symbols of evil, an assessment confirmed by their utter destruction.

It appears then that חרם is associated particularly with the conquest and the destruction of the occupants of the land in the DtrH.[3] The last time Israel engages in חרם against her enemies occurs in 1 Samuel 15. This limits the particular mode of warfare to the distant past when Israel took possession of the land. The point is made clearly by the epoch marker in 1 Kgs 9.20-21:

> All the people who were left of the Amorites, the Hittites, the Perizzites, the Hivites, and the Jebusites, who were not of the people of Israel—their descendants who were left after them in the land, whom the people of Israel were unable to destroy utterly (לא־יכלו לחרימם)—these Solomon enslaved unto this day.

This passage shows that חרם is intended for these peoples from the distant past. While a more detailed discussion of the nation lists is required at a later stage, it can be noted that the only two instances of these lists in Deuteronomy are directly linked to חרם (Deut. 7.1-5; 20.16-18), in which they denote the primaeval occupants of the land. Therefore, it seems that חרם is included in a schema that describes the fate of the occupants of the land, marking the period of conquest.[4]

At the same time it functions as a test. This is evident in Joshua 6–7, 1 Samuel 15 and in 1 Kgs 20.42 where King Ahab is to be punished because he releases Ben-hadad. He is condemned for this failure to practise חרם. The logic of the story is the same as that in 1 Samuel 15. There are also further nuances to the concept of חרם which require exploration.

---

1. Parallel passages are Isa. 37.11; 2 Chron. 32.14.
2. In contrast, the prophetic texts often have YHWH as subject, Isa. 34.2, 5; Jer. 25.9, etc.
3. Schmitt, *Du sollst keinen Frieden schliessen*, p. 144.
4. Cf. W. Richter, *Die Bearbeitungen des 'Retterbuchs' in der Deuteronomischen Epoche* (BBB, 21; Bonn: Peter Hanstein, 1963), p. 43).

g. חרם *as an Offering*

The words which occur in 6.17, והיתה העיר חרם וכל־אשר־בה ליהוה, could be understood as describing an offering. Indeed, the fact that some of the property is given to the Lord suggests that the destruction of this first city to be conquered could be perceived as a first fruits offering.[1] The ideology informing this could be that the Lord as creator and owner of all is to be thanked for giving victory.[2] This would help to explain why Jericho in particular is destroyed. A modified form of this argument is that חרם is simply an offering to express gratitude for the victory.[3]

This interpretation is supported elsewhere in the Hebrew Bible when חרם is used as 'gift' (Lev. 27.21, 28; Num. 18.14; Ezek. 44.29), and the text in Micah 4.13, where gift and warfare are combined.[4] In Num. 21.1-3, Israel vows to practise חרם against the king of Arad and his people if YHWH grants victory. On the strength of this text, Brekelmans concludes that the 'oorlogsherem' is primarily a gift to YHWH.[5]

Similarly, other ancient Near Eastern texts show that conquered territories are emptied of their inhabitants and consecrated to the gods. A solemn curse is made against anyone who resettles in the area, thereby withdrawing it from the god's use.[6] The language of the Mesha inscription also strongly suggests that the slaughter is understood as sacrifice. The slaughter of all the people is 'as satiation (intoxication) for Chemosh and Moab',[7] and they are החרים לכמש. This

---

1. Greenberg, 'HEREM', p. 437.

2. On the relationship between חרם and the doctrine of creation, cf. Brekelmans, *De Herem*, pp. 169-70.

3. F. Schwally, *Semitische Kriegsaltertümer I. Der heilige Krieg im alten Israel* (Leipzig: Dieterich'sche Verlagsbuchhandlung, 1901), pp. 37-39.

4. In Deut. 13.17, the burning of the city and its spoil is called כליל ליהוה, a sacrificial term (cf. Lev. 6.16; Ps. 51.21). However, it cannot be called a terminus technicus. Thus Judg. 20.40 has כליל־העיר השמימה (cf. Josh 8.20, which has עשן instead of כליל). In addition, offerings need to be unblemished. It is therefore safer to say that כליל is used when describing an act of complete burning, cf. Dekkers, 'Der Kriegsherem', pp. 56-60.

5. Brekelmans, *De Herem*, pp. 67-70.

6. A. Goetze, 'Warfare in Asia Minor', *Iraq* 25 (1963), pp. 124-30 (129). For examples, cf. S. Gervitz, 'Jericho and Shechem: A Religio-Literary Aspect of City Destruction', *VT* 13 (1963), pp. 52-62 (59-60).

7. W.F. Albright's reading רוה in *ANET*, p. 320. For full discussion and

idea of satisfying a bloodthirsty divinity goes beyond what the destruction in Joshua 6 could possibly mean. Nevertheless, there is a functional similarity between the phrases החרים לכמש and . . . חרם היא ליהוה (6.17) and קדש הוא ליהוה (6.19). While an understanding of offering may well be implied in Joshua 6, it has to be borne in mind that elsewhere the contrast between חרם and sacrifice is made very clear, most notably in 1 Samuel 15.

The story in 1 Samuel 15 establishes a clear distinction between the act of חרם where man is the executor of divine will and gives to God what belongs to him, and where man presents an offering from what he has to God. Yet, at the same time, the slaughter of Agag is described in sacrificial language: he is cut into pieces לפני יהוה (1 Sam. 15.33). It does seem that there is a certain amount of ambiguity surrounding the notion of חרם as an offering in both Joshua 6 and 1 Samuel 15.

What still requires examination is that characteristic which seems to be a property of an object that is חרם, and its ability to affect whatever comes into contact with it so that it, in turn, becomes חרם.

h. חרם *as Taboo*

A. Malamat has tried to demonstrate the similarities of Joshua 6–7 to the command in the Mari texts not to take the *as-akku* of a god or a king on the penalty of a monetary fine.[1] He argues that both passages utilize the notion of a taboo on spoils of war which, he says, is originally imposed to prevent individual looting during a campaign, a problem that confronts the leaders of non-professional armies. Such an historical hypothesis is plausible but difficult to demonstrate. The value of Malamat's study is that it draws attention to the fact that booty could be dedicated to a god and that there are sanctions against removing it. In this regard, the Mari text is similar to Joshua 6.

The idea that all the property of an idolator is contaminated and must be destroyed, which is evident in the rules for the destruction of the apostate city in Deuteronomy 13 and in the destruction of Achan in Joshua 7, is not evident in Joshua 6. Here, some of the property is not contaminated as it can be given to the Lord, and it is brought into his house. All the silver, gold and other precious metals are to be

support of this reading, cf. Dekkers, 'Der Kriegsherem', pp. 138-45.

1.   A. Malamat, 'The Ban in Mari and in the Bible', *Mari and the Bible: A Collection of Studies* (Jerusalem: Hebrew University Press, 1975), pp. 52-61.

brought into the temple because קדש הוא ליהוה (6.19). Therefore, there
is a contrast between קדש and חרם. What is holy becomes חרם when
handled incorrectly.

According to one idea of holiness in the Hebrew Bible, the holy is
charged with a mysterious physical power (e.g. Exod. 29.37; 30.39),
and, when approached irreverently or misused, it can have disastrous
consequences (e.g. Num. 19.1-10). Thus, the idea of something
becoming חרם coincides with such a thought complex.[1] At the same
time, it needs to be recognized that more is involved. What makes
something חרם is not some idea of 'primitive taboo' but the fact that
the act of possession is an act of disobedience. This appears to be the
fundamental understanding of חרם in the account of the conquest of
Jericho.

Therefore, when Josh. 6.18 states that the 'camp of Israel' will
become חרם as a consequence of taking forbidden goods, the primary
meaning is not that the camp is contaminated, but that Israel is being
punished.

i. חרם *as Punishment*

Undoubtedly, there is a connection in the annals between the severity
of the destruction and the extent of the crime, particularly the crime
of rebellion. In Deuteronomy, one of the reasons for the conquest of
Canaan is the wickedness of the residents (Deut. 9.5).[2] The prophetic
writings also make it clear that the Lord can use war to punish a
nation.[3] The accounts of the destruction of Sihon and Og in
Transjordan suggest that they are punished as aggressors. The
Amalekites' reputation for aggression (Deut. 25.19), and the fact that,
apart from Jericho, the only cities in Joshua whose destruction is
emphasized are those who took aggressive action against Israel (Ai
and Hazor), suggest the notion of punishment. Finally, the accounts of
חרם being employed against Israel always contain the notion of
punishment (Deut. 13.16, 18; Josh. 7; Judg. 21.11).

Yet ch. 6 carries no hint of this in the case of Jericho. While the
account in 24.11 records Jericho coming out to attack Israel, ch. 6

1. Cf. N.H. Snaith, *Distinctive Ideas of the Old Testament* (London: Epworth,
1945), pp. 21-50, on the integral relationship between the two concepts.
2. Cf. Gen. 15.16; Lev. 18.24; Deut. 12.29-31.
3. R.M. Good, 'The Just War in Ancient Israel', *JBL* 104 (1985), pp. 385-
400).

emphasizes that Jericho is destroyed simply as an act of obedience. Although the account does not mention a divine command, and the decision appears to be taken on Joshua's initiative, later it is expressly stated that the command is from the Lord (10.40; 11.12). This is the understanding of the legislation in Deuteronomy as well as in much of the remaining DtrH: obedience and not punishment in the heat of the moment. The primaeval occupants of the land are to be exterminated because they are in the land that Israel must occupy, and because they are symbols of primordial evil.

While ch. 6 does not contain the idea that חרם is used against Jericho as punishment, there is no doubt that חרם is used as a punishment in the Achan story. It is so close to Joshua 6 that it must colour the understanding of the destruction of Jericho. Hypotheses like these have merit, but it can be asked whether the whole affair does not have a much simpler explanation.

j. חרם *for Dramatic Emphasis*

In a perceptive study of the battle of Gibeon in Josh. 10.1-11, E. Noort demonstrates how exaggeration is used for dramatic effect in the development of the story.[1] Both forces in the conflict are presented in dimensions much larger than life, and the outcome of the battle is a total victory in which the enemy is completely annihilated. Therefore, it is possible to explain חרם in these terms as a dramatic element in the story of the conquest of Jericho.

This solution carries merit but does not explain all the functions of חרם, particularly why such an issue is made of the failure to destroy completely. There appears to be more than one level of meaning.

k. *Conclusions on the Function of* חרם *in Joshua 6*

As a result of this brief survey, I conclude that, while the idea of an offering is hinted at and there is possibly a notion of punishment, the primary functions of חרם in Joshua 6 are dramatic and as a test of obedience. Unlike Deuteronomy, the destruction of the nations is not justified as the destruction of a pernicious cult in Joshua 6. Even so, the destruction of the city occurs in the context of a detailed cultic ceremony, and the connection cannot be ignored. Furthermore, חרם

---

1.   E. Noort, 'Zwischen Mythos und Rationalität: Das Kriegshandeln Yhwhs in Josua 10.1-11', in H.H. Schmid (ed.), *Mythos und Rationalität* (Gütersloh, 1988), pp. 149-61.

means much more than the outcome of a battle. Within an individual story of a battle it is simply a descriptive element. However, the technical connotations of the word signify another dimension to the story. Crucial as it might be, חרם is not the only word for destruction in Joshua 6.

1. Further Language of Destruction in Joshua 6

The command is to engage in חרם against the city. The details of how this is to be operationalized are then disclosed. All the animals are 'put to the sword' (6.21).[1] The city is then burned, a fate which also befalls Ai (8.8) and Hazor (11.11, 13). Although burning a conquered city is well attested in the literature and archaeological remains of the ancient Near East,[2] it is likely that, to some extent, the meaning of the burning of Jericho needs to be analysed in association with the account of the destruction of Achan which follows, and which includes the use of fire to destroy what is contaminated. While it is true that חרם is a technical term for the most radical form of destroying a foreign cult,[3] this use is absent here. The act is not explained as being necessary because of a cultically contaminated city. It is simply an act of obedience.

Finally, a solemn curse is uttered by Joshua: anyone rebuilding the city is ארור לפני יהוה. This wording makes YHWH the effective agent of the curse,[4] an interpretation which is confirmed by the fact that, in the wider DtrH, Josh. 6.26 functions as a prophecy of events recorded in 1 Kgs 16.34. This curse on a city, not unknown in the ancient Near East, is virtually unique in the Hebrew Bible. The only parallel is the salting of Shechem (Judg. 9.45). Both ceremonies appear in ancient Near Eastern literature as acts of consecration to a deity.[5]

In the context of the chapter, the curse on the future rebuilder

---

1.   The expression לפי־חרב appears regularly in association with חרם, Deut. 13.16 × 2; 20.13; Josh. 6.21; 10.28, 35, 37, 39; 11.11; 1 Sam. 15.8. The relationship to חרם is also established through assonance (Lohfink, *ThWAT*, III, p. 196).

2.   P.D. Miller, 'Fire in the Mythology of Canaan and Israel', *CBQ* 27 (1965), pp. 256-61.

3.   Hoffman, *Reform und Reformen*, pp. 225, 345.

4.   W. Schottroff, *Der altisraelitische Fluchspruch* (WMANT, 30; Neukirchen–Vluyn: Neukirchener, 1969), p. 52.

5.   Gervitz, 'Jericho and Shechem', pp. 52-62.

emphasizes חרם, giving it a permanent character. This appears to be the sense in Deut. 13.17 where, after חרם has been exercised against the apostate city, it is declared תל עולם. The link between חרם and the destruction of a city appears again in Josh. 8.28, in which Ai is ruined and deserted, and in 11.13, in which Hazor is ruined. Heaps of stones, as reminders of the past, are said to remain עד היום הזה:

7.26	stones heaped over Achan
8.28	Ai is a heap of ruins
8.29	stones heaped over the King of Ai
10.27	stones sealing off the caves where the five kings are buried.

Thus, the destruction is presented as having a lasting effect. The two concepts, חרם and curse, seem to have an integral connection, even though the only clear textual indication lies in Jer. 48.10, in which the curse is part of holy war.[1]

In a study of the language used to describe the destruction of undesirable entities in the Hebrew Bible and in ancient Near Eastern literature generally, C.T. Begg notes how acts of destruction are accumulated although their fulfilment on a single object is a practical impossibility.[2] He concludes that there are fixed formulations concerning destruction which are accumulated in order to emphasize the thoroughness of the destruction. These accounts often form the climax of the story.

The combined use of all this language in Joshua 6 serves to make a very strong statement about the destruction of the city. This destruction is paralleled simultaneously with the description of the survival of Rahab. The two contrasting elements are intertwined.[3]

Although Rahab and her family are set outside the camp of Israel (6.23), there is no sense in which they are a threat. The danger to Israel's existence lies within the camp. The story of Achan that follows does not say anything directly about the nations. However, it does provide a contrast to the story of Rahab and, at the same time, expands the understanding of חרם in Joshua.

1. Schottroff, *Der altisraelitische Fluchspruch*, pp. 211-17.
2. C.T. Begg, 'The Destruction of the Calf (Exod. 32, 20/Deut. 9, 21)', in N. Lohfink (ed.), *Das Deuteronomium: Entstehung, Gestalt und Botschaft* (BETL, 68; Leuven: University Press/Peeters, 1985), pp. 208-51.
3. Cf. below, Chapter 8.

3. The Achan Story (7.1-26)

a. *Divine Anger*

The audience is provided with information not available to the actors. This heightens the sense of drama because it introduces an atmosphere of foreboding. The Lord is angry with Israel because there has been a breach in the instructions regarding חרם (7.1).[1] For the first time in the book, there appears a pattern which is familiar in the DtrH: Israel provokes the Lord—divine anger: divine punishment.[2] Tension mounts as the audience awaits the inevitable outcome. Joshua, in the mean time, is unaware of all of this as he prepares to conquer Ai.

b. *A First Attack on Ai*

The spies who are sent out report that only a portion of the army is required to ensure victory.[3] The emphasis on the smallness of Israel's army usually demonstrates that the victory is from the Lord.[4] However, instead of the expected outcome, a convincing defeat occurs. This is all the more shocking after the complete victory at Jericho.[5] The limited force sent is not to be perceived as a tactical error that gives rise to the defeat. Defeat is inevitable, and it is through this defeat that the Lord reveals his anger. Serious soul searching follows a defeat.[6] This is a natural consequence to the common belief that the

---

1.　There is assonance between the anger formula, ויחר־אף יהוה, and חרם, cf. also Deut. 7.4; 13.18.

2.　Cf. D.J. McCarthy, 'The Wrath of Yahweh and the Structural Unity of the Deuteronomistic History', in J.L. Crenshaw and J.T. Willis (eds.), *Essays in Old Testament Ethics. J. Philip Hyatt, In Memorium* (New York: KTAV Publishing House, 1974), pp. 99-110. He notes how the theme of divine anger appears at key points, serving to reinforce the thrust of the narrative.

3.　The activity of the spies establishes a parallel between the Jericho and Ai stories, cf. M. Noth, 'Bethel und Ai', *PJ* 31 (1935), pp. 7-29, and M. Noth, *Aufsätze zur biblischen Landes- und Alterumskunde, vol. 1* (ed. H.W. Wolff; Neukirchen–Vluyn: Neukirchener, 1971), pp. 210-28 (226).

4.　Cf. particularly Gideon's army in Judg. 7.

5.　The irony of the defeat is that the small number of the enemy is stressed (7.3). Usually, it is the enemy's heart which melts (2.11; 5.1); however, in this instance, it applies to Israel (7.5). 'This vividly expresses the fact that Israel has become the enemy rather than the people of God' (Butler, *Joshua*, p. 84).

6.　Cf. J.A. Soggin, 'The Prophets on Holy War as Judgement against Israel',

Lord decides the outcome of a battle, and that he can use warfare to punish his disobedient people. This is consistent with the account of Joshua humiliating himself (7.6). A twist in the tale occurs when Joshua makes a statement expressing a desire to reverse the process of conquest. He employs language that is almost identical to the faithless response of the people to the spies' report in Deut. 1.27:

> Alas, O Lord God, why have you brought this people over the Jordan at all, to give us into the hands of the Amorites, to destroy us. Would that we had been content to dwell beyond the Jordan (7.7).

Joshua's complaint draws YHWH into a legal case in which, as a covenant partner, he has to prove his innocence.[1] The Lord's response is to explain the cause of the disaster, and to outline the route to divine blessing.

c. *Israel's Guilt*

The gravity of the crime of taking from what is חרם is demonstrated by being paralleled in five other charges:

> Israel has sinned;[2] they have transgressed my covenant which I commanded them; they have taken some of the devoted things; they have stolen, and lied, and put them among their own possessions (7.11).

This duplication of charges appears again in 7.15 in which the one who has taken from the devoted things is said to have transgressed the covenant and to have done a shameful thing in Israel (עשה נבלה בישראל).[3] The focus is on one particular crime, which is described in such a way as to demonstrate its gravity. At the same time, it is drawn

---

in *idem*, *Old Testament and Oriental Studies* (BibOr, 29; Rome: Biblical Institute Press, 1975), pp. 67-71.

1. For this interpretation of the text cf. G.C. Macholz, 'Gerichtsdoxologie und israelitisches Rechtsverfahren', *DBAT* 9 (1975), pp. 52-69. It is also possible to understand 7.6-9 as a 'Klagegebet' from the exilic period, cf. T. Veijola, 'Das Klagegebet in Literatur und Leben der Exilsgeneration am Beispiel einiger Prosatexte' in J.A. Emerton (ed.), *Congress Volume Salamanca 1983* (VTS, 36; Leiden: Brill, 1985), pp. 286-307 (299-305).

2. In 7.20, Achan admits to having sinned against the Lord, the God of Israel. In both instances, the verb חטא is employed.

3. At best, נבלה means a stupid action; at worst, it is something scandalous which threatens the fabric of society and endangers the whole community (Gen. 34.2; Deut. 22.21; Judg. 19.23; 20. 6-10; 2 Sam. 13.12; Jer. 29.23). For a fuller discussion, cf. Brekelmans, *De Herem*, p. 96.

into a broader field of meaning by being described as a breach of the covenant, עבר ברית יהוה (7.11, 15). The formula ברית יהוה describes the complete relationship between the Lord and Israel and, even when employed in the sense of a set of laws, it always implies the relationship between the Lord and his people Israel, a covenant being formed with the people as a whole.

The crime that is most often described as forsaking the covenant in Deuteronomy and the DtrH is that of seeking other gods (Deut. 17.3; 29.24; 31.20; Josh. 23.16; Judg. 2.19 f.; 1 Kgs 11.10 f.; 2 Kgs 17.35, 37f.; cf. Jer. 11.10; 22.9).[1] In this text (Josh. 7.11, 15) the act of removing items that are declared חרם is to break the covenant. As has been noted earlier, one has to wait for ch. 23 to be warned of the danger of foreign gods. This omission is all the more noticeable in relation to 23.16 which uses almost identical language to that in 7.11, עברו את־בריתי אשר צויתי. The presence of the idea of covenant raises the possibility of viewing the subsequent punishment as a covenant curse.[2] The consequence of taking from what is forbidden is that one becomes oneself חרם, a thing for destruction. The idea does not seem necessarily to be one of contamination because, throughout the encounter, the Lord is the one who decides what is to be destroyed. Thus the state of חרם in ch. 7 is more like a juridical decision.

d. *The Solution*
The solution is to eliminate the cause of the trouble; namely, החרם מקרבכם (7.12, 13 × 2).[3] The verbs used are השמיד (7.12) and הסיר (7.13). Both are exceptionally strong expressions of rejection. In Joshua, השמיד relates to the complete destruction of the inhabitants of

---

1. Contexts which describe Israel's going after other gods often include the anger formula. The only occasion in Joshua is in 23.16, but elsewhere in Deut. 6.12-14; 7.4; 11.16; 29.24-27; 31.16-17; Judg. 2.19-20; 3.7-8; 10.6-7; 2 Kgs 17.15-18, etc.

2. Butler, *Joshua*, p. 73, entitles his discussion of 7.1–8.29 'Consequence of Covenant Curse'.

3. The language and the concept are similar to the command in Deuteronomy ובער הרע מקרבך (e.g. 13.6; 17.7, 12; 21.21; 22.21, 24; cf. also 1 Kgs 14.10; 16.3; 21.21). Usually 'in the midst of' is used of the whole community of Israel. The concern is to preserve the integrity of the community by ensuring that the evil is thoroughly removed. For a fuller discussion, cf. the excursus in Rose, *Der Ausschliesslichkeitsanspruch Jahwes*, pp. 33-38.

the land (9.24; 11.14, 20) and of those in Transjordan (24.8),[1] and of what will happen to the Israelites if they should pursue other gods (23.15 f.).[2] The other verb הסיר is used of the complete removal of foreign gods (24.14, 23) and of Joshua not deviating from the commands of the Lords (11.15).[3] Both words have associations with the language of cultic reform.[4] The plural personal object that השמיד usually carries is viewed by B.J. Alfrink as an indication that החרם to be destroyed in 7.12b is the remnant of a version of the story which concerns a particular group of Israelites being guilty of the crime.[5] The evidence for this is slight, and החרם is used throughout this story to refer to the forbidden objects themselves (7.11, 12b, 13ab, 15). The only exception is 7.12a where Israel's military defeat is explained on the ground that the children of Israel היו לחרם. The curious fact is that Achan himself is not described as having become חרם.[6] Equally puzzling is the use of the plural in 7.11-13 which finds all Israel as being guilty of the crime. Either we have a version of a story in which *all* the people helped themselves to the forbidden goods, or the narrator has chosen a particularly vivid manner to illustrate Israel's corporate guilt for the crime of an individual.[7] The latter seems prob-

1. Cf. Deut. 2.12, 21, 22, 23; 7.23, 24, etc.

2. Cf. Deut. 4.26; 6.15; 7.4 etc. Later in the DtrH, it is used of the destruction of certain dynasties, 1 Kgs 13.34; 15.29; 16.12; 2 Kgs 10.17.

3. In its use in Deut., and the rest of the DtrH, it describes the act of removing something and not necessarily an act of physical destruction. In the cult reform texts סור (hiph) is characteristic, cf. Judg. 10.6; 2 Sam. 28.3; 1 Kgs 15.12, 13; 2 Kgs 3.2; 18.4, 22; 23.19.

4. Hoffman, *Reform und Reformen*, pp. 347-48.

5. B.J. Alfrink, 'Die Achan-Erzählung (Jos. 7)', in A. Metzinger (ed.), *Miscellanea Biblica et Orientalia. R.P. Athanasio Miller O.S.B. Completis LXX Annis Oblata* (StAns; Rome, 1951), pp. 114-29.

6. However, this is consistent with ch. 6 where the *camp* of Israel is said to become חרם if any of the חרם is taken (6.18).

7. One way of understanding this is through the idea of 'a corporate personality', cf. H.W. Robinson, *Corporate Personality in Ancient Israel* (Edinburgh: T. & T. Clark, rev. edn, 1981), pp. 1-20. However, J.R. Porter, 'The Legal Aspects of the Concept of "Corporate Personality" in the Old Testament', *VT* 15 (1965), pp. 361-80, demonstrates that the guilt resides with a single individual, as is the case with Old Testament law in general, even though all suffer as a result. The overall impression of the story, with its resolution in the death of Achan, does support this notion; nevertheless, the use of the plural in 7.11-12 does seem to include Israel in the actual guilt. This idea of corporate guilt should not come as a surprise, given the

able, as the editor does not suppress the paradox in the introduction to the story in which Israel is said to have broken faith with the Lord בחרם, *and* that Achan took מן־החרם (7.1). The disaster to the community is explained and a way forward is presented as the narrative progresses.

The Lord says to Joshua, 'Arise, sanctify the people, and say, "Sanctify yourselves for tomorrow" ' (7.13a). This procedure is a preparation for a theophany (e.g. Exod. 19.10, 14).[1] This can include a physical washing of people and clothing as well as the abstention from sexual contact (Exod. 19.10 ff.; Lev. 15.19 ff.). It can also involve the removal of cultically offensive objects (Gen. 35.1-4). While it is possible that התקדשו in 7.13 is meant to be understood as removing החרם,[2] the procedure is presented as a preparation for the following day when this will take place. The time delay creates suspense and reveals how the Lord is in control of the situation.

The attention of the audience is ensured as the awesome and terrifying account of the discovery of the offender is narrated.[3] When it is disclosed that Achan is the guilty party, Joshua calls on him to give glory (כבוד) and praise (תודה) to the Lord and thereby eliminate the past deed.[4] Achan explains how he took the forbidden goods (7.21):

> When I saw among the spoil a beautiful mantle from Shinar, and two hundred shekels of silver, and a bar of gold weighing fifty shekels, then I coveted them, and took them; and behold they are hidden in the earth inside my tent, with the silver underneath.

If these goods are related to the instructions in ch. 6 then it does seem that they would be understood as those things that are reserved for the Lord's temple (6.19, 24), even though the beautiful mantle from

---

context of covenant breaking where the curse affects the whole community, cf. J. Scharbert, *Solidarität in Segen und Fluch im Alten Testament und in seiner Umwelt. I. Väterfluch und Vätersegen* (BBB, 14; Bonn: Peter Hanstein, 1958).

1. Cf. Müller, 'קדש', pp. 590-610 (605).

2. Alfrink, 'Die Achan-Erzählung', p. 121.

3. The procedure is not explained, but it can be assumed that it occurs by sacred lot, cf. 1 Sam. 10.20-21; 14.42.

4. Usually appearing in cultic context, תודה, may be used by the guilty party to acknowledge and praise the correctness of God's judgement, for example, Ps. 26.7; Ezra 10.11; cf. H.-J. Hermisson, *Sprache und Ritus im Altisraelitischen Kult zur 'Spiritualisierung' der Kultbegriffe im Alten Testament* (WMANT, 19; Neukirchen–Vluyn: Neukirchener, 1965), esp. pp. 39-42 which refers to Josh. 7.

Shinar does not strictly fall into the category of metals. Again, in this instance, there are no obvious associations of the goods with a foreign cult. The beautiful mantle merely shows that they are understood as valuable. It is worth noting that until this juncture the forbidden goods are referred to as החרם, and now whenever they are mentioned it is as the silver, gold and the mantle (7.21, 22, 23, 24). This would hardly be significant were it not for the fact that they are laid before the Lord in 7.23. There are two possibilities of what becomes them: according to the MT they are destroyed along with Achan and all his possessions, but according to the LXX there is no mention of their destruction. Even if this second reading is not adopted the story suggests that the goods are only objectionable when used illegitimately. Another noteworthy feature of the description of the forbidden goods is that Achan says that he saw them בשלל. This clever use of language is an attempt on his part at legitimizing his action because throughout the rest of the book שלל is used in the sense of legitimate booty.[1] Be that as it may, we must return to the story.

Joshua sends messengers running to the tent (7.22).[2] They discover everything as it has been described. Then they convey the goods to Joshua where they are laid before the Lord, ויצקם לפני יהוה (7.23), possibly as an act of consecration.[3] The main concern of the story is however elsewhere: the destruction of Achan.

e. *The Punishment*
Then Joshua and 'all Israel' *take* Achan to the valley of Achor.[4] 'The silver and the mantle and the bar of gold (according to MT), and his

1.   Alternatively, the account of the destruction of an apostate city in Deut. 13.12-18 demonstrates that both החרם and שלל are to be destroyed and there is no significant distinction.

2.   LXX adds 'into the camp' which reminds of the whole community being polluted, cf. 6.18 where the camp is said to become חרם.

3.   Note that יצק is not a technical cultic term, cf. 2 Kgs 4.5.

4.   The verb לקח is repeated throughout the story and functions as part of a somewhat ironical compositional structure:

    7.1   Achan takes
    7.11   Israel takes
    7.21   Achan takes
    7.23   messengers take
    7.24   Joshua and all Israel take Achan.

sons and daughters, and his oxen and asses and sheep, and his tent, and all that he had' goes with him. The idea seems to be that everything close to him is contaminated and needs to be destroyed. The systematic listing of everything serves to show the completeness of the destruction.

In an aside, Joshua sums up the judgment by a word-play on עכר. This word rarely occurs. It denotes an act that seriously threatens the continued existence of a community.[1] Just as Achan brought trouble on Israel, so the Lord will bring trouble on him (7.25). Undoubtedly, there is also a play on Achan's name which sounds and looks familiar.[2] The name of the valley where he is destroyed is repetitive and a little confusing, but there is no question that the job has been thoroughly accomplished. Although חרם does not appear in the account of the destruction, the concept is present.

The question of the destruction of Achan's family has been reviewed by G.R. Driver.[3] He demonstrates that different verbs are used of the stoning. In the singular רגם is usually employed in cases where the affront is a direct offence to God, and סקל in the plural is regularly used of less serious crimes where the stoning is intended to drive the person out of the community. He says that a distinction in the treatment meted out to Achan on the one hand, and to his family on the other, is confirmed by 22.20b. Rather than give the customary translation, 'And he [Achan] did not perish alone for his iniquity', Driver's version reads, 'And he perished only for his iniquity.' This

---

1.   The fairly restricted range of meaning is soon evident:

Gen. 34.30: Jacob says that his sons have brought *trouble* on the family from the inhabitants of the land who will destroy them.

Josh. 6.18: The *trouble* is parallel to the camp of Israel becoming חרם.

Judg. 11.35: The *trouble* caused by Jephtah's daughter when she meets him after he has made a vow to offer as a human sacrifice the first person to meet him on his arrival home.

1 Sam. 14.29: Jonathan says that Saul has caused *trouble* by placing an oath with a curse of death on anyone who eats before the end of the battle.

1 Kgs 18.17, 18: Ahab and Elijah consecutively call each other *troublers* of Israel.

1 Chr. 2.7 reminds the reader of Achar, the *troubler* of Israel, who transgressed in the matter of the חרם.

Prov. 11.29; 15.27 of an individual bringing *trouble* on his family, and 11.17, the only instance not applying to a community, of an individual bringing *trouble* on himself.

2.   LXX calls him Αχαρ and the Peshitta, *'akar*, and in 1 Chron. 2.7 his name is עכר.

3.   G.R. Driver, 'Affirmation by Exclamatory Negation', *Journal of the Ancient Near Eastern Society of Columbia University* 5 (1973), pp. 107-13.

makes use of the grammatical possibility of affirmation by exclamatory negation. While this is a possible hypothesis, the argument appears somewhat contrived. If any contrast is present in 22.20, it should appear between Achan and all the congregation of Israel, who are described as having been under the wrath of God because of Achan. Furthermore, סקל does not always have mild connotations. It can feature in instances of the most wicked apostasy, for example, in violating the sacred mountain (Exod. 19.12-13), worshipping false gods (Deut. 13.10; 17.5-7) and blasphemy (2 Kgs 21.9-15). Finally, its use in the plural does not necessarily imply a reference to his family as distinct from Achan. As has been observed earlier, there is a tendency to heap up the epithets in accounts of destruction. There is therefore no compelling reason for viewing רגם and סקל as anything other than parallel.

An explanation for the destruction of Achan's family together with Achan has been sought in the notion of corporate personality. This has been contested by J.R. Porter who suggests that a more plausible explanation concerns the idea of holiness, 'a mysterious, quasi physical force', which affects everything with which it comes into contact. There are dire consequences when this contact is illegitimate. Therefore, the presence of holy objects in the household of Achan would have affected all of the household.[1]

Porter proposes other possible explanations in which a man could be understood as the owner of the family, or where the destruction of all is applicable in cases of exceptional crimes. A further suggestion relates to the idea of the solidarity of the family in the instance of a curse.[2] The several layers of meaning in the story produce several explanations. However, the most likely explanation resides elsewhere.

If the account is related to the wider context of the conquest of the nations, then Achan's family receives exactly the same treatment as the doomed cities of the land. The battle reports contain a catalogue of the destruction of women and children. The similarity between the treatment consigned to apostate Israelites and the nations is focused in the contrast between the treatment given to Rahab the Canaanite and Achan the Israelite.

Even though accounts of destroying the nations can be very brutal, they cannot match those describing the treatment of fellow Israelites.

1. Porter, ' "Corporate Personity" in the Old Testament', esp. p. 369.
2. For this interpretation of Josh. 7. cf. Scharbert, *Solidarität*, pp. 115-19.

The closest comparison to the Achan story is to be found in the regulations concerning the destruction of an apostate city in Deuteronomy 13.

f. A Comparison with Deuteronomy 13.13-19
The prominence given to this catalogue of destruction is without parallel in the Hebrew Bible. After ascertaining that the inhabitants are guilty of having pursued other gods, the sentence is pronounced in detail:

> You shall surely put the inhabitants of that city to the sword, destroying it utterly, all who are in it and all its cattle, with the edge of the sword. You shall gather all its spoil into the midst of its open square, and burn the city and all its spoil with fire, as a whole burnt offering to the Lord your God, it shall be a heap forever, it shall not be built again. None of the devoted things shall cleave to your hand; that the Lord may turn from the fierceness of his anger. . .

In both Deuteronomy 13 and Joshua 7 חרם is employed against fellow Israelites with a severity and thoroughness unparalleled in the accounts of it being used against the nations. The repetition of all that is to be destroyed emphasizes the severity of the punishment and the extent of the abhorrence. In Deuteronomy 13 the crime is that of worshipping foreign gods and the destruction could be compared to the accounts elsewhere in Deuteronomy of the destruction of forbidden cult objects.[1] It is noteworthy that the Achan story contains no references of this; it is primarily a case of disobedience. In both Deuteronomy and Joshua, warfare involving חרם is reserved for a particular class of enemy. In the instance of the apostate Israelites in Deuteronomy 13, the Lord wages war against them. In Joshua 7 the Lord wages war against all Israel (7.12), as well as against Achan. Both narratives of apostasy (Deut. 13 and Josh. 7) have their logical conclusion in the statement that the Lord turns from his fierce anger (Deut. 13.17; Josh. 7.26).

Achan is punished for disobedience. The extent of the destruction is an expression of abhorrence for apostasy and thereby places Israel in

---

1. The act of apostasy is described as תועבה (Deut. 13.15) which is used when speaking of the things that the Lord particularly hates. In particular, this applies to the cult of the nations in the land (e.g. Deut. 18.9, 12). The term can be used in parallel to החרם (Deut. 7.26). Further, on תועבה, cf. Hoffman, *Reform und Reformen*, p. 359; Bächli, *Israel und die Völker*, pp. 53-55.

the same category as the nations. The theological schema underwriting
the story is that of disobedience: national disaster: removal of the
cause of the the punishment: divine favour on the nation. Therefore,
the disaster is explained, and a way forward presented.[1]

4. *The Second Attack on Ai (8.1-29)*

A second attack on Ai is launched. The strategy presents a limited
force making an apparent attack on the city. They pretend to flee
thereby enticing the defenders of the city to pursue them. This leads
the pursuers into an awaiting ambush.[2] Meanwhile, another group of
Israelites has entered the city and set it ablaze. There is a great
slaughter.

There are noticeable parallels to the abortive attack on Ai, particularly by means of a play on the concept of flight. A factor in Israel's
earlier humiliation is that of turning their backs and fleeing before the
men of Ai (7.4). Here Israel's pretence at fleeing is described in elaborate detail (8.5, 6 × 2, 15).[3] The similarity to the first attack is not
obscured. The people of Ai are portrayed as saying, 'They are fleeing
from us, as before' (8.6).[4] The moment of truth dawns, and those who
are fleeing turn around and confront their pursuers who now have
nowhere to flee (8.20). The irony is also evident in the fact that while
not a remnant of those who attack Israel is left in the city (8.17), so no
remnant is left after the slaughter (8.22).

In contrast to the former battle, this battle is preceded by the divine
command to attack and destroy the city, along with the statement not
to fear because the city has been given into their hand (8.1, 18). If one
considers the two accounts (omitting the Achan story), then their main
point is to illustrate the relationship between obedience and success.

1.   On the significance of this for an exilic or post-exilic community cf. Butler,
Joshua, p. 88.

2.   For a remarkably similar story, cf. Judg. 20.30-46.

3.   In the battle reports, as is the case here, the expression is normally, וינסו לפני,
followed by the name of the victor. It is one of the ways of describing the
completeness and the humiliation of the defeat.

4.   Z. Zevit, 'Archaeological and Literary Stratigraphy in Joshua 7–8', *BASOR*
251 (1983), pp. 23-35, is surely correct in pointing out that ambush and feigned
retreat are part of ancient military practice. However, this does not explain why the
second attack on Ai is described in this way: the careful literary formulation makes it
more than the coincidence of a preserved tradition.

This lesson is further emphasized by the interweaving of the Achan story into the two battles. Therefore, it is abundantly clear that the first defeat is the consequence of disobedience.

The second battle assumes greater status by the portrayal of the size of the enemy. In the first account, they are considered small enough for the deployment of an Israeli force of only two or three thousand (7.3-4); while, in the second account, the large numbers of Israelites are mentioned. The ambush group alone consists of thirty thousand (8.3), and the slaughtered inhabitants number twelve thousand (8.25). The account of the complete eradication of the inhabitants, the burning and reduction of the city to a heap of rubble, the humiliating death of its king and the heap of stones raised over his corpse are all features of battle reports elsewhere in Joshua. Another feature common to many battle reports is the mention of booty. Before enquiring into the particular function of this in the conquest of Ai, we need to examine the general employment of the booty motif.

5. The Issue of Booty

In the context, booty taking is an economic reality in Israel and amongst her neighbours. It is part of an economic system which enables a king to pay for his military escapades, his bureaucracy, his building projects, and to honour his gods with gifts.[1] This economic import requires meticulous recording practices, and every detail is reported to the king.[2] Apart from their practical value, the booty lists also serve to emphasize the grandeur of a particular victory and, by implication, the status of the king and the national gods. An illustration of the ideological function of the booty report is that when earlier inscriptions are used as a source for later compositions, the figures relating to booty, numbers of enemy taken and cities conquered are increased in subsequent editions.[3] The literary function of booty is

1.   Elat, 'The Impact of Tribute and Booty', pp. 224-51.
2.   For details of the quantities of booty and surrender tribute, cf. the tables in M. Elat, *Economic Relations in the Lands of the Bible (c. 1000–539 BC)*, (Jerusalem, 1977), pp. 23, 24, 30, 50.
3.   Grayson, 'Assyria and Babylonia', pp. 167-68. An example is Sargon's letter concerning the booty of Musasir which includes 1,235 sheep in the early version (D.D. Luckenbill, *Ancient Records of Assyria and Babylonia* [Chicago: University of Chicago Press, 1926], I, p. 647), and 100,225 sheep in a later version

developed even further in Hebrew Bible narrative.

Although the booty issue leads to the first defeat in the land of the downfall of Israel's first king, there has been a dearth of scholastic interest in the literary function of 'booty'. Obviously it is not possible within the compass of this book to examine all the functions of booty taking in the Hebrew Bible. There is no reason to suppose that the Israelites did not practise booty taking in its wars as an accepted right of the conqueror. In their literature, the idea of gaining benefit from foreigners can be regarded as a positive merit. Booty is seen as a gift from God that is to be enjoyed (Deut. 20.14; Judg. 5.30; 1 Sam. 30.16; Isa. 9.2; Ps. 119.162). Nevertheless, booty is never the goal of victory but the consequence. In some battle reports it is simply a part of the story, usually helping to illustrate the significance of the victory (e.g. Judg. 8.24, 25; 2 Sam. 3.22; 12.30). However, it can also be turned against an apostate Israel and be the means of illustrating the horror of defeat at the hands of an avaricious enemy (e.g. Isa. 8.1-4).[1]

The most common words used for booty are שלל and בז.[2] Usually they are synonymous, and sometimes they appear together in parallel. In Deuteronomy and Joshua, and nowhere else in the DtrH, is שלל the object of בז, 'to take booty as spoil' (Deut. 2.35; 3.7; 20.14; Josh. 8.2, 27; 11.14).[3] These are all passages in which booty taking is legitimate, and the only such passage not employing this construction is Josh. 22.8, in which שלל appears on its own. The formula, וכל־הבהמה ושלל הערים תבזזו להם, is found in all these passages, although there are minor variations. This illustrates the use of שלל to describe inanimate movable objects as distinct from cattle. The distinction is evident in those texts which stress the destruction of everything and everyone. Thus, in Deut. 13.12-18, the spoil is to be gathered

---

(D.D. Luckenbill, *Ancient Records of Assyria and Babylonia* [Chicago: University of Chicago Press, 1927], II, p. 22).

1. Much of the rare scholarly discussion on the function of booty in the Hebrew Bible is found in commentary on this text, cf. E. Vogt, 'Einige hebräische Wortbedeutungen', *Bib.* 48 (1967), pp. 57-74 (63-69).

2. For a study of the usage, cf. H. Ringgren, בז, *ThWAT*, I, pp. 585-88; H. Stoebe, 'Raub und Beute', in *idem* (ed.), *Hebräische Wortforschung: Festschrift für Walter Baumgartner* (VTS, 16; Leiden: Brill, 1967), pp. 340-54.

3. The formula is found elsewhere in a completely different set of texts, 2 Chron. 20.25; 28.8; Esth. 3.13; 8.11. Stoebe, *Hebräische Wortforschung*, p. 352, tentatively raises the possibility of an ideological function for the formula in Deuteronomy–Joshua.

together and burnt along with the city, whereas all living things are 'put to the sword'. Likewise, in Joshua 6, the city is burnt and living things are 'put to the sword'.

There is no idea in the booty concept itself for people because all the inhabitants of the land are meant to be destroyed. An exception is Deut. 20.14, in which women and children from conquered cities *outside* the land are regarded as booty.[1] However, the broader meaning of שלל found in Deut. 20.14 is in deliberate contrast to the application חרם, the fate of the occupants of the land (20.16). Later in Joshua the nations remaining in the land are said to be enslaved. Therefore, they are an afterthought in the sense that their inclusion justifies their continued presence in the land. Nevertheless, they are never regarded as 'booty'.

Another feature of booty language in Deuteronomy and Joshua is that שלל is always part of a formula linking it to the enemy, whether together with the name of particular city or more generally as שלל העיר or שלל איביך.[2] This genitive construction makes the point that the spoil once belonged to someone else but now belongs to the victor.[3]

If the usage of שלל is traced through the DtrH, it is evident immediately that, apart from a few scattered occurrences, they are clustered at certain points.[4] In Deuteronomy and Joshua they occur at regular intervals, almost always together with חרם, as the following table of all the instances of חרם and שלל will indicate:

חרם		שלל	
Deut.	2.34	Deut.	2.35
	3.6 × 2		3.7
	7.2, 26 × 2		
	13.16, 18		13.7 × 2
	20.17		20.14 × 2
Josh.	2.10		
	6.17, 18 × 4, 21		
	7.1 × 2, 2, 11, 12, 13, 15	Josh.	7.21
			8.2

1. At a superficial level, this is the same as the understanding of *shallautu* in the Annals where it is employed of captive humans, animals and material objects, cf. Ringgren, 'בז', p. 586.

2. This is also found elsewhere, 2 Sam. 8.12; 12, 30, but these are also exceptions as שלל is not usually in the genetive.

3. Stoebe, *Hebräische Wortforschung*, p. 347.

4. בז only occurs in the rest of the DtrH in 1 Sam. 14.36 and 2 Kgs 7.16.

8.26	8.27
10.1, 28, 35, 37, 39, 40	
11.11, 12, 20, 21	11.14
	22.8
22.20	

The evidence demonstrates that whenever שלל appears it is in relation to חרם; the only exception is Josh. 22.8. However, this passage serves as a concluding statement to the conquest as a whole, and is therefore not really an exception.[1]

There are several references to שלל in the remainder of the DtrH. These usually occur in battle reports but are never related to חרם (Judg. 5.30 × 3; 8.24, 25; 2 Sam. 3.22; 8.12; 12.30; 2 Kgs 3.23). However, in 1 Samuel 14–15, together with one instance of בז, it occurs four times and is contrasted with חרם; and, finally, in 1 Samuel 30 it occurs six times in what appears to be a legitimization of the policy of a fair distribution of spoil.[2] While there is no trace of any notion of חרם in that passage, it is hardly insignificant that the enemy in question is the Amalekites!

Therefore, it does seem reasonable to conclude that the frequent correlation between שלל and חרם in the DtrH is noteworthy.[3] In the DtrH the notion of booty taking has a variety of functions, ranging from a joyously received gift of God to the worst possible crime. The booty reports are concentrated around the accounts of the destruction of the pre-Israelite nations and the Amalekites. Usually, these occur in theological interplay with חרם. The function of booty taking is particularly noticeable because not only does it link שלל to חרם, but it also uses the distinctive formula וכל־הבהמה ושלל הערים תבזזו להם.

The reference to booty can hardly go unnoticed because it is placed directly after the Achan story. It is emphasized by being included not only in the report of the outcome of the battle, as might be expected (8.27), but also in the initial command (8.2), which is very unusual. Furthermore, in both cases the contrast with the treatment of the

---

1. On the return of the Transjordanian tribes as a signal that the epoch of conquest is over, cf. below.

2. Stoebe, *Hebräische Wortforschung*, p. 343.

3. Other terminology for booty taking, שסה and שסס, is usually translated as 'plunder' (Judg. 2.14 × 2, 16; 1 Sam. 14.48; 17.53; 2 Kgs 17.20), with the possible exception of 1 Sam. 14.48, is not used in relation to חרם; cf. Richter, *Bearbeitungen*, pp. 29-30.

human is highlighted by being introduced with רק.[1] Yet, even with the divine mandate, the reader is unlikely to forget that the first example of booty taking in the book leads to a national disaster, or that the first to mention the word שלל is Achan.

6. Conclusion

I have undertaken an examination of sufficient battle language to enable me to comment on the heuristic value of comparisons with the campaign reports of the Assyrian annals together with the battle reports from elsewhere in the Hebrew Bible. The evidence suggests that although the battles in Joshua have elements in common with the others, here they are put to a particular usage.

The key concept in chs. 6 and 7 is חרם, which is first employed to describe the complete destruction of Jericho and its inhabitants. However, if it is read along with ch. 7, it serves as a test of obedience. No reason for the extent of the destruction is offered apart from the fact that it is commanded. In the story of Achan, a new aspect to the meaning of חרם emerges, in that the systematic destruction of Achan, his family and possessions suggests the idea of abhorrence and perhaps cultic contamination as well. When this is concatenated to the accounts of the destruction of the nations, an explanation for their fate surfaces.

The survival of Rahab and her family is not only in contrast to the destruction of Jericho but to the destruction of Achan, which appears in the following chapter. Another contrast is that directly after Achan has suffered the most severe punishment for taking booty, the Israelites are expressly told to do the very same thing. No attempt is endeavoured to lessen this contrast, rather the reverse is evident, and attention is drawn to it. The juxtaposition of חרם and שלל is evident elsewhere in the DtrH, particularly in 1 Samuel 15 where the interplay is also an essential element of the story.

If חרם, strengthened by the idea of destroying enemy property as a sign of rejection and abhorrence, is meant to advocate maintaining a social distance from foreigners, then the 'undermining' of this view, by means of contradiction, probably indicates a modification to the isolationist perspective. However, because חרם has more than one

---

1.   This technique is employed with a similar intent in Deut. 2.35 and 20.14.

function in the text, there has to be fluidity in explanation, and no single factor is adequate.

The fact remains that, for a moment during the stories of the defeat of the Israelites at Ai and the thorough destruction of Achan, Israel is treated no differently from the occupants of the land. In an oblique manner, this raises the status of the nations. This conclusion is unavoidable because of the symmetry between the narratives concerning Rahab the Canaanite and Achan the Israelite.

Chapter 3

'YOU SHALL DO TO THE CITY AND ITS KING AS YOU DID TO JERICHO AND ITS KING' (8.30–12.24)

1. *Introduction*

The second battle at Ai secures Israel's part once more in the divine plan to destroy the cities. However, the momentum is immediately slowed down by the accounts of the covenant on Mount Ebal and the intrigues of the Gibeonites in chs. 8 and 9. Then, in chs. 10–12, we are led from battle to battle without interruption.

The overriding concern of the narrative in chs. 8–12 is to demonstrate that Jericho marked the beginning of the thorough destruction of all the occupants of the land. The fate of cities and kings is central to the stories, and is also noticeable in the compositional structures.

2. *Compositional Structures Connecting the Battle Reports*

The formula 'and he did to city B and its king as he had done to city A and its king' serves to connect the accounts of slaughter and destruction by linking a battle to its predecessor.[1]

8.2   You shall do to Ai and its king as you did to Jericho and its king.
10.1   Doing to Ai and its king as he had done to Jericho and its king.
10.28 He did to Makkedah and its king as he had done to the king of Jericho.
10.29 He did to Libnah and its king as he had done to the king of Jericho.
10.32 Lachish. . . as he had done to Libnah.
10.35 Eglon. . . as he had done to Lachish.
10.37 Hebron. . . as he had done to Eglon.
10.39 Debir and its king. . . as he had done to Hebron and to Libnah and its king.

---

1.   The same structure is evident in the conquest of Transjordan:

Deut. 3.2: . . . you shall do to him (Og) as you did to Sihon the king of the Amorites.
Deut. 3.6: And we utterly destroyed them, as we did to Sihon the king of Heshbon.

The destruction of Jericho and its king serves as the major paradigm for the subsequent accounts. It is referred to in the first four instances of the formula.[1] Without exception, all these instances serve as a means of reinforcing the interest in the complete destruction of cities and their kings. Often they are situated in parallel to other language of destruction.

This organization of material can be related to the wider compositional structure, which introduces a battle story by describing the enemy hearing about the previous victory.[2] Therefore, after the momentum gained from the victory at Ai, one would expect the introduction of the next battle. However, the scene shifts to Mount Ebal.

3. *An Interlude on Mount Ebal (8.30-35)*

The narrative of conquest is interrupted by the story of a covenant ceremony on Mount Ebal.[3] The manner is unusual in that the account of the nations fearing when they hear of an Israelite victory (9.1-2) does not appear after the battle but after the ceremony. Another strange feature is the geographical setting in as yet unconquered territory at Shechem. The scene of the next story is back at Gilgal (9.6).

The mountain top location, the legal discourse and the sacrificial practices all focus attention on Israel's relationship to the Lord. The incident supplies the ground for the fear of the pre-Israelite monarchs, and the participation of the גרים in the congregation serves as a prelude to the ensuing story of the Gibeonites.[4]

---

1.   The expression 'Jericho and its king' does not appear in the actual account of the destruction in ch. 6 which does not mention a king at all. However, the king and his messengers are introduced as the opposition by the story of Rahab and the spies in ch. 2.

2.   Cf. below, Chapter 7.

3.   The Samaritan Pentateuch reads Gerizim. Polemic between Samaritans and Jews no doubt influenced the text tradition. Gerizim would make more sense as it is traditionally the place of blessing. For a fuller discussion, cf. H. Seebass, 'Gerizim und Ebal als Symbole von Segen und Fluch', *Bib* 63 (1982), pp. 22-31.

4.   Polzin, *Moses and the Deuteronomist*, pp. 116-17.

4. *A Covenant with the Gibeonites (9.1-27)*

The account of the kings hearing, fearing and gathering together to fight (9.1-2) is paralleled in the next verse (9.3) in which the inhabitants of Gibeon hear but respond with guile. The point of the deception is to impress upon the Israelites that they have come from 'far away':

9.6	מארץ רחוקה
9.9	מארץ רחוקה
9.13	מרב הדר מאד
9.22	רחוקים מאד

The legislation in Deut. 20.10-18 constitutes a definite distinction between the treatment given to nations that are far away from those residing in the land. The latter are consigned to חרם. This is the context of the intrigue. It is almost as though the Gibeonites have read the text in Deuteronomy in which the crucial distinction appears between הערים הרחקת ממך מאד and ערי הגוים־האלה (Deut. 20.15).[1] In Joshua 9 the same contrast is described as existing between אתם בקרבנו ישבים and רחוקים אנחנו מכם מאד (9.22).[2]

The appeal to allow them to survive (Josh. 9.15, 20, cf. 24) is also a reflection on this חרם legislation. The shock at discovering that Israel has made a covenant with the inhabitants of the land is even more understandable in the light of the command in Deut. 7.2 not to enter into any covenants with these people. While the explanation for the destruction of the inhabitants as a religious threat is absent in Joshua 9, it is possible that the Gibeonites' impeccable confession of faith is stimulated by this idea.[3]

On the one hand, a convincing argument could be presented that the story is an interpretation of the Deuteronomic חרם legislation.[4] On the

1.   In a subsequent chapter it will be shown that הגוים האלה is a technical term for the doomed occupants of the land.

2.   The reasons for the distinctive formulas in Joshua will be discussed in Chapter 8.

3.   Cf. particularly Exod. 34.11-17 and Deut. 7.1-5, in which the prohibition against forming covenants with the pre-Israelite nations is linked to intermarriage with them and worshipping their gods.

4.   C. Schäfer-Lichtenberger, 'Das gibeonitische Bündnis im Lichte deuteronomischer Kriegsgebote. Zum Verhältnis von Tradition und Interpretation in Jos. 9', *BN* 34 (1986), pp. 58-81.

other hand, it must be recognized that Joshua 9 is not unique in this regard, and that the idea of destroying all the inhabitants of the land is a central theme in Joshua as a whole, particularly in the immediate context of ch. 9. At the same time, one observes that the Gibeonites introduce the legislation with a clarity that has not appeared before. In this respect, they are similar to Rahab, who is the first to mention the word חרם. These notable exceptions remind the reader of the existence of the legislation.

It is evident that the covenant is established against the חרם legislation in Deuteronomy. This is explicit in Deut. 7.2, לא־תכרת להם ברית, and implied in Deut. 20.10-18. The latter instance permits a contrast between the treatment given to cities close at hand and those far away who are offered terms of peace, שלום.[1] The only way the Gibeonites have been able to avoid their fate is by deceitful conduct. The narrative continues with the accounts of destruction.

5. Destruction of the Southern Kings (10.1-43)

The story commences by employing the now familiar narrative device of depicting Adonizedek, king of Jerusalem, listening to an account of what has happened and being filled with fear. He responds by forming a coalition together with Hoham, king of Hebron; Piram, king of Jarmuth; Japhia, king of Lachish; and Debir, king of Eglon. Their magnitude is emphasized by a repetition of the list (10.3, 5). The group is called 'the five kings of the Amorites'.[2] In their terror, the Gibeonites exaggerate and claim that they are being attacked by 'all the kings of the Amorites that dwell in the hill country'. Israel intervenes with the assistance of YHWH, and there is a great slaughter of the enemy at Gibeon. The five kings are first imprisoned in the cave at Makkedah in which they have been hiding. Then they are hanged from five trees and their corpses are returned to the cave. There follows a stylized account of the destruction of the cities, some of which are identical to those of the five kings (10.28-39). Lachish,

---

1.   Elsewhere the prohibition against a covenant with occupants of the land: Exod. 23.32; Exod. 34.12, 15; Deut. 7.2 (list of pre-Israelite nations); Judg. 2.2. For discussion of these texts, cf. J. Halbe, *Das Privilegrecht Jahwes*, particularly pp. 230-55 on כרת ברית as 'obligation'.

2.   The 'five kings' is possibly a stereotype, cf. 'the five rulers of the Philistines' (13.3).

Eglon and Hebron are the same, while Debir is the name of a city and not king Debir of Eglon as in 10.3, 5.

The story set at Makkedah (10.16-27) is generally seen as being based on an aetiology of the burial place of the five kings.[1] This has been attached to the account of the battle at Gibeon by situating the five kings at the beginning of the account. The different locations do suggest different stories. However, the total destruction of the enemy is a perennial theme in Joshua, and legitimates the inevitable sequel concerning the kings hearing about what has happened to their neighbours. This suggests that the stories are best understood as a corpus.[2] Of particular interest is the manner in which the battle of Gibeon has been integrated with ch. 9.

a. *The Fear of the Kings (10.1-5)*

The prototype in 5.1, 9.1, 10.1 and 11.1 suggests that the kings are fearful because they hear about the awesome activity of the Lord and his people. In 10.1-2, an additional reason is offered. Their fear is compounded because of the covenant between Israel and the Gibeonites. Israel attacks the enemy as a loyal partner in the covenant. Nevertheless, once the battle commences, initiative is completely in Israel's hands, or, more accurately, under divine control.

b. *The Battle at Gibeon (10.6-15)*

The cause of the enemy's defeat is divinely inspired panic. The Lord instructs Israel not to be afraid because he has given the enemy into their hand (10.8). In 10.10, he throws them into panic before Israel. This function of המם is found in other battle reports which emphasize the Lord's intervention (cf. Exod. 14.24; 23.27; Judg. 4.15; 1 Sam. 7.10).[3] In the insertion of a poetic description of the Lord pelting the enemy with stones from heaven, the hailstones account for more deaths than the Israelite swords, according to the narrator (10.11). This demonstrates that YHWH is the victor.

The idea that gods unleash natural phenomena against their enemies

---

1. Cf. M. Noth, 'Die fünf Könige in der Höhle von Makkedah', *Aufsätze*, pp. 281-93.

2. Cf. Noort, *Mythos und Rationalität*, pp. 149-61, for a convincing argument that sources have been so thoroughly reworked that it is virtually impossible to extricate them.

3. Cf. Richter, *Untersuchungen*, pp. 52-53.

is not uncommon in the battle reports in the ancient Near East.[1] There are also examples of this in the first part of the DtrH, and David's battles against the Philistines provide the final examples.[2] G. von Rad has also shown that the concept of the 'Day of the Lord' in the prophetic literature draws together the idea of divine intervention through natural phenomena, and the complete annihilation of the enemy, on occasions, described as an act of חרם (cf. Isa. 34.2; Mic. 4.13).[3]

The centre of interest in our story is the act of God. This is further emphasized when Joshua, as the Lord's representative, commands the sun and the moon, perceived to be the gods by Israel's neighbours, to stand still (10.12). Time is halted in order to enable Israel 'to take vengeance on her enemies' (10.13). This is the only instance that נקם appears in Joshua. The word is employed of the legitimate vengeance performed by the highest authority, which means a king or God. The context is when the normal juridical institutions of society are ineffective.[4]

The enemy is in desperate flight. They are smitten by the Israelites as far as Azekah and Makkedah (10.10); and, while proceeding down Beth-horon, the Lord attacks them from heaven (10.11).[5] The story appears to be over when the Israelites return to their camp at Gilgal (10.15); however, the scene retrogresses in time and links what follows to the theme of flight.

c. *The Flight of the Kings (10.16-27)*
In the desperate flight the five kings hide away in a cave at Makkedah, a subterfuge that is discovered, and they find themselves sealed inside.

---

1. Cf. M. Weinfeld, ' "They fought from Heaven"—Divine Intervention in War in Ancient Israel and in the Ancient Near East', *ErIs* 47 (1978), pp. 23-30.

2. Richter, *Untersuchungen*, p. 53.

3. G. von Rad, 'The Origin of the Concept of the Day of Yahweh', *JSS* 4 (1959), pp. 97-108. He says that the concept originated in the tradition of the holy wars of YHWH, in which he appears personally to annihilate his enemies; and that the universal and even cosmic dimension to the events has been introduced in correspondence to a growing measure of political danger experienced by Israel.

4. G.E. Mendenhall, 'The "Vengeance of Yahweh" ', in *idem* (ed.), *The Tenth Generation: The Origins of the Biblical Tradition* (Baltimore/London: Johns Hopkins University Press, 1973), pp. 60-95.

5. Cf. J. Blenkinsopp, *Gibeon and Israel* (Cambridge: Cambridge University Press, 1972), p. 44, who states that two different routes are being described, which suggests multiple traditions.

There is no respite in the pace of the story, and once again the enemy is in disorderly flight (10.19). Joshua has urged that none be allowed to return to their cities and the slaughter is עד־תמם.[1] However, simultaneously a remnant manages to reach their fortified cities (10.20). This establishes a narrative link with 10.28-39, in which enemy cities are systematically and thoroughly destroyed, while, at the same time, increasing the impact of the story by means of a dramatic pause.

Once again the Israelites 'return to their camp', this time at Makkedah (10.21). This typical phrase, which often marks the conclusion of a battle, serves to shift the narrative back to the five kings who are once more listed by name. Their humiliation and slaughter is described in detail. They are brought out of the cave and Joshua instructs the people to place their feet on the necks of the enemy, which is a sign of triumph.[2] Then, in the midst of this occurrence, Joshua exhorts the people not be afraid because the Lord will accord the same treatment to all their enemies. Joshua smites them, and they are further humiliated by being hanged from five trees, the same fate as the king of Ai (8.29). At sundown their bodies are taken down and thrown into the cave 'where they had hidden themselves', a somewhat ironical observation. Great stones are set over the mouth of the cave which remain 'unto this day'.[3] The stones used are אבנים גדלות, which are the very objects used to pelt the fleeing Amorites in 10.11,[4] and not the regular גל־אבנים גדול used in burying the victims of חרם (7.26; 8.29).[5]

The narrative has moved backwards and forwards with a relentless persistence. In the end the enemy is destroyed, a message highlighted

1. Usually עד־תמם means that a particular action has been completed, cf. Deut. 31.24; 1 Kgs 8.54; 9.1.
2. Exod. 23.27; 2 Sam. 22.41; Isa. 51.23; Ps. 18.41. Cf. G. Schmuttermayr, *Psalm 18 und 2 Samuel 22: Studien zu einem Doppeltext* (StANT, 25; Munich: Kösel, 1971), p. 169.
3. Noth, 'Die fünf Könige', *Aufsätze*, pp. 282-83, states that there are two versions of the aetiology of the stones. The first has the kings sealed in the cave presumably dying of hunger (cf. 10.18), while the second has them killed first and the cave serves as a burial place.
4. Parallel to אבני הברד, hailstones.
5. Noort, *Mythos und Rationalität*, p. 159, who draws attention to the phenomenon, concludes that the use of אבנים גדלות in 10.11 and in 10.27 indicates a thoroughly integrated story.

by the clearly outlined stages in the process. The flight only increases the drama and draws attention to the inevitable conclusion. The destruction of the kings is finalized by the destruction of the cities.

d. *The Systematic Destruction of Cities and Kings (10.28-39)*

A carefully formulated schematic summary of the destruction of cities and kings is included in the narrative:[1]

a. Verbs of military activity (לחם × 4, לכד × 5) followed by the name of the city.

b. Verbs of slaughter (נכה לפי־חרב × 6, נכה × 1, חרם × 4).

c. Statement about the identity of the victims:

  i. The name of a city × 6, on two occasions supplemented by 'and all its towns'.

  ii. 'And its king' × 4, the kings of Lachish and Eglon not being mentioned presumably because they are in the cave at Makkedah; in addition Horam king of Gezer includes himself by coming to the aid of Lachish.

  iii. ואת־כל־הנפש אשר־בה × 7.

d. A statement of completeness (לא השאיר שריד × 6).

e. A statement that the city (and its king) have received the same treatment as the previous city (and its king).

f. Verbs of movement, at the end of one report and introducing the next (שוב, עלה, עבר × 3).

There is little doubt that the interest of these battle reports resides in the complete destruction of the enemy. At this juncture, the emphasis does not lie in the Lord's involvement or in the heroism of the battle, rather, the accounts of destruction are repeated and the same pattern is echoed with only minor variations in language.[2] The fate of Horam, king of Gezer, who assists Lachish, which is destroyed until nothing remains (10.33), is added to the tale of six destroyed cities.

---

1. For a table demonstrating which formulas are used in relation to each particular city, cf. B.J. Alfrink, *Het 'Stil Staan' van Zon en Maan in Jos. 10, 12-15* (StC, 24; Nijmegen, 1949), pp. 12-13.

2. R. Borger, *Einleitung in die Assyrischen Königsinschriften. I. (Das zweite Jahrtausend V. CHR)* (HO, 1; Leiden: Brill, 1961), p. 125, notices that the scribes of the annals who normally follow a set form occasionally vary the formulas in order to overcome monotonous repetition.

The statement that 'not a remnant remained' is reproduced in these accounts. The language of a remnant is derived from roots שאר and יתר, and is used in a variety of senses in Joshua, most significantly to emphasize the accomplishment of the slaughter (8.22; 10.28, 30, 33, 37, 39, 40; 11.8, 11, 14, 22). The use of the language of remnant to impress the completeness of the slaughter is a feature of most of the battle reports in Joshua, but is rarely found elsewhere in this connection.[1]

Joshua 10 makes it apparent that there are no survivors. The way in which the various stories are connected portrays the destruction of a remnant in a vivid manner: the enemy is slaughtered in a major battle and while fleeing there is a further slaughter; the five kings hide only to be found and slaughtered; and, finally, the cities to which any of the survivors could have fled are thoroughly destroyed, without a remnant remaining.

e. *Conclusion to the Southern Annihilation (10.40-43)*
The important themes are drawn together in the conclusion. The destruction of the kings is referred to on a further two occasions. The explanation for the mighty victory is that 'the Lord God of Israel fought for Israel', and the impression of pace is confirmed by the statement that all this happened 'at one time'.

A novel aspect now enters the narrative. This is the emphasis on the land. Until now, land has not featured in the battle reports. Most of the attention is devoted to the destruction of the kings, people and cities. Often the verb נכה has been used of kings and people, but here, for the first time, it is employed of כל הארץ (10.40). Similarly, לכד, which has been used repeatedly of the conquest of cities is now used of 'all these kings *and their land*' (10.42). Joshua defeats them 'from Kadesh-barnea to Gaza, and all the land of Goshen, as far as Gibeon'. The formula 'from... to' appearing in battle reports to demonstrate the greatness of the victory[2] can place the emphasis on one of several aspects: on the flight of the enemy (Josh. 10.10; 11.8), the extent of a victory (Num. 21.24; 1 Sam. 14.31) or on the extent of the land

1. Cf. Exod. 14.28; Deut. 2.34; 3.3; 1 Sam. 11.11. The discussion in Richter, *Untersuchungen*, p. 54, makes it clear that the statement about no remnant remaining is a particular feature of the book of Joshua.
2. Richter, *Untersuchungen*, p. 53.

conquered (Judg. 11.13, 22). Here, the last receives prominence in the light of the growing interest in the land.[1]

Although land has been conquered, there is no sense in which it is occupied. The concluding refrain 'and Joshua returned, and all Israel with him, to the camp at Gilgal' makes this obvious. After each battle report there are verbs of movement, either of Israel moving on to new conquests or returning to the camp, usually at Gilgal.

The destruction in ch. 10 has been located in the south, now the north is to receive the same treatment.[2]

6. Destruction of the Northern Kings (11.1-23)

The king of Hazor hears of Israel's deeds in the south and responds by gathering together a coalition to engage in warfare against Israel (11.1-5). The various geographical areas from which the kings are drawn,[3] along with a list of pre-Israelite nations, serve to indicate the size of the opposition. The impact is entrenched by the statement that the kings came out 'with all their troops, a great host, in number like the sand that is on the seashore, with very many horses and chariots'.

Meanwhile, the Israelites have made their way northwards. They have received both an assurance of victory from the Lord, and a command to hamstring the horses and burn the chariots of the enemy with fire (11.6). In the ensuing battle, the enemy is humiliated. They

---

1. Significantly, the structure עד. . . מן is used in 13.3, 4, 5, 6, 9 in territorial descriptions, and מן introduces several territorial descriptions, 15.3; 16.2; 19.34; cf. O. Bächli, 'Von der Liste zur Beschreibung. Beobachtungen und Erwägungen zu Jos. 13–19', *ZDPV* 89 (1973), pp. 1-14.

2. There are similarities between the accounts of the battle at Gibeon (10.1-15) and that by the waters of Merom (11.1-15). The structured parallel is apparent in the employment of similar language:

10.1 and 11.1	ויהי כשמע
10.5b and 11.5b	ויחנו
10.8a and 11.6a	ויאמר יהוה אל־יהושע אל־תירא
10.9 and 11.7	ויבא...יהושע...פתאם

Cf. V. Fritz, 'Das Ende der spätbronzezeitlichen Stadt Hazor Stratum XIII und die Biblische Überlieferung in Joshua 11 und Richter 4', *UF* 5 (1973), pp. 123-39, esp. 132-33.

3. Major geographical regions included are ערבה, נגב and שפלה, which hardly confines the kings to the northern regions.

flee, and even the remnant is slaughtered. Then, their horses are hamstrung and their chariots are burned.[1] The reader is reminded that this action accords to the Lord's command. Presumably, all these events take place in the field. The attention now shifts to the cities themselves, in order to magnify the completeness of the destruction.

The first to be destroyed is Hazor, the prime target. It is the only city to be mentioned by name and is said to have been 'formerly head of all those kingdoms'. There is no question as to its importance. Perhaps more significant is the fact of Hazor having been the seat of Jabin, the legendary king of the Canaanites who oppressed the Israelites through his chariotry-based military force and was defeated in an epic battle of cosmic dimensions (Judg. 4 and 5; Ps. 83).[2] Thus a city whose greatness is emphasized becomes an example of glorious waste. Possibly, this is the reason why it alone is singled out for burning, a fact that is noted by the narrator (11.11, 13).[3] A further reason could be that this great city is wasted because it is disobedient to the Lord. Finally, the destruction could be an act of punishment for inciting the opposition. However, Jerusalem is not dealt with in this manner in the previous chapter, even though it is responsible for initiating the southern coalition.

The now familiar formulae for destruction are repeated: all people are put to the sword, an act described as חרם. This is said to be in obedience to the command of Moses. For the first time since ch. 8, the battle report includes a statement about booty captured. This is followed immediately by the assurance 'but every man they smote with the sword, until they had destroyed them, and they did not leave any that breathed' (11.14). Again there is the reminder that all this is done in obedience to the Lord's word through Moses, and that Joshua left none of it undone. Any qualms which the reader might have are quashed.

---

1.   There is a prejudice against these weapons of war, cf. Deut. 17.16; 2 Sam. 8.4; Isa. 2.7; 31.1; etc.
2.   On the relationship of these traditions to each other, and to Josh. 11, cf. Fritz, 'Das Ende der spätbronzezeitlichen', pp. 123-39.
3.   1 Kgs 9.15 records the rebuilding of Hazor.

7. *Conclusion to the Northern Annihilation (11.15-23)*

The significance of the preceding events is stated by ויקח יהושע את
כל־הארץ הזאת , and is followed by a description of the northern and
southern regions (11.16). The focus of the battle reports has been on
destruction. The cities and kings are taken, an act expressed by לכד
(cf. 6.20; 8.19, 20; 10.1, 28, 32, 35, 37, 39, 42; 11.10, 12, 17; 15.16,
17; 19.47), only to be destroyed. Another verb is employed, לקח, in
order to speak of something that is captured and retained. In Joshua it
has several functions. This includes the taking of the land in the sense
of it becoming Israel's inheritance (11.16, 23; 13.8; 18.7).[1] Its
appearance here is another sign of a shift of interest to the issue of
land. However, the destruction of the Anakim returns the attention to
the destruction of enemies for a moment.

a. *Destruction of the Anakim (11.21-22)*
Joshua wages war against the Anakim. חרם is used on them, and even
the remnant is destroyed. However, a few manage to survive in Gaza,
Gath and Ashdod, traditional Philistine territory.

The Anakim are associated with the legendary giants who so
terrified the Israelites when the spies reported them (Num. 13.22, 28,
33; Deut. 1.28; 2.10, 11, 21; 9.2) and now their presence in Gath
prepares them for the introduction of the formidable Goliath (1 Sam.
17.4; 2 Sam. 21.18-22).[2] This is no commonplace enemy, as is evident
from the traditions concerning them (cf. further, esp. Deut. 9.2).[3]
Therefore, reference to them in Joshua 11 serves to associate the
nations in general with the symbols of primordial evil.

The account has switched the scene to the south, and appears to be
in some sense a duplication of other conquest material in the previous
chapter. The Anakim who are eliminated are said to be those from
areas that include three town names, Hebron, Debir and Anab, but the
earlier reports have made it apparent that all the occupants of Hebron

1.   The difference between the two verbs is not absolute. In 10.42, לכד is used
of taking kings and their land, and in 11.19, לקח, of taking all the enemy in battle.
2.   However, there is no text making explicit a connection between Goliath and
the Anakim.
3.   It is possible, according to Soggin, *Joshua*, p. 141, that the Anakim also
existed historically as they are mentioned in the Egyptian execration texts, cf. *ANET*,
p. 328f.

and Debir have already been destroyed (10.28-39). The reader had been left with the impression that the population of the south has been completely wiped out.[1] The Anakim, who are usually associated with Hebron, are still to be driven out by Caleb (Josh. 14.12-15; 15.13-14; Judg. 1.20). However, in its present context, Josh. 11.21-22, with its account of the destruction of the Anakim, provides a commentary on the conquest as a whole, and recalls the legendary power of an enemy that has been destroyed with such ease.

After their destruction, the consequences are summed up again in the formula (11.23) ויקח יהושע את־כל־הארץ. The changes in the language employed are further indication that the conquest is in the past. Whereas 10.42 contains references to 'the kings and their land', now the territory is linked to the new owners, and the text speaks of 'the hill country of Judah', 'the hill country of Israel' and 'the land of the people of Israel' (11.21-22).

There follows a summary describing Joshua as the one who allocates the inheritance of Israel. Finally, a statement marks the completion of conquest, and the retaining of an interest in the land, והארץ שקטה ממלחמה (11.23; cf. 14.15; Judg. 3.11, 30; 5.31).

b. *'The Lord Hardened Their Hearts'*
The overwhelming interest of the narrative has been on the destruction of the kings of the northern coalition. At one point it appears as though this is not the only option for the occupants of the land because it is said that 'there was not a city that made peace with the people of Israel, except the Hivites, the inhabitants of Gibeon' (11.19). Access is granted, only to be repealed in the next sentence:

> For it was the Lord's doing to harden their hearts that they should come against Israel in battle, in order that they should be utterly destroyed, and should receive no mercy but be exterminated, as the Lord commanded Moses.

A noteworthy similarity to the battle reports of Deuteronomy 1–3 is apparent. They all follow a regular pattern. They open with an Israelite request for peaceful transit, and this is met until the borders

---

1.   The most likely explanation for this is that we are dealing with an independent tradition of the Anakim which has been inserted into its present position; cf. for example, Soggin, *Joshua*, p. 141, who suggests that it reflects a very ancient independent tradition.

of Transjordan are reached. In the meantime, the Lord has promised this land to Israel (Deut. 2.24; 3.2). From this point onward, the normal request for transit is met by aggression. The cause is that the nations' hearts have been hardened by the Lord, leading them to initiate their own destruction (Deut. 2.30).[1] In summary it is the Lord who makes it easier for the Israelites to obey his command to exterminate the inhabitants by leading them to resist.

The reminder that the command to exterminate the inhabitants in the land is 'as the Lord commanded Moses', and the observation concerning the Lord hardening their hearts makes 11.29-30 an exceptionally strong statement about חרם, even though the Gibeonites are noted as an exception. The account is brought to a climax in the next chapter where the defeated kings are listed one after the other.

8. *The List of Defeated Kings (12.1-24)*

The conclusion to the narrative of conquest is presented in two sections, with the conquest of Cisjordan being set in parallel to that in Transjordan.

The first section (12.1-6) opens with the words: 'Now these are the kings of the land, whom the people of Israel defeated and took possession of their land.' There follows a territorial description of Transjordan, a statement about King Sihon and his territory, then a statement about King Og and his territory, and, finally, there is a note about their defeat and the fact of their land having been given by Moses as a possession to Reuben, Gad and the half-tribe of Manasseh.

The second section (12.7-24) opens in a similar manner: 'Now these are the kings of the land whom Joshua and his people of Israel defeated on the west side of Jordan.' A territorial description of Cisjordan is given, followed by a note that Joshua has given their land to Israel as a possession, then a further territorial description and a statement that it is 'the land of. . . ', a list of pre-Israelite nations, and, finally, a list of the kings concerned.

The kings are included in a schema, מלך...אחד. The impact of their number is made unavoidable by the concluding statement 'in all thirty-one kings'. While it is possible that the list has its origin as an

---

1. Characteristic of one with a hardened heart is that he/she acts in an irrational way against his/her own interests; cf. F. Hesse, *Das Verstockungsproblem im Alten Testament* (Berlin: Töpelmann, 1955), p. 40.

administrative document,[1] in its present context it serves to provide a powerful summary of the conquest which unites the events of Joshua 6–11.[2]

Joshua 12	Joshua 6–11
Jericho	Jericho (ch. 6)
Ai	Ai (chs. 7–8)
Southern coalition	
Jerusalem, Hebron	Jerusalem, Hebron
Jarmuth, Lachish	Jarmuth, Lachish
Eglon, Gezer, Debir	Debir, king of Eglon
	(10.3, 5, 23)
Libnah	Libnah (10.29-30)
Makkedah	Makkedah (10.28)
	King of Gezer (10.33)
	Debir (10.38-39)
Northern coalition	
Madon, Hazor, Shimron-meron	Hazor, Madon, Shimron,
Achshaph	Achshaph (11.1)
Geder, Hormah, Arad, Adullam,	
Bethel, Tappuah, Hepher, Aphek,	
Lasharon, Taanach, Megiddo,	
Kedesh, Jokneam, Dor,	
Goyim, Tirza	

All the cities which have been conquered in the preceding narrative are included.[3] They are arranged chronologically: first, the campaign in the south, then the campaign in the north. The lists of southern kings in 10.3, 5, 23 is followed in much the same order and supplemented by additional cities listed in 10.28-29. The list of northern kings is the same as 11.1, with only one change in order. The kings of sixteen towns included in the list, which are not mentioned in the earlier accounts of conquest, create the impression of

1. V. Fritz, 'Die sogenannte Liste der besiegten Könige in Josua 12', *ZDPV* 85 (1969), pp. 136-61. He points out that the towns are all strategically placed in an economic and military sense during the period of the Solomonic empire.

2. Therefore, it is not surprising that Josh. 12.1-24 has generally been regarded as part of the deuteronomistic redactional framework; cf. Noth, *Josua*, p. 9.

3. An exception is Anab which is one of the cities of the destroyed Anakim (11.21). In this instance, however, the interest is not in cities or kings but in the destruction of a people. The exception can also be explained by the fact that 11.21-22 does seem to reflect an independent tradition.

a victory on an even grander scale then at first envisaged.

The aim of this conclusion to the summary of conquest presented in
ch. 12 is to demonstrate the total destruction of the enemy kings.
Simultaneously, there is a noticeable shift of interest to the land itself
which assumes the idea of the land as possession (ירשה) in Transjordan
and duplicates it in Cisjordan (12.6; 12.7-8). This marks a return
for the first time to the language of the land promise characteristic of
ch. 1.

9. *Concluding Remarks on Chapters 8–12*

After the victory at Ai the pace of conquest suddenly diminishes with
a scene at Mount Ebal, and then the trickery of the Gibeonites and the
resultant covenant. However, this story establishes that all nations in
the land are doomed. The pace is renewed again with vigour in chs.
10–12. The main concern is to demonstrate that all the occupants and
their kings, south and north, have been killed, and no remnant
remains. The inclusion of the legendary Anakim in the list of the
fallen adds an ideological dimension to the narrative. There is an
unusually high concentration of the language of destruction in chs.
10–12 and expressions particularly associated with the conquest are
employed repeatedly, for example, חרם and נכה לפי חרב. The focus on
total destruction is not only a feature of the individual stories but also
of the compositional structures in which the stories are arranged. This
is evident particularly in the repetition of 'and he did to city B and its
king as he did to city A and its king'. The phrase summarizes the
demise of the enemy kings and is usually used together with a battery
of destruction terminology. The razing of Jericho serves as the
paradigm for the subsequent destruction. Therefore, in Joshua there
can be no doubt that conquest is understood as the destruction of kings
and their cities.[1]

Although the concentration has been on destroying the enemy, there
is a discernible shift of attention in chs. 11–12 to the occupation of the
land itself, and the language of ch. 1 returns. Thus the reader is
prepared for the ensuing chapters.

---

1. Similarly, the conquest of Transjordan, which is recorded in Deut. 1.3, is
encapsulated in the destruction of the kings of that region, Sihon and Og.

Chapter 4

'THERE STILL REMAINS MUCH LAND TO BE OCCUPIED' (13.1–22.9)

The material in chs. 13–21 is very diverse. Two somewhat contradictory statements emerge: (1) the period of warfare is over; and
(2) there has been a partial failure to conquer and settle.

1. *The Period of Warfare is Over*

In chs. 1–12, the war is separated from the occupation of the territory
by repeated references to the Israelites at the camp of Israel, or
returning to the camp after each battle (4.19, 20; 5.9, 10; 9.6; 10.6, 7,
9, 15, 43; cf. 14.6),[1] a feature of the composition structure.[2] In chs.
6–11, Israel's energies are devoted almost entirely to the eradication
of the occupants of the land. From ch. 13 onward, the accounts of the
destruction of the enemy are no longer dominant. A new state of
affairs is signalled in several ways.

a. *Language of Land Allocation and Settlement*
The most significant activity in chs. 13–19 is the allocation of the land
to the tribes of Israel. It is emphasized that every tribe, except the
Levites, is given its own territory.[3]

1. According to Y. Kaufmann, *The Biblical Account of the Conquest of
Palestine* (Jerusalem, 1953), p. 92, this is a well-conceived strategy for preventing
the disintegration of the army by premature land occupation. He adds that this is the
hidden reason for the destruction and curse of Jericho. Alternatively, Ottosson,
Erövring och fördelning av Land, demonstrates that a theological explanation of the
circular movement of Israel is possible. There is the circular movement (סבב) of
Israel in the wilderness (Deut. 2.2), the circling of the walls of Jericho in Josh. 6,
and the movement of the ark in 1 Sam. 4.
2. P. Weimar, 'Die Jahwekriegerzählungen in Exodus 14, Josua 10, Richter 4
und 1 Samuel 7', *Bib* 57 (1976), pp. 38-73 (51).
3. It is generally agreed that the bulk of the material is made up of a combination

Unlike the narratives in chs. 1–12, in which the cities are normally part of a construction 'the king of. . . ', the following section lists the cities on their own, demonstrating that the kings are there no longer.[1] In a study of the role of cities in Joshua, M. Ottosson points out that of the 746 city names listed in the Hebrew Bible, 358 occur in the book of Joshua, and that of these 199 are *hapax legomena*.[2] The high concentration of city names in Joshua is because cities are symbols of power and, along with their kings, the most spectacular objects of war. He then proceeds to study the function of the city lists in the territorial descriptions of the Israelite tribes. Judah has 144 (85 of which are *hapax legomena*), Benjamin 38 (13 of which are *hapax legomena*), and the other tribes have 22-25 each. From this information he concludes that the cities have an ideological function, and that the number mentioned in each case is in relation to the 'orthodoxy' of the tribe. This reveals a clear prejudice in favour of Judah.

The attention focused on the land is sustained throughout by the long lists of place names and boundaries denoted by listing the most important boundary places. If two tribes share the same boundary, there is a repetition of the names (cf. 15.2ff.; 16.1ff.; 17.7ff.; 18.11ff.). The descriptions of territory allocated to each tribe are so comprehensive that A. Alt can comment that they leave 'kaum ein Fleckchen Palästinischer Erde westlich vom Jordan frei'.[3] The theologically important word ארץ can apply to all of the area west of the Jordan (13.2, 7; 14.1, 4, 5, 7; 18.2, 4, 6, 8 × 2, 9, 10; 19.49, 51), or to a particular stretch of territory (13.4, 5, 21, 25; 15.19; 17.5, 12, 15, 16). Similarly, נחלה appears in chs. 13–19 some 44 times. While it is possible to translate it as 'place of residence' rather than 'property',[4] it is evident that like ארץ it has additional theological

of lists of tribal boundaries and geographical localities. This helps to explain why the narrative of settlement is fraught with literary, historical and geographical problems: cf. on these issues, particularly, M. Noth, 'Studien zu den historisch-geographischen Dokumenten des Josua-Buches', *ZDPV* 58 (1935), pp. 185-255; Z. Kallai, *Historical Geography of the Bible: The Tribal Territories of Israel* (Jerusalem: Magnes Press, 1986).

1. Josh. 24.11 describes the earlier situation when it refers to 'the rulers of Jericho'.

2. Ottosson, *Erövring och fördelning av Land*.

3. Alt, *Kleine Schriften I*, p. 195.

4. G. Gerleman, 'Nutzrecht und Wohnrecht. Zur Bedeutung von אחזה und נחלה, *ZAW* 89 (1977), pp. 321-25 (313-25).

dimensions in Joshua because it is situated within the concept of the Lord's gift of the land. Three verbs are prominent in this activity, נתן, חלק and נחל.[1]

Although the subject of נתן is the Lord, the verb also describes Moses' act of allocating Transjordan to the tribes living there (1.14, 15; 12.6; 13.8 × 2, 15, 24, 29; 14.3; 17.4 × 2; 18.7; 22.7). Moses' gift of Transjordan is intended to parallel Joshua's activity. This is obvious because the two are placed side by side (12.6-7; 22.7). Joshua's only action after ch. 12 is to allocate the land (12.7; 14.12, 13; 15.13; 17.14; 22.7). Caleb also apportions land to his family (15.19 × 4). The people of Israel allocate land to Joshua (19.49, 50), cities for refuge (ch. 20) and cities for the Levites (ch. 21). The reminders that the Levites are not allocated any further territory also serve to maintain interest in the issue of land allocation (13.14, 33; 14.3, 4).

Similarly, with regard to Transjordan (13.32; cf. 1.14, 15), Moses is the subject of נחל, 'to give an inheritance', and, directly afterwards, Joshua, together with Eleazer and the leaders of the people, distributes the territory (14.1; cf. 1.6; 19.51). The verb also denotes the tribes receiving what has been allocated to them (14.1; 16.4; 17.6; 19.9, 49).

The verb חלק (13.7; 14.5; 18.2, 5, 10; 19.51) is another expression prominent in texts describing the allocation of land to the tribes. This verb, which means 'apportion', is most commonly utilized in connection with land distribution (cf. 2 Sam. 19.30; 1 Kgs 18.6) and of the distribution of שלל after a battle (cf. Gen. 19.27; Exod. 15.9; Josh. 22.8; Judg. 5.30; 1 Sam. 30.24-26). The only other instance in the DtrH is 2 Sam. 6.19 in which David distributes food. The fact that in Josh. 22.9 חלק is used in the context of the distribution of the spoils of victory makes it possible to understand the distribution of land in Josh. 13.1 ff. in similar terms. It occurs *after* a victory.

The climax of land allocation is the settlement. The key verb in this regard is ישב. A despondent Joshua wishes to settle in Transjordan (7.7). The land has been allocated to the Transjordanian tribes. However, they are only described as dwelling there when they return after the conquest (22.33). The Levites are given cities in which to

1. M. Wüst, *Untersuchungen zu den siedlungsgeographischen Texten des Alten Testaments. I. Ostjordanland* (Beihefte zum Tübinger Atlas des Vorderen Orients, 19; Wiesbaden: Reichert, 1975), pp. 199-201. He refers to 'Die zwei Verteilungsprinzipien und-termini חלק und נחל.' As will be demonstrated below, נתן is no less important than the other two.

dwell (14.4; 21.2). The climax of the conquest by the Danites is their
settlement (19.47). Joshua settles in the land allocated to him (19.50),
and the Israelites are said to settle in the land after the conquest
(21.43). For Israel, settlement succeeds conquest. The new state of
affairs is expressed in 24.2-13. The account rehearses the Lord's
mighty deeds and is concluded by the settlement. In Joshua 24, the
settlement is the climax of a series of divine acts which are regarded
as complete and they underwrite Joshua's exhortation for a faithful
response from the people.

These statements about Israel's settlement serve as a counterpoint to
the frequent references to the nations who dwell in the land, references which, incidentally, confirm the sequential relationship between
ירש and ישב (13.13; 15.63; 16.10; 17.11-13).

The amount of attention given to land allocation and settlement in
chs. 13–19 creates the overwhelming impression that the period of
warfare is over. Specific statements confirm this impression.

b. *Statements that the Period of War is Over*
i. *The enemy annihilated.* The final chapters of Joshua 6–12 convey
the impression that the enemy has been completely annihilated. This
interpretation is confirmed by the words in 10.40, ויכה יהושע
את־כל־הארץ, and those in 11.16, ויקח יהושע את כל־הארץ.

ii. *The land at rest.* The formula, 'and the land had rest from war',
והארץ שקטה מלחמה, appears in 11.23 and 14.15. A similar formula,
ותשקט הארץ plus a stated period of years, is a feature of the narrative
structure in the early chapters of Judges. It appears there in 3.11, 30;
5.31; 8.28.[1]

The formula in Josh. 14.15 is confirmed by being preceded by an
account of how Kiriatharba, named after Arba, the greatest of the
Anakim, has its name changed to Hebron after Caleb's conquest, cf.
Judg. 1.10. The renaming of conquered sites in the conquest traditions
serves to mark a transition.[2]

---

1. Cf. Richter, *Bearbeitungen*, p. 65, who demonstrates how the formula is part
of the structure, sin: punishment: cry for help: help: land has rest from war.
2. Cf. A. Malamat, 'The Danite Migration and the Pan-Israelite Exodus-
Conquest: A Biblical Narrative Pattern', *Bib* 51 (1970), pp. 1-16 (14-16). Further
examples are:

iii. *The land subdued.* Josh. 18.1 has a unique manner of describing the consequences of conquest and land allotment, 'and the land lay subdued before them', והארץ נכבשה לפניהם. The similarity of the wording to Gen. 1.28, פרו ורבו ומלאו את־הארץ וכבשה, is significant, in that it could suggest a link between the process of conquest and settlement, and creation. Thus the allotment of land would be perceived as the fulfilment of the command to fill the earth and subdue it.[1]

However, כבש (*niph*) also appears in military contexts and, more specifically, as part of a description of the occasion when the Transjordanian tribes may return at the conclusion to the conquest in Num 32.22, 29 (הם) ונכבשה הארץ לפני. The phrase appears as an epoch marker in 1 Chron. 22.18 where it occurs together with a statement that 'the Lord had given rest'. It indicates the period when the temple is to be built.

iv. *The Lord has given rest.* Most noteworthy as an epoch marker is the statement that the Lord has given rest:

21.44	וינח יהוה להם מסביב
22.4	ועתה הניח יהוה אלהיכם לאחיכם
23.1	הניח יהוה לישראל מכל איביהם מסביב

In all these contexts the idea of 'rest'[2] plays a significant role as an epoch marker signalling the time when the promises are fulfilled. The words הניח יהוה לישראל מכל־איביהם מסביב function in the DtrH as a time signal which serves as a prelude to something new. Thus it marks the time when the temple may be built (Deut. 12.10; 2 Sam. 7.1, 11 [without מסביב]; cf. 1 Chron. 22.9) and the occasion when Amalek is to be exterminated (Deut. 25.19). Right at the outset in the book of Joshua there is the promise of 'rest' as something that will follow conquest (1.13, 15).

Num. 21.3; cf. Judg. 1.17. . . Zephat becomes Hormah.
Josh. 14.15; cf. Judg. 1.11. . . Kirjath-sepher becomes Debir.
Judg. 1.23; cf. Gen. 28.19. . . Luz becomes Bethel.
Judg. 18.29. . . Laish becomes Dan.

1.   J. Blenkinsopp, 'The Structure of P', *CBQ* 38 (1976), pp. 275-92 (290). Also, cf. Lohfink, *Gewalt und Gewaltlosigkeit*, pp. 76-106, in which he argues that 'P' represents a tradition of non-violent conquest. Passages so designated are Josh. 4.19; 5.10-12; 14.1 f.; 18.1; 19.51.

2.   On the meaning of 'rest', cf. von Rad, 'Es ist noch eine Ruhe vorhanden dem Volke Gottes', pp. 104-11.

Together in the Land

v. *The fulfilment of promise.* This is an important compositional theme in Joshua, and the reference in 21.43-45 deserves scrutiny. The conquest and settlement of the land is presented as the fulfilment of the divine promise. This connection is exhibited by the return to the language of ch. 1. In the table that follows, the text of 21.43-45 appears in the left-hand column, and the parallel texts from ch. 1 are arranged in the right-hand column.

Ch. 21	Ch. 1
ויתן יהוה לישראל את־כל־הארץ אשר נשבע לתת לאבותם	אל־הארץ אשר אנכי נתן להם... כאשר דברתי אל־משה (1.2-3)
	תנחיל ... את־הארץ אשר־נשבעתי לאבותם לתת להם (1.6)
וירשוה וישבו בה	לבוא לרשת את־הארץ אשר יהוה אלהיכם נתן לכם לרשתה (1.11)
וינח יהוה להם מסביב	יהוה אלהיכם מניח לכם (1.13)
	יניח יהוה לאחיכם ככם וירשו את־הארץ אשר־יהוה נתן (1.15)
ככל אשר־נשבע לאבותם	
ולא־עמד איש בפניהם מכל־איביהם את כל־איביהם נתן יהוה בידם	לא־יתיצב איש לפניך (1.5)
לא־נפל דבר מכל הדבר הטוב אשר־דבר יהוה אל־בית ישראל הכל בא	

The central concern of 21.43-45 is to demonstrate that the promises have been fulfilled, not simply in terms of land possession, but in victory over the enemies. The thoroughness of this fulfilment is illustrated by the sixfold use of כל:

1. *all* the land
2. according to *all* that he promised
3. none of *all* the enemy was able to stand before Israel
4. *all* their enemies given into their hand

5.   none of *all* the promises failed
6.   *all* came true.

The wording in 21.43-45 is re-employed in 23.14, and then, once again, in 1 Kgs 8.56 to mark another epoch which is the occasion of the building and dedication of the temple:[1]

Josh. 21.44a, 45	1 Kgs 8.56
וינח יהוה להם מסביב	נתן מנוחה לעמו ישראל
לא־נפל דבר	ככל אשר דבר לא־נפלדבר אחד
מכל הדבר הטוב	מכל דברו הטוב
אשר־דבר יהוה אל־בית ישראל	אשר דבר ביד משה עבדו
הכל בא	

Yet another epoch marker is provided by the movement of the Transjordanian tribes.

vi. *The return of the Transjordanian tribes*. This demonstrates that the period of warfare is over. Again, there is a noticeable similarity to ch. 1 because the wording of 1.15 is echoed in 22.4. This is established by a comparison of the terminology:

22.4	1.15
ועתה הניח יהוה אלהיכם לאחיכם	עד אשר־יניח יהוה לאחיכם ככם
כאשר דבר להם	וירשו גם־המה את־הארץ אשר־יהוה
	אלהיכם נתן להם
ועתה פנו ולכו לכם לאהליכם	ושבתם לארץ ירשתכם וירשתם אותה
אל־ארץ אח זתכם	
אשר נתן לכם משה עבד יהוה	אשר נתן לכם משה עבד יהוה
בעבר הירדן	בעבר הירדן מזרח השמש

The return of Reuben, Gad and the half-tribe of Manasseh, therefore, establishes the end of the period of warfare. Their presence in the introductory chapters having introduced a military mood into the narrative, now signals an end to the period of war. The movement of these tribes creates a symmetry between chs. 1 and 22. This helps to explain the curious reference to taking provisions in 1.10. Just as provisions are taken from Transjordan, so the Transjordanians return with much booty! In a farewell blessing Joshua says:

---

1.   Cf. the next chapter, in which Josh. 21.45 and 23.14 are compared.

> Go back to your homes with much wealth, and with very many cattle, with silver, gold, bronze and iron, and with much clothing; divide the spoil of your enemies with your brethren.

This booty report does not only draw more attention to the return of the tribes, it also functions as another mark of the end of the campaign, because, customarily, the booty report occurs when the fighting ceases. The return of the Transjordanians is reinforced by a dramatic quarrel which occupies the remainder of the chapter.

The numerous epoch markers in the second half of the book of Joshua indicate that the period of conquest is over. These statements constitute the bulk of the theological reflection to be found in chs. 13.1–23.1. At the same time, the failure to conquer and settle is also part of the compositional structure.

2. The Failure to Conquer and Settle

Israel's failure in this regard is indicated in several ways:

a. Transjordan as a Model
A vanquished Transjordan serves as a model and as a rebuke. This is particularly striking in ch. 13, in which a survey of unconquered land on the west bank (13.2-6) is followed by a description of the complete conquest of the east bank (13.18-33). In the midst of these accounts resides a terse statement that Israel has failed to conquer the Geshurites and the Maacathites (13.13). The irony is made evident by the reference two verses earlier to the conquest of these very peoples in Transjordan.

b. Statements of Failure
In a very matter-of-fact way, a list of unconquered territories appears in a speech by Joshua (13.2-6).[1] Similarly, the reader encounters unconquered peoples in 23.1-16. While 13.2-6 is about 'the remnant of the land', 23.1-16 is concerned about the 'remnant of the nations'. These texts present such a vivid contrast to their contexts that R. Smend has concluded that they are part of a subsequent deuteronomistic redaction, DtrN.[2]

---

1. Judg. 3.1-6 has a similar list of unconquered nations. The theological significance is made explicit both as a punishment and as a test.
2. Smend, *Probleme biblischer Theologie*, pp. 494-509.

The notes about the continued presence of nations in Israel's midst, with a preamble to say that Israel failed to conquer them (13.13; 15.63; 16.10; 17.11-13), are no less surprising. The manner in which they contradict their context leads A.G. Auld to conclude that these notes are also part of the work of DtrN.[1] Although 13.13 places culpability on all of Israel, the remaining references place the blame in the hands of individual tribes. The point is therefore clearly made that Israel has only partially succeeded in conquering and settling the land.

c. *Exhortations to Conquer the Land*
There are several explicit exhortations to conquer the land. Chronologically they occur well after conquest is supposed to have been an event of the past:

13.1	והארץ נשארה הרבה־מאד לרשתה
18.3	לבוא לרשת את־הארץ
23.5	וירשתם את־ארצם

In each case the exhortations come as a surprise. The exhortation in 13.1 is preceded in ch. 12 by a lengthy list of defeated kings which demonstrates comprehensive conquest. Ch. 18 begins with a statement about the land lying subdued before Israel. Similarly, ch. 23 is introduced by a statement that 'the Lord had given rest to Israel from all their enemies round about'.

In these instances, it is not at all evident whether ירש (*qal*), combined syntactically with ארץ, is intended as an exhortation to go to war or not.[2] As has been noted, the *hiph'il* form is usually used in battle reports, and the *qal* form, when associated with the land promise as it is here, always appears in speeches with a focal interest in the land. It is worth noting that along with ירש (*qal*) in 13.1 and 23.5 where Israel is the subject, ירש (*hiph*) appears with YHWH as the subject in 13.6 and 23.5. In other words, the final promised conquest of the nations is reserved for YHWH!

Even though 13.2-6, 13 details a failure to conquer, there is no longer the interest in destroying enemy kings but in occupying unconquered territory. The immediate response to the exhortation in

1. Auld, *Joshua, Moses and the Land*, pp. 64-65, 67.
2. W. Rudolf, *Der 'Elohist' von Exodus bis Josua* (BZAW, 68; Berlin, 1938), p. 211, explains ירש in 13.1 as a conquest without weapons.

18.1-3 is that a team is sent out to survey the land. A lot is then cast to allocate the land (chs. 18–19). The exhortation to conquer the land in ch. 23 is succeeded by instructions about retaining a social and religious distance from the nations remaining in the land. Therefore it would appear that the exhortations are not concerned with renewing the military conflict at all.

However, the context presents the possibility of understanding the localized accounts of conquest as responses to the exhortation to conquer the land.

a.   Caleb conquers his own territory (14.6-15; 15.13-19). This is an account inserted into the territorial description of Judah. The link between Caleb and Judah is clarified by the manner in which the story is introduced:

> Then the people of Judah came to Joshua at Gilgal; and Caleb the
> son of Jephunneh the Kenizzite said to him. . .

In other words, Judah receives the credit for the regional conquest, which is in keeping with the concern to present Judah in a most favourable light.

b.   The story of 'the tribe of Joseph's' dissatisfaction about the size of their territory, and about how they receive permission to conquer more territory (17.14-18), is inserted into the territorial description of Ephraim and Manasseh (chs. 16–17). This explains why the exhortation in 18.2-3 is specifically applied to the remaining seven tribes who have been hesitant in occupying the land.

c.   Finally, the Danites conquer their own territory (19.47), but this is perceived as a reconquest because their land has been lost to them (cf. also Judg. 1.34). Their action is presented as an example to the more hesitant tribes.

This survey of the context of the exhortations has not brought us much closer to a solution to the question of their precise significance. On the one hand the immediate response to the exhortations is never military conquest, while on the other hand military escapades are inserted into the narrative in such a way that the participants are commended for their actions. It is apparent that as exhortations they stand in some tension to the statements about the complete conquest of the land.

3. *Conclusion*

While the contradiction between statements of complete conquest and incomplete conquest is easily explained as the result of a variety in the source or redactional contribution, the issue cannot be settled until it is possible to relate it to the contradictions running through the book of Joshua as a whole.

The overwhelming impression in chs. 13–22 is that the days of warfare are past, although there are scattered exhortations to conquer the land and reports of minor engagements in battle. The number of epoch markers indicates that a new situation prevails. The drama recedes, and the battles against enemy kings abate. The nations remain in the land. In chs. 13–22 other interests are dominant, and the nations are not recorded as doing anything apart from occupying small parcels of land. However, as the book of Joshua draws to a close, the fate of the nations once more becomes an issue because it serves as a warning to Israel.

Chapter 5

'AND YOU SHALL PERISH QUICKLY FROM OFF THE GOOD LAND'
(22.1–24.33)

Three scenes conclude the book of Joshua. Each in its own way presents the possibility that Israel could experience the same fate as the nations: the destruction and loss of the land.

1. *A Drama of Apostasy (22.1-34)*

The Transjordanian tribes return home in great honour. Then they are discovered to have committed the most terrible apostasy by building an altar on the way. The main body of Israelites believes that they are guilty of rebellion,[1] and liken this to the crime of Achan (22.20). This explicit thematic link to ch. 7 is reinforced by the language which is noticeably similar to the opening words of the Achan story:

7.1   וימעלו בני־ישראל מעל בחרם ויקח עכן . . . מן־החרם
ויחר־אף יהוה בבני ישראל

22.20   הלוא עכן . . . מעל מעל בחרם
ועל־כל־עדה ישראל היה קצף . . .

Both texts are concise theological summaries of the Achan story, and present a meditation on the nature of divine wrath. Particularly striking is the reappearance of מעל in ch. 22, usually translated as 'breaking faith', and a key word in the story (22.16 × 2, 20 × 2, 22, 31 × 2). This in itself would be unremarkable were it not that apart from ch. 7 מעל only occurs on one other occasion in the DtrH.[2] There does therefore seem to be a structural connection between chs. 7 and 22, a connection which is established at a fundamental theological level.

---

1.   מרד appearing in 22.16, 18, 19 × 2, 22, 29.
2.   Deut. 32.51.

The Israelites remind the reader that Achan's sin caused the whole nation to come under divine wrath, 'and wrath fell upon all the congregation of Israel; and he did not perish alone for his iniquity' (22.20). Therefore, they are justifiably anxious about the action of the Transjordanians.

Their concern is compounded by observing that, in a similar fashion, the rebellion at Peor had caused a plague to fall upon the whole community (22.17; cf. Num. 25.1-9; Deut. 4.3). These parallels with the potentially illicit altar and apostasy at Peor bring the question of חרם into association with the worship of foreign gods for the first time.

The intention of the Israelites is 'to make war against them, to destroy the land (לשחת את־הארץ)[1] where the Reubenites and Gadites were settled' (22.33). Fortunately, before this occurs messengers are sent, a misunderstanding is resolved and there is a happy ending.[2] Nevertheless, the message of the story is clear: if they were guilty the ending would be very different! This message is repeated in the final scenes of the book of Joshua.

2. These Nations as a Temptation (23.1-16)

The main theme of Joshua's speech—the need to retain a social distance from the remaining occupants of the land—is something of a surprise because it occurs directly after statements about a comprehensive victory. It is set at a time when 'the Lord had given rest to Israel from all their enemies round about' (23.1).

The Lord's role in creating the new situation is left in no doubt by the twice-repeated phrase כי יהוה אלהיכם הוא הנלחם לכם (23.3, 10). No explanation is offered for the continuing presence of the nations except that the Lord will deal with them, יהדפם מפניכם והוריש אתם[3] (23.5).

The nations are the focus of attention in ch. 23. Those having been conquered and those remaining are said to be the נחלה of Israel's

---

1. An expression not used elsewhere in Joshua.
2. The basis of the story is possibly an earlier tradition of the Transjordanians building an altar, which has been reworked so as to declare them innocent on deuteronomistic terms, cf. N.H. Snaith, 'The Altar at Gilgal: Joshua XXII 23-29', *VT* 28 (1978), pp. 330-35.
3. In the DtrH, הדף is used in this sense in Deut. 6.19; 9.4; and in a mundane sense in 1 Kgs 4.27.

tribes (23.4). This is a new use of the term which, up to this point, has applied to territory.

Israel's responsibility is twofold:

1. To conquer the land, וירשתם את־ארצם (23.5). If this were a call to battle, then it would be somewhat indirect. The first part of 23.5 makes it clear that it is the Lord who will deal with the nations. YHWH is the subject of הוריש.

2. To obey the command to keep away from the nations. This command is the main theme of the speech and גוים appears six times; either it refers to the nations which have been destroyed or to those which remain.

Juxtaposed at various points in the speech are (a) prohibitions against contact with the nations and their gods; (b) an appeal to gratitude by pointing to the gracious acts of the Lord; and (c) a solemn warning about the consequences of disobedience.

a. *Prohibitions*

While the RSV translation of the first of the list of prohibitions לבלתי־בוא בגוים האלה (23.7) is 'you may not be mixed with these nations', it can be argued that the expression has sexual if not matrimonial connotations.[1] This is followed by four other prohibitions against having anything to do with the gods of the nations, 'or make mention of the names of their gods, or swear by them, or serve them, or bow down yourselves to them'. Instead, Israel is to 'cleave to the Lord your God', כי אם־ביהוה אלהיכם תדבקו (23.8).

A few verses later in 23.12, the word דבק, which can have decided sexual and relational connotations, is used as part of a warning against 'cleaving to the remnant of the nations'. This is defined as 'to make marriages with them, so that you marry their women and they yours'.[2]

Finally, in 23.16, serving other gods (והלכתם ועבדתם אלהים אחרים והשהחויתם להם),[3] is described as breaking the covenant (בעברכם

---

1. Schmitt, *Du sollst keinen Frieden schliessen*, p. 149 n. 41. However in Exod. 23.23 the angel of the Lord will bring (... אל והביאך) Israel to the Amorites, the Hittites, the Perizzites, etc., but here the nations are more a geographical location, and בוא is used as a conquest word. (The dual function of בוא in Joshua will be discussed below in Chapter 8 in relation to the Rahab story.)

2. In 1 Kgs 11.2, דבק is used of Solomon's marriages to foreign women, an act which is paralleled by the prohibition, מן־הגוים . . . לא־תבאו בהם והם לא־יבאו בכם.

3. Verbs used to describe the apostate worship of other gods include הלך

אֶת־בְּרִית).[1] This is the first occasion that the danger of worshipping foreign gods is clearly stated. Neither has this been offered as an explanation for the extermination of the nations. The danger of their gods is not the justification for killing them, but it is a sufficient cause for retaining a social distance.

An obvious question that comes to mind is how to reconcile the promise that YHWH will destroy (הוריש) the nations (23.5)[2] with a prohibition against social contact. It could be that the situation is analogous to Deut. 7.1-5 in which a command to destroy the nations, החרם תחרים אתם, is accompanied by a series of commands to retain a social distance. This puzzle might be solved if חרם is understood as a literary device for advocating a strict separation from the nations.[3] It is possible that the military term הוריש in Joshua 23 is a means of reinforcing the prohibition to keep separate through vivid metaphor. However, the logical problem is partially solved in 23.13 by making Israel's separation from the nations the *condition* for YHWH להוריש the nations. Yet even so, the destruction of the nations and separation from them remain in tandem because the punishment is in the fraternization itself (23.3b). The logic of the call for separation is not based on any threat, but on the gracious acts of the Lord.

b. *Gracious Acts of the Lord*
Both the conquest of the land and the final removal of the remnant of the nations are viewed as the work of YHWH. The reappearance in

(Deut. 29.25; Judg. 2.19; 1 Kgs 11.10), עבד (Deut. 29.25; 31.20; Judg. 2.19; 2 Kgs 17.35), שחה hithpael (Deut. 29.25; Judg. 2.19; 2 Kgs 17.35). These verbs appear together also in Deut. 8.19; 11.16; 17.3; etc.

1. The connection between serving other gods and breaking the covenant is made elsewhere in the DtrH (Deut. 29.24; 31.16, 20; Judg. 2.20; 1 Kgs 11.11; 2 Kgs 17.15, 35, 38; cf. Jer. 11.8, 10; 22.9). For fuller discussion of the relationship between illicit worship and breaking the covenant, cf. L. Perlitt, *Bundestheologie im Alten Testament* (WMANT, 36; Neukirchen–Vluyn: Neukirchener, 1969), pp. 36-38. Particularly significant as cross-references are Exod. 34.11-17 and Deut. 7.1-5 where the prohibition against intermarriage with the pre-Israelite nations is linked to prohibitions against forming covenants with them and worshipping their gods.

2. The conquest up to that point is described in similar terms, ויורש יהוה מפניכם גוים (23.9).

3. Cf. above in the Introduction, the discussion of Welch's interpretation of Deut. 7.1-5.

23.14 of the words of 21.45 conveys the Lord's faithfulness to the foreground.[1]

21.45	23.14
לא־נפל דבר מכל הדבר הטוב	לא־נפל דבר אחד מכל הדברים הטובים
אשר־דבר יהוה אל־בית ישראל	אשר דבר יהוה אלהיכם עליכם
הכל בא	הכל באו לכם
	לא־נפל ממנו דבר אחד

The adjective טוב is also used in connection with the land (23.13, 15, 16); and throughout this speech it serves to emphasize the gracious gifts of the Lord. At the same time the goodness of the Lord's gifts introduces a sense of poignancy into the survey of potential disobedience.

c. *The Consequences of Disobedience*

After the warning against illicit contacts with the nations remaining in the land, the consequences of disobedience are spelled out in 23.13:

> Know assuredly that the Lord your God will not continue to drive out these nations before you; but they shall be a snare and a trap for you, a scourge on your sides, and thorns in your eyes, till you perish from off this good land which the Lord your God has given you.

The image of a snare, מוקש, appears in a set of texts which all have a similar function: to describe the dangers which proceed from contact with the occupants of the land and their gods (Exod. 23.33; 34.12; Deut. 7.16; Josh. 23.13; Judg. 2.3; Ps. 106.36; cf. also the verbs from נקש in Deut. 7.25; 12.30).[2] In Josh. 23.13 this basic metaphor is supplemented by parallel metaphors not found in the other texts; namely, 'a trap', 'a scourge on your sides' and 'thorns in your eyes'. The combination of punishment terminology in ch. 23 functions as a powerful deterrent. Contact with the nations will itself constitute divine punishment—*they* are the trap, the scourge, etc. However, the consequences of fraternization are more severe and involve being destroyed and removed from the land.

The judgment on a potentially disobedient Israel is pronounced three times:

---

1. Cf. the previous chapter where 21.45 is compared to 1 Kgs 8.56.
2. For discussion of מוקש in these texts, cf. Halbe, *Das Privilegrecht Jahwes*, pp. 127-34.

23.13	עד־אבדכם מעל האדמה הטובה הזאת אשר נתן לכם יהוה אלהיכם
23.15	עד־השמידו אותכם מעל האדמה הטובה הזאת אשר נתן לכם יהוה אלהיכם
23.16	וחרה אף־יהוה בכם ואבדתם מהרה מעל הארץ הטובה אשר נתן לכם

Thus the link between the land promise and obedience is clearly established. Disobedience ensures the loss of the land. This tragedy is emphasized by the use of the term 'the good land' in the judgment formulas. The anger formula concludes the speech (23.16), and dispels any doubt about the consequences of disobedience.

The anger formula in 23.16, חרה אף־יהוה, is the same as that which frames the Achan story (7.1, 26). The first part of the verse also employs language similar to that in the Achan story:

| 7.11 | וגם עברו את־בריתי אשר צויתי אותם |
| 23.16 | בעברכם את־בריח יהוה אלהיכם אשר צוה אתכם |

In ch. 7, disobedience regarding the question of חרם is described as breaking the covenant which leads to divine wrath. In ch. 23, associating with the nations is described in exactly the same way![1] Therefore, these two stories are related at a fundamental level with regard to theology and composition.[2]

3. The Choice of Whom to Serve (24.1-33)

Unlike ch. 7, in which decisive action is taken against apostate Israelites, here we discover an *appeal* to Israel to serve the Lord. The concept of legitimate and illegitimate worship had been introduced into the narrative in 22.5, 27, and then stated unambiguously in 23.16. In ch. 24 the word עבד serves as the pivot on which the argument moves, either referring to the worship of YHWH (24.14 × 2, 15 × 2, 18, 19, 21, 22, 24, 31) or to the illicit worship of gods (24.2, 14, 15 × 2, 16, 20).[3] Serving other gods is equivalent to forsaking YHWH, עזב את־יהוה (24.16, 20).[4]

---

1. Note the assonance between חרם and חרה אף־יהוה, also in Deut. 7.4 and 13.18 (Lohfink, 'הרם', p. 198).

2. Cf. McCarthy, *Essays*, pp. 99-110.

3. Use of the same contrast is made in Exod. 23.24-25; Deut. 11.13-17; 13.3-5; Judg. 10.6-16; 1 Sam. 12.10; Ezek. 20.39-40.

4. Cf. further on this formula, J.P. Floss, *Jahwe Dienen—Göttern Dienen: Terminologische, literarische und semantische Untersuchungen einer theologischen Aussage zum Gotterverhältnis im Alten Testament* (BBB, 45; Köln/Bonn: Peter Hanstein, 1975), pp. 94-107.

The gods to be avoided are characterized in several ways:

24.2, 16	אלהים אחרים[1]
24.20, 23	אלהי (ה)נכר[2]
24.14, 15, cf. 2	אלהים אשר עבדו אבותיכם בעבר הנהר (ובמצרים)
24.15	אלהי האמרי אשר אתם ישבים בארצם[3]

While the expression 'other gods' appears frequently to describe Israel's apostasy, 'foreign gods' adds a further dimension to the concept of illicit worship by linking the practice to other peoples.[4] This link is confirmed by the references to gods worshipped in three different geographical regions, Mesopotamia, Egypt and Canaan.[5] It is not the Egyptians or the Amorites themselves who are a threat, but their gods.[6] The days of physical battles are past, and the occupation by the nations of the land is also a thing of the past. The cities, houses, orchards of the former inhabitants are now occupied by Israelites (24.13).[7] The audience is warned about serving 'the gods of the Amorites in whose land you dwell' (24.15). Israel occupies a land that had belonged to others. This concept is implied by the expression, 'land of Canaan' (Josh. 5.12; 14.1; 21.2; 22.9, 10, 11, 32; 24.3),

---

1. Cf. Deut. 5.7; 6.14; 7.4; 8.19; 11.16, 28; 13.3, 7, 14; 17.3; 18.20; 28.14, 36, 64; 29.25; 30.17; 31.18, 20; Josh. 23.16; Judg. 2.12, 17, 19; 10.13; 1 Sam. 8.8; 26.19; 1 Kgs 9.6, 9; 11.4, 10; 14.9; 2 Kgs 5.17; 7.35, 37, 38; 22.17. Elsewhere some 18 times in Jeremiah and 7 times in the remainder of the Hebrew Bible.

2. Cf. Gen. 35.2, 4; Deut. 31.16 ('of the land'); Judg. 10.16; 1 Sam. 7.3; Jer. 5.19.

3. Elsewhere only in Judg. 6.10.

4. Cf. E. Nielsen, *Shechem: A Traditio-Historical Investigation* (Copenhagen: Gad, 1959), p. 103, נכר has a distinctly *political* meaning, which cannot be said of אחרים'.

5. Hoffmann, *Reform und Reformen*, p. 304, has drawn attention to the amount of geographical language in ch. 24: Mesopotamia (24.2, 3, 14, 15); Egypt (24.4, 5, 6, 7, 14); Canaan (24.8, [11], 15, [18]). In 24.17 Egypt is referred to as the 'house of bondage'; cf. Exod. 13.3, 14; 20.2; Deut. 5.6; 6.12; 7.8; 8.14; 13.6, 11; Judg. 6.8; Jer. 34.13; Mic. 6.4. Particularly in the context of Josh. 24 where עבד describes the worship of foreign gods, the phrase בית עבדים also serves to draw attention to the illicit worship. For a full discussion of the formula, cf. the excursus in Floss, *Jahwe Dienen*, pp. 56-63.

6. Perlitt, *Bundestheologie*, p. 255.

7. Cf. Deut. 6.10-11; Neh. 9.25.

which is, perhaps, analogous to 'booty of. . . ' in the battle reports.[1] While the former occupants are no longer a concern in Joshua 24, their gods are an issue. In contrast to the previous chapters there is *no* mention of surviving nations.

Israel's involvement is minimized in the account of the conflict with the nations in Egypt and in Canaan. This exalts the might and grace of YHWH, which is also emphasized by the novel presentation of the Amorites and leaders of Jericho coming out in aggressive war. Another innovation to the book of Joshua is the explanation that the Lord 'sent a hornet before you, which drove them out before you, the two kings of the Amorites' (24.12).[2] Whenever גרש (*pi*) is used in relation to the conquest, YHWH is the subject (Exod. 23.28-31; 33.2; Josh. 24.12, 18; Judg. 2.3; 6.9).[3] Elsewhere, 'to be driven out' means to lose one's rights to something (Judg. 11.2; 1 Sam. 26.19; 1 Kgs 2.27). Likewise, this is the implication of the account in Joshua 24 of YHWH banishing the occupants of the land. The description is very similar to that promised in Exodus:

Exod. 23.28	ושלחתי את־הצרעה לפניך וגרשה . . . מלפניך
Exod. 33.2	ושלחתי לפניך מלאך וגרשתי . . .
Josh. 24.12	ואשלח לפניכם את־הצרעה ותגרש אותם מפניכם

Apart from the verbal similarities, all three texts are accompanied by a list of the pre-Israelite nations. The image of the hornet, הצרעה,

1. This implication is not always the case. The expression occurs most often in the latter chapters of Genesis (35 times as opposed to 27 times elsewhere in the Hebrew Bible) where the 'land of Canaan' is distinguished from the 'land of Egypt'. Similarly it is used to distinguish Cisjordan from the 'land of Gilead' notably in Josh. 22 and in Num. 34; for discussion on the usage in Num. 34, cf. Wüst, *Untersuchungen*, pp. 110-12.

2. If the narrative sequence is followed then these two kings are from Cisjordan. Exactly the same appellation is however used of Sihon and Og in Josh. 2.10 and 9.10, שני מלכי האמרי. Although Sihon and Og are many times called 'kings of the Amorites' it is only here in Josh. 24 that one has the expression standing on its own in this way. The verbal similarities to the kings of the Transjordan serve possibly to create a parallel between the east and west banks. The LXX appears to treat the reference in a reflective way, and reads 'the *twelve* kings of the Amorites'. According to E. Tov, 'Midrash-Type Exegesis in the LXX of Joshua', *RB* 85 (1978), pp. 50-61 (60-61), the number represents a summary of conquest of Cisjordan: the kings of Jericho and Ai together with the five kings of the south (10.5) and the five kings of the north (11.1).

3. Cf. Halbe, *Das Privilegrecht Jahwes*, pp. 140-42.

occurs only in conquest texts (Exod. 23.28; Deut. 7.20; Josh. 24.12), and serves further to underwrite the power of the Lord.[1]

It is emphatically stated that 'it was not by your sword or by your bow' (24.12). This gracious initiative serves as the basis of the appeal for the gratitude of Israel. The exhortation to a response is introduced by. . . ועתה (24.14), and follows a long recitation of the acts of YHWH (24.2-13).

The Israelites are called to put away the gods which, presumably, they have brought with them.[2] The verb which is employed, סור *hiph* (24.14, 23), is characteristic of the cult-reform texts from Joshua to 2 Kings.[3] They are warned that, if they should continue to serve foreign gods, then YHWH 'will turn and do you harm, and consume you, after having done you good' (24.20). In 8.24 and 10.20, כלה (*piel*), 'to consume or finish', concerns the utter destruction of the nations. In this manner Israel is threatened with the same fate as befell the nations. Nevertheless, the strategy of the argument is not to obtain a response to a threat but a response of gratitude.

This is an unambiguous call to repentance, even though the 'appeal' in Joshua 24 is far less aggressive than is usually found in the cult-reform texts.[4] H.W. Wolff[5] and, more recently, J.P. Floss[6] have demonstrated that an important theme of the DtrH is a call to repentance functioning as an interpretative key to the theology of Israel's history. Joshua's speech in ch. 24 is a call to repentance and, as the final statement of the book it transforms the whole work into a prelude to this call.

---

1.   The image could be analogous to the plagues of Exodus, cf. E. Blum, *Die Komposition der Vätergeschichte* (WMANT, 57; Neukirchen–Vluyn: Neukirchener, 1984), p. 53.

2.   Blum, *Die Komposition*, p. 51.

3.   Judg. 10.16; 1 Sam. 7.3, 4; 28.3; 1 Kgs 15.12, 13; 2 Kgs 3.2; 18.4, 22; 23.19. Cf. Hoffmann, *Reform und Reformen*, p. 346.

4.   Cf. J. van Seters, 'Joshua 24 and the Problem of Tradition in the Old Testament', in W.B. Barrick and J.R. Spencer (eds.), *In the Shelter of Elyon: Essays on Ancient Palestinian Life and Literature in Honor of G.W. Ahlström* (JSOTSup, 31; Sheffield: JSOT Press, 1984), pp. 139-58 (146).

5.   Wolff, 'Das Kerygma', pp. 171-86.

6.   Floss, *Jahwe Dienen*.

4. Conclusion

Chapter 23 presents a parallel conclusion to the work. Differences between the two lend support to the thesis that ch. 24 is part of a subsequent composition.[1] A pertinent difference is that while the nations are a prevalent threat in ch. 23, they form part of history in ch. 24. Nevertheless, the common denominator of the three stories which conclude the narrative is the warning that illicit worship will result in the reversal of the conquest, and Israel will share the fate of the nations. Therefore, the nations serve as symbols of extreme danger for Israel, whether remembered as past history or as present reality.

1.   The fundamental differences between chs. 23 and 24 have long been recognized by scholarship; for a recent discussion cf. Blum, *Studien zur Komposition des Pentateuchs*, pp. 288 ff.

Part II
THE IMAGE OF THE NATIONS

Chapter 6

'ALL THE OCCUPANTS OF THE LAND'

The development of the narrative in Joshua passes through three distinct phases: the conquest, the settlement, and the concluding reflection. The ways in which the nations are characterized are slightly different in each of these phases. In the first phase they are presented in comprehensive categories.

1. *Comprehensive Titles for the Nations*

There is a concern to present the nations as a totality throughout the conquest narrative of Joshua 1–12. Several titles are used to achieve this effect.

a. *'All the Occupants of the Land'*

In the DtrH, יֹשְׁבֵי הָאָרֶץ is used consistently to describe the pre-Israelite occupants (Josh. 2.9, 24; 7.9; 9.11, 24; Judg. 1.32, 33; 2.2; 11.21; 1 Sam. 27.8; 2 Sam. 5.6).[1] On occasions the formula is parallel to 'Canaanites', 'Amorites', or one of the other primaeval nations (Josh. 7.9; Judg. 1.32, 33; 11.21; 1 Sam. 27.8; 2 Sam. 5.6).

The formula has a distinctive function in Joshua. It always appears as כָּל־יֹשְׁבֵי הָאָרֶץ, a formulation which is found only in Joshua, and is due to the concern to present the nations as an aggregate. Further, it is significant to note that these occupants of the land in Joshua are always *doing* something, even if it is only hearing and trembling.[2] The remainder of the DtrH simply records their destruction or continued presence in the land.

When the term יֹשְׁבֵי (or יוֹשְׁבֵי) is combined with a city name it is

1. Cf. also Exod. 23.31; 34.12.
2. Cf. below, the next chapter for discussion on 'hearing' as a compositional structure.

employed to describe the occupants of a particular city, for example, in Josh. 8.24, 26; 9.3; 10.1; 11.19.[1] This nomination designates all the people of the enemy, and is mentioned to record either their destruction or continued presence in the land. The Gibeonites are the exception from this appellation. The expression has an unusually important function in the book as a whole because the issue of the land occupation is central, and ישב is the climax of the conquest. In a set of texts which will be discussed in Chapter 8 (13.13; 15.63; 16.10; 17.12-13), the continued presence of the nations, which is noted by the verb ישב, is preceded by a statement about Israel's failure to conquer. Thus it can be argued that ישבי has suggestions of political power and land ownership.[2]

This establishes that, while 'occupants of. . . ' is usually an adequate translation for ישבי, the expression needs to be understood in relation to the conquest. Therefore it has political, juridical and military connotations.

It is possible to conclude that the comprehensive title, כל־ישבי הארץ presents the combined force of resistance to Israelite occupation of the land. As rival claimants to the land they hear, fear and fight. This unique appearance of the title demonstrates that the occupation occurs on a grand scale. A similar function is served by the lists of pre-Israelite nations in Joshua.

b. *Lists of Pre-Israelite Nations*
Six of these lists are presented in Joshua (3.10; 5.1; 9.1; 11.3; 12.8; 24.11). The first is in 3.10:

> Hereby you shall know that the living God is among you, and he will not fail to drive out from before you the Canaanites, the Hittites, the Hivites, the Perizzites, the Girgashites, the Amorites, and the Jebusites.

Twenty-eight lists of pre-Israelite nations are distributed in Israel's

1. For a discussion of the formulas, cf. C. Schäfer-Lichtenberger, *Stadt und Eidgenossenschaft im Alten Testament: Eine Auseinandersetzung mit Max Webers Studie 'Das antike Judentum'* (BZAW, 156; Berlin: de Gruyter, 1983), pp. 204-208.
2. N.K. Gottwald, *The Tribes of Yahweh: A Sociology of the Religion of Liberated Israel 1250–1050 bce* (London: SCM Press, 1980), pp. 512-34, argues that when used in the accounts of the conquest ישבי can be translated as 'rulers of'. Gottwald's thesis can be demonstrated in 12.2-5 where it is used of Sihon and Og, with ישב being parallel to משל, but all that can be said for the remainder of the instances in Joshua is that it is possible to understand them in this way.

descriptions of its early history.[1] The variety of number and order of
the nations is a problem which has exercised scholars. Attempts have
been made to assign the various lists to different literary sources or
redactional stages. Thus, for example, F. Langlamet has noticed that
the four instances where the Hittites head the list occur in
Deuteronomy and Joshua. This leads him to conclude that they belong
to a 'Deuteronomistic type' and, further, that the lists beginning with
the Canaanites are of a 'Yahwistic type'.[2] However the textual basis of
these conclusions is too slender. The number of exceptions occlude
any neat explanations. The only significant pattern that emerges is that
24 of the 28 begin with either Canaanites, Hittites or Amorites. These
titles are often employed as comprehensive descriptions of all the pre-
Israelite occupants of the land.

A novel historical explanation for the differences between the lists
is offered by T. Ishida. He demonstrates that the meaning of these
terms is fluid and changing during the period of the monarchy, and
suggests that this is the reason for the differing emphases between the
lists.[3] His thorough examination of the texts is undermined by the
stated assumption that the lists are transmitted independently of their
literary context. Therefore, there is a consequent lack of attention to
their literary function.

I shall argue that the concern with the order and number of the
nations listed is less important than a study of the way in which the
lists function in their literary contexts. The literary functions of the
lists of pre-Israelite nations in the Hebrew Bible may be summarized
as follows:

---

1. Cf. below, Appendix, on the lists of pre-Israelite nations.
2. F. Langlamet, *Gilgal et les récits de la traversée du Jourdain* (CRB, 11; Paris:
Gabalda, 1969), p. 110. M. Noth, 'Nu 21 als Glied der "Hexateuch"-Erzählung',
ZAW 58 (1940–41), pp. 161-89 (= M. Noth, *Aufsätze zur biblischen Landes- und
Altertumskunde*, I [ed. H.W. Wolff; Neukirchen–Vluyn: Neukirchener, 1971],
pp. 75-101 [100]), has come to similar conclusions. He however links the Hittites to
the Priestly writer, the Yahwist to the Canaanites and the Elohist to the Amorites.
3. T. Ishida, 'The Structure and Historical Implications of the Lists of Pre-
Israelite Nations', *Bib* 60 (1979), pp. 461-90. Richter, *Bearbeitungen*, pp. 41-44,
says that the differences are due to different schools having differing versions of
these lists which were used in historical-geographical education.

a. Ethno-geographical descriptions of the inhabitants of the
    world (Gen. 10.15-18; and an identical copy in 1 Chron.
    1.13-16).

b. The pre-Israelite inhabitants of the land in which Israel is
    sojourning, in both cases the Canaanites and the Perizzites
    (Gen. 13.7; 34.30).

c. As part of the Lord's promise of land, 'the land of. . . ', the
    lists serve, along with other devices, to emphasize the
    geographical size of the land (Gen. 15.19-21; Exod. 3.8, 17;
    13.5; Neh. 9.8).

d. The nations that are to be destroyed. Paradoxically there is
    the accompanying exhortation not to intermingle because of
    the danger of syncretism. The Lord is usually the speaker,
    and their number serves to emphasize the power of the Lord
    and the extent of the temptation (Exod. 23.23, 28; 34.11;
    Deut. 7.1; 20.17).[1] The failure to destroy these nations and
    the consequent intermingling is bewailed in Judg. 3.5.

e. Recorded simply as those who will be destroyed (Exod. 33.2;
    Josh. 3.10; 5.1; 9.1; 11.3; 12.8; Judg. 1.4, 5; 1 Sam. 27.8) or
    as those who had been destroyed (Josh. 24.11). Their number
    emphasizes the power of the Lord in being able to deal with
    them. The exact opposite is presented in the faithless report
    of the spies in which Israel fears their numbers (Num.
    13.29). Amalek's inclusion both here and in 1 Sam. 27.8
    appears significant because to be on the list is to be a
    candidate for destruction.

f. For the remainder of the DtrH they are recorded in the
    census (2 Sam. 24.7) and the matter finally is settled when
    they are reduced to slavery under Solomon and never
    mentioned again (1 Kgs 9.20; cf. 2 Chron. 8.7).

g. In Ezra 9.1 the list is used again in order to emphasize the
    horror of intermingling. Here it is augmented by the
    Ammonites, Moabites and Egyptians to make it a
    contemporary statement.

The lists of pre-Israelite nations present a variety of literary functions. They are included in a carefully devised plan as part of a
schema involving the fulfilment of the land promise in the DtrH.

---

1. Deut. 7.1 introduces the list with, גוים רבים.

According to W. Richter, the lists in Exod. 3.8, 17; 13.5; 23.23, 28; 33.2; 34.11; Deut. 7.1; 20.17; Josh. 3.10; 9.1; 11.3; 12.8; 24.11; (Judg. 3.5); 1 Kgs 9.20, follow the theological schema of land promise and conquest. He labels this deuteronomistic.[1] The argument has been criticized on the grounds that a single redactional level is insufficient to explain the differences in detail between the lists.[2] However, the criticism is unsatisfactory because it does not allow for variations in style within a composition. The lists in Joshua all have a similar literary function, while differing in particular details.

The narrative presents a far more active role for these pre-Israelite nations than one encounters anywhere outside the book of Joshua. Elsewhere they play no active role in the narrative at all.[3] The lists in Joshua are unparalleled because they are given a human face by serving as part of the expression 'the king(s) of. . . ' (5.1; 9.1; 11.1-3; 12.7-8),[4] or, together with the phrase בעלי־יריחו, 'the leaders of Jericho',[5] who take the initiative in fighting against Israel (24.11). The only exception is 3.10 which lists the nations in the normal impersonal way.

The lists in Joshua are part of the narrative structure, and serve as a constant reminder of the presence of the enemy. These nations hear of the mighty acts of the Lord at regular intervals. They are part of the narrative structure introduced ויהי כשמע (5.1; 9.1; 11.1ff.). The only exceptions are in 3.10 and 12.8 where their destruction is simply recorded, and 24.11 in which they come out to fight against Israel.

Most of the lists begin with 'Canaanites', 'Amorites' or 'Hittites'. These nations can also appear on their own as comprehensive titles of all the pre-Israelite occupants of the land.

c. 'The Canaanites'
The Canaanites appear in most of the lists in Joshua. The title can apply to all the doomed inhabitants of the land (7.9), or to groups

---

1. Richter, *Bearbeitungen*, p. 43.
2. Halbe, *Das Privilegrecht Jahwes*, pp. 140-46.
3. The only possible exception being Gen. 34.30 where Jacob fears that the action of his sons will make him odious to the Canaanites and the Perizzites.
4. The list in 12.8 is introduced by ואלה מלכי הארץ in 12.7.
5. On the use of בעלי העיר as a designation for the leaders of Canaanite cities, cf. Schäfer-Lichtenberger, *Stadt und Eidgenossenschaft*, pp. 213-22.

remaining in the land after the conquest (13.3-4; 16.10; 17.12, 13).[1]
They can be distinguished from the Amorites, and limited to the plains
(5.1; 11.3; 13.3, 4; cf. Deut. 1.7).[2] M. Noth explains the texts which
limit the Amorites to the hill country and the Canaanites to the plains
as pre-deuteronomistic elements which have not been incorporated
into the ideological and literary categories which see all the nations in
the land as a unity.[3] However, when they are geographically so distinguished in Josh. 5.1 and 11.3 the Canaanites of the plains and the
Amorites of the hills are *part* of a list of pre-Israelite nations and
therefore also serve as comprehensive ideological categories. In con-
tradistinction to the rest of the DtrH, 'Canaanites' are not presented as
a religious threat in Joshua.

In the DtrH the Canaanites are prominent as enemies who continue
to dwell in the land and a religious threat up to the period of the
monarchy. There are only two further references to them (2 Sam.
24.7; 1 Kgs 9.16[4]), and in neither instance are they Israel's enemies or
a religious threat. After the report of their enslavement in 1 Kgs 9.20-
21 they are not mentioned again. Thus they always are conceived of as
living in the distant past, and reference to them usually performs an
ideological function.

It has been argued that there are traces of an understanding of the
Canaanites as an upper-class group in the conquest narratives.[5] The
term can have this function in other contexts, but the only direct
evidence in Joshua is 17.16, 18 in which the Canaanites of the plain
are said to have chariots of iron. It can be argued that this is a form of
military technology based on wealth.

The reference to 'chariots of iron' certainly does introduce a
powerful negative prejudice against Canaanites.[6] J.F.A. Sawyer

1. The use of 'Canaanites' as a particular designation for those who continue in
the land is also evident in Judges, cf. 1.28, 29, 30, etc.
2. But elsewhere they are said to occupy the plains and the hill country
(17.16, 18).
3. Noth, 'Nu 21 als Glied', *Aufsätze*, pp. 95-97.
4. In recording that there were still Canaanites in Gezer the DtrH is being very
consistent with itself as the continued presence of Canaanites is recorded in Josh.
16.10; cf. Judg. 1.29, 'However they did not drive out the Canaanites that dwelt in
Gezer: so the Canaanites have dwelt in the midst of Ephraim to this day but have
become slaves to do forced labour.'
5. Cf. particularly, Gottwald, *The Tribes of Yahweh*, pp. 499-500.
6. Cf. above, Chapter 3, the discussion on the destruction of horses and

demonstrates that *iron* has 'peculiarly ugly or frightening associations' and is 'an emotive term, suggesting, in almost all its occurrences, foreign aggression and brutality'.[1] However, the Amorites are associated with aggressive warfare to a greater degree than the Canaanites.

d. *'The Amorites'*

While the Canaanites are regularly listed as those remaining in the land, the Amorites have a more active role in the narrative of Joshua. They are introduced as the pre-Israelite occupants of Transjordan who are destroyed by Moses, and often are listed together with their kings Sihon and Og.[2] The reason for mentioning them on each occasion is to record the fact of their death at the hand of the Israelites who occupied their land (2.10; 9.10; 12.1-2; 13.8-12; 13.21; 24.8). The same can be said of the other references to the Transjordanian Amorites that are scattered in several parts of the Hebrew Bible (cf. Deut. 1.4; 3.2; Judg. 11.19-23; Ps. 135.10-11; Ps. 136.18-19).[3] Their destruction always is associated with the Lord's gift of their land to Israel.[4]

In Joshua these references to what happened in Transjordan serve as a model for the conquest of Cisjordan.[5] The fact that Israel's enemy is on both sides of the Jordan is another means of portraying the unity of Israel's territory, east and west.

The term is used of an enemy in Cisjordan that will engage in aggressive warfare against Israel (7.7; 10.5-6)[6] and yet be defeated

chariots in 11.6, 9 which is understandable in its ideological dimensions.

1. J.F.A. Sawyer, 'The Meaning of *barzel* in the Biblical Expressions "chariots of iron", "yoke of iron", etc.', in J.F.A. Sawyer and D.J.A. Clines (eds.), *The History and Archaeology of Late Bronze and Iron Age Jordan and North-West Arabia* (JSOTSup, 24; Sheffield: JSOT Press, 1983), pp. 129-34 (129, 133).

2. Cf. Noth, 'Nu 21 als Glied', *Aufsätze*, pp. 94-101, for a thorough study of the literary functions of 'Amorite' in the Hebrew Bible.

3. In 1 Kgs 4.19 they are simply part of a geographical description of Transjordan, as the former inhabitants.

4. The Transjordanian Amorites are mentioned in Josh. 13.4, but simply as a neutral geographical description although it could be significant that the unconquered territory extends to their border.

5. The pattern of using the conquest of the Amorites in Transjordan as a model also appears in Deut. 3.2 and Judg. 11.19-23.

6. Cf. Deut. 2.16–3.11, where the Transjordanian Amorites also have a reputation for being the aggressors.

thoroughly (10.12; 24.12, 18). The 'gods of the Amorites' are perceived as an ongoing religious threat (24.15; Judg. 6.10). Their connection with forbidden religious practices appears in the course of an account of the destruction of the kings of Transjordan in which there is a reference to the slaying of 'Balaam, son of Beor, the soothsayer' (Josh. 13.22). Significantly, the parallel text in Num. 13.8 makes no mention of Balaam's soothsaying, a practice which is condemned in Deut. 18.9-14.[1]

In the remainder of the DtrH the name 'Amorites' reappears in 1 Sam. 7.14, in which the Philistines are connected with them as the prime enemies of the Lord,[2] and in 2 Sam. 21.2, in which the Gibeonites are characterized as 'the remnant of the Amorites'. The question of their destiny is solved by their inclusion in the list of the nations enslaved by Solomon (1 Kgs 9.20-21). Finally, they are *remembered* for their abominable religious practices in 1 Kgs 21.26 and 2 Kgs 21.11 (cf. Gen. 15.16).

The fact that they are always referred to as dwelling in the distant past suggests that they were regarded as symbols of primordial evil.[3] The references in the Psalms to their kings in Transjordan, Sihon and Og, serve the same function (Pss. 135.11; 136.19 f.). In Deut. 1.27-28 the Amorites are associated with giants and, particularly, with the Anakim,[4] who in turn are linked to the Rephaim in Deut. 2.10-11, 20. Og of Bashan is described as 'one of the remnant of the Rephaim, who dwelt at Ashtaroth and Edrei' in Josh. 12.4 and 13.12.[5] Rephaim are included in the list of pre-Israelite nations in Gen. 15.19-21. The ideological dimensions to the title 'Rephaim' are made even more vivid by the fact that they can be equated with the shades of the dead, for

1. E. Noort, 'Transjordan in Joshua 13: Some Aspects', in *idem* (ed.), *Studies in the History and Archaeology of Jordan III* (Amman/London: Department of Antiquities, 1988). pp. 125-29 (129).

2. Van Seters, 'The Terms "Amorite" and "Hittite" in the Old Testament', p. 75, suggests that 'Amorites' has the same ideological function as 'Philistines'. Although the Philistines are mentioned in Josh. 13.3, at this stage there is no mention of warfare with them.

3. M. Liverani, 'The Amorites', in D.J. Wiseman (ed.), *Peoples of Old Testament Times* (Oxford: Clarendon, 1975), pp. 100-33 (126).

4. Cf. Above, the discussion on the Anakim in Chapter 3.

5. Both cities are understood as being part of the land of *Rp'um* in Ugaritic texts. For a comprehensive bibliography and discussion, cf. Noort, *Studies in the History and Archaeology of Jordan III*, pp. 128-29.

example Ps. 88.11 in which מתים and רפאים are parallel. The giants among the Philistines are also linked to the legendary Rephaim (2 Sam. 21.15ff.; 1 Chron. 20.4-8). The battle with Goliath in 1 Samuel 17 illustrates how the giant is the epitome of defiance against the Lord.[1] The association of legendary giants with the Amorites appears only obliquely in Joshua by references to Anakim in 11.21ff.; 14.6, 14. The conquest of the Rephaim is implied by the reference to the boundaries of Judah and Benjamin passing along the 'Valley of Rephaim' (15.8; 18.16). However, the Rephaim are amongst those who remain unconquered in 17.14-18.

Undoubtedly, the 'Amorites' is one of the most significant titles for the nations in the narrative of Joshua, referring as it does to the ideological enemy on both sides of the Jordan.

e. 'The Hittites'

The name 'Hittites' appears in most of the lists of pre-Israelite nations in Joshua (all except 5.1). On only one occasion is it employed independently in the sense of all the inhabitants and that is 1.4 in which it functions more like a geographical than an ethnological description. The word can also have derogatory connotations (cf. Ezek. 16.3).[2]

In the subsequent DtrH, the Hittites are amongst the enslaved nations (1 Kgs 9.20). After this there are a further three references to Hittites as a group but they are presented as being outside of Israel (1 Kgs 10.29; 11.1; 2 Kgs 7.6). There are two people, Ahimelech the Hittite, who is only mentioned once (1 Sam. 26.6) and Uriah the Hittite, who is the key figure in the drama with David and Bathsheba (2 Sam. 11.3, 6, 17, 21; 12.9, 10; 23.39; 1 Kgs 15.5). His heritage is not an accidental detail because, with irony, he is presented in contrast to David as an ideal Israelite who stringently follows all the holy war regulations. It seems reasonable to conclude that 'Hittites' does have something of an ideological function in the DtrH.

f. The Ideological Significance of 'Canaanites', 'Amorites' and 'Hittites'

The names 'Canaanites', 'Amorites' and 'Hittites' all serve as symbols of primordial opposition to YHWH. They appear usually in passages

---

1. Cf. van Seters, 'The Terms "Amorite" and "Hittite"', pp. 74-75.
2. Van Seters, 'The Terms "Amorite" and "Hittite"', p. 80.

which have a kerygmatic or confessional character. As such, they serve the same function as the lists of nations.

The Canaanites, Amorites and Hittites are well known in biblical and extra-biblical sources,[1] where they sometimes appear together as a list.[2] Throughout the second and first millennia the titles are used with a certain fluidity and, at least by the eighth century BCE, they are virtually synonymous archaic terms for the inhabitants of Syria-Palestine.[3]

Their inclusion in the lists of pre-Israelite nations, along with other nations whose existence is nowhere attested outside the Bible,[4] indicates their character as a literary creation. All the nations mentioned in the lists are imbued with particular ideological import by their literary contexts, and are much more than ethnological designations.[5] A great deal of caution is necessary before the DtrH can be used as a source of ethnological information. The term 'Canaanites', in particular, has been used frequently by scholars as an historical designation with scant recognition of the very precise literary function that it performs in the DtrH.[6]

Had the survey only dealt with selected references in the DtrH to 'Canaanites', 'Amorites' or 'Hittites', the conclusion would have been less convincing. It has been possible to demonstrate that these names

1. Cf. A.R. Millard, 'The Canaanites', in D.J. Wiseman (ed.), *Peoples of Old Testament Times* (Oxford: Clarendon Press, 1975), pp. 29-52; Liverani, 'The Amorites', pp. 100-33; H.A. Hoffner, 'The Hittites and Hurrians', in Wiseman, *Peoples*, pp. 197-228.

2. Cf. Ishida, 'Lists of Pre-Israelite Nations', p. 472 n. 19 for bibliography.

3. Cf. van Seters, 'The Terms "Amorite" and "Hittite"', p. 66.

4. With varying degrees of plausibility several attempts have been made at identifying the Jebusites as a sub-unit of the Hittites, the Girgashites as a sub-unit of the Teucrians, the Perizzites as a sub-unit of the Philistines, and the Hivites as Ahhijawa; for discussion and bibliography, cf. O. Margalith, 'The Hivites', *ZAW* 100 (1988), pp. 60-70.

5. Cf. R. de Vaux, 'Les Hurrites de l'Historie et les Horites de la Bible', *RB* 74 (1967), pp. 481-503, who says that neither the Hurrians nor the Hittites in the Bible can be linked to groups outside the Bible, as these terms have an ideological function in the Hebrew Bible. The same argument is employed in relation to the other pre-Israelite nations by several scholars, notably, Liverani, 'The Amorites', pp. 100-33; van Seters, 'The Terms "Amorite" and "Hittite"', pp. 64-81.

6. Cf. A. Haldar, 'Canaanites', *IDB*, I, pp. 494-98, for an example of the indiscriminate combination of literary and archaeological material that has characterized much of the discussion.

are loaded with distinctive ideological connotations in almost every instance.

The references to the nations that remained after the conquest are usually explained as an attempt to bridge the gap between the claims of absolute destruction and the reality of these nations continuing to exist in the land.[1] However, the historical basis for this supposition has in recent years been the source of considerable discussion amongst scholars. In demonstrating that Alt's theory of Samaria as a 'Canaanite' city is based on insufficient evidence, G. Buccellati emphasizes that Samaria was as much Canaanite and as much Israelite as any other city in Israel.[2]

It is difficult to find any 'nations' in the land during the final days of the monarchy through to the post-exilic period, the most likely setting of the book of Joshua, that could be likened to those described in Joshua. If a 'referent' is necessary then J. van Seters's solution is more plausible.[3] He views the nations described in the accounts of the conquest as reflecting the situation of non-Israelites living in the land after the exile, or a situation of diaspora during the author's day. By making everything archaic, authority is given to the rules relating to the nations.

The evidence shows that the terms 'Canaanite', 'Amorite' and 'Hittite' in the DtrH refer to all the pre-Israelite occupants of the land, and function primarily as ideological categories. In Joshua these titles are included in the action of the narrative by appearing as part of the formula 'the kings of the. . . ', a feature almost unique to Joshua.[4]

g. *Lists of Defeated Kings*
The kings of the nations feature prominently not only in individual stories but are part of significant compositional structures. There is a repeated pattern denoting kings *hearing*, particularly, with reference

---

1. Cf. Otto, *Das Bundes-Mazzotfest von Gilgal*, pp. 216-17.
2. G. Buccellati, *Cities and Nations of Ancient Syria: An Essay on Political Institutions with Special Reference to the Israelite Kingdoms* (Rome: Istituto di Studi del Vicino Oriente, 1967), esp. pp. 228-33; and more recently, Schäfer-Lichtenberger, *Stadt und Eidgenossenschaft*, esp. pp. 396-417.
3. Van Seters, 'The Terms "Amorite" and "Hittite"', p. 68.
4. Cf. elsewhere 'the kings of the Amorites' is a standard appellation when referring to Sihon and Og, Deut. 1.4; 3.2; Judg. 11.19; Ps. 135.10-11; Ps. 136.18-19.

to what had happened to other kings described in the previous story.[1]
Another pattern relates to the destruction of King B in the fashion of
King A.[2] Therefore, the *hearing* and the final destruction of the kings
serve as the introduction and the inevitable conclusion to the
individual stories of conquest.

The kings play a central role in the stories themselves as symbols of
what is to be destroyed. In chs. 10–11 the kings emerge as the opposition, organize a conspiracy and are soundly defeated. Their personal
destruction receives considerable attention. The concern is to demonstrate the comprehensiveness of the enemy ranged against Israel and
its subsequent destruction, first in the south and then in the north. The
record of all the defeated kings on both sides of the Jordan in ch. 12,
introduced by ואלה מלכי הארץ (12.1, 7), is detailed and covers the
whole land. The cities listed in Joshua 1–12 are normally part of a
formula, 'the king of. . . ,[3] and ch. 12 makes the point that *all* were
destroyed.

h. *Conclusion*
A concern to demonstrate the comprehensiveness of the nations is
evident in the titles used of the nations in Joshua 1–12, 'all the
occupants of the land', lists of pre-Israelite nations, 'Canaanites',
'Amorites' and lists of kings.[4] This combination produces an overwhelming impact on the reader. The conclusion of the conquest
signals, for a moment, an end to the comprehensive titles for the
nations.

2. *The Transition from All the Nations to Single Nations*

The detailed description of the destruction in ch. 12 causes the statement in ch. 13 about unconquered land and remaining nations to come
as an unexpected surprise. The differences between chs. 1–12 and

1.   Cf. the next chapter.
2.   Cf. above, Chapter 3.
3.   Usually all the attention is on an individual city or king yet the meaning can
be fluid, particularly in the case of Jericho which can be understood as representing
all the enemy; cf. 24.11 where the list of pre-Israelite nations is added to the men of
Jericho who fight the Israelites.
4.   Two further comprehensive titles, 'all peoples' (4.24) and 'all their enemies'
(10.25), appear also in chs. 23–24, and will be discussed below.

13.1ff. often are explained with respect to differing origins.[1] While there are considerable differences between the two sections, there are also noticeable continuities, particularly with regard to the way in which new information is introduced into the narrative with the use of headings:[2]

12.1	ואלה מלכי הארץ אשר הכו בני־ישראל וירשו את־ארצם בעבר הירדן מזרחה השמש
12.7	ואלה מלכי הארץ אשר הכה יהושע ובני ישראל בעבר הירדן ימה
13.2	זאת הארץ הנשארת
14.1	ואלה אשר־נחלו בני־ישראל בארץ כנען
Judg. 3.1	ואלה הגוים אשר הניח יהוה לנסות בם את־ישראל

At a thematic level the settlement only begins from 14.1 onwards, where it is introduced by 'and these are the inheritances'.[3] This introduction forms part of the same compositional framework which introduces the destruction of all the kings of Transjordan and Cisjordan, 'and these are the kings of the land' in 12.1, 7.

The transition from all the nations to single nations appears to be a carefully constructed feature of the composition. It is no accident of the redactional process that the occasional references after 13.1 to groups that remain in the land are to *isolated* groups which are no longer part of a united opposition. A title like 'the Canaanites' no longer applies to the combined opposition, but to individual groups

---

1. Noth, *Josua*, is a representative example of this approach: chs. 1–12 consist largely of aetiological traditions, while 13.1ff. largely of a combination of city lists and territorial boundaries.

2. G. Seitz, *Redaktionsgeschichtliche Studien zum Deuteronomium* (BWANT, 93; Stuttgart: Kohlhammer, 1971), p. 31, who draws attention to these 'Überschriften', has also outlined a similar structure in Deuteronomy:

1.1	אלה הדברים
4.44	וזאת התורה
4.45	אלה העדת והחקים והמשפטים
6.1	וזאת המצוה החקים והמשפטים
12.1	אלה החקים והמשפטים
28.69	אלה דברי הברית
33.1	וזאת הברכה

However, whether it is possible to speak of a 'system' in Deuteronomy is another question; cf. N. Lohfink, 'Die *huqqîm ûmišpatîm* im Buch Deuteronomium und Ihre Neubegrenzung durch Dtn 12, 1', *Bib.* 70 (1989), pp. 1-30 (1 n. 2), who points out that these 'Überschriften' differ slightly from each other in their literary functions.

3. Ottosson, *Erövring och fördelning av Land*.

which have managed to survive the onslaught. Their loss of power is illustrated by the omission of any reference to surviving kings in relation to these groups. The names of cities, which abound in Joshua, are no longer part of the formula 'the king of. . . ' but appear on their own.[1] Indeed, most city names in chs. 13–19 have no relationship at all to the nations.

3. *Individual Nations Listed in Chapters 13–19*

As Israel divides and settles the territory, the impression is created that the territory is deserted in chs. 13–19. Therefore reference to surviving nations comes as a surprise to the reader, and appears to contradict the context. The continued presence of the nations is recorded in a variety of ways.

a. *Occupants of Unconquered Territory*

The specific purpose in 13.2-6 is to list the extent of 'the land that remains'. This is not achieved by the kind of town and territorial listing that is a feature of the settlement accounts, but by recording a list of nations, each in a genitive construction. Those listed are Philistines (13.2, 3),[2] Geshurites (13.2), Avvim (13.3), Canaanites (13.3, 4), Sidonians (13.4, 6), Amorites (13.4) and Gebalites (13.5). The Lord promises to conquer, יָרַשׁ (*hiph*), these nations (13.6).

The land to be conquered by the tribe of Joseph is also linked by means of genitive constructions to Perizzites, Rephaim and Canaanites (17.14-18). While it is possible to understand some of these references in the sense 'the land that had once belonged to. . . ', as in 'the land of the Canaanites', the list in 13.2-6 leaves no doubt that the nations named continue to occupy sections of the land.[3]

Judg. 3.1-6 lists the nations that continue to live in the land. The

---

1. For the sake of exactness it should be noted that in the listing of unconquered territory in 13.2-6 'the five rulers of the Philistines', חֲמֵשֶׁת סַרְנֵי פְלִשְׁתִּים, are associated with the names of five cities; cf. the same formulation in Judg. 3.3.

2. The towns of the five rulers of the Philistines are Gaza, Ashdod, Ashkelon, Gath and Ekron. Surprisingly Ekron, Ashdod and Gaza are later included in Judah's territory (15.45-47). The same tension appears in Judges where the towns are conquered by Judah (Judg. 1.18-19), but later the five rulers of the Philistines are included amongst the nations who remain (Judg. 3.3).

3. Soggin, *Joshua*, p. 181.

passage offers a theological reflection which links the period of conquest to the period of the judges by commenting that the nations that remain are there to test Israel's faithfulness. Although there is not the same stated interpretation of history in Josh. 13.2-6, it also serves as a key statement in the narrative of Joshua.[1]

b. *Part of a Territorial Description*
Several nations are mentioned in the course of geographical descriptions. The territories of the Archites and Japhletites are included amongst town names and geographical areas in the territory of the tribe of Joseph (16.3). The boundary of Judah passes the 'Shoulder of the Jebusite' (explained as Jerusalem) and the 'Valley of Rephaim' (15.8). The boundary of Benjamin also passes the 'Shoulder of the Jebusite' and the 'Valley of Rephaim' (18.16). The nations in these descriptions are little more than geographical entities.

Some of these references might be explained as pre-deuteronomistic remnants of earlier tradition. However, there are references to individual nations which are included in a carefully constructed compositional framework, and which require another kind of explanation.

c. *Nations Listed as Part of a Formula 'And They Dwelt in the midst of Israel unto This Day'*
The language which reports the nations surviving after the conquest presents common features:

> 6.25 the family of Rahab
> 9.7, 16, 22, 27; 10.1 Gibeonites
> 13.13 Geshurites and Maacathites
> 15.63 Jebusites
> 16.10 the Canaanites of Gezer
> cf. 17.12-13 the Canaanites of Bethshean, Ibleam, Dor, Endor, Taanach, Megiddo and all their villages.

A subsequent analysis of these texts will demonstrate that they form an important element in the structure of Joshua.

---

1. Cf. below Chapter 8 for fuller treatment of this text.

d. *Conclusions*

The nations are listed individually in the course of the settlement narrative. There is no longer any thought of a united opposition to the new owners of the land. The language returns to general categories for describing the occupants of the land from 21.44. These references only occur in the *past* tense![1]

4. *A Return to Comprehensive Titles*

a. *'All Their Enemies'*

When the nations are viewed as military opponents they can be called the enemy. The phrase כל־איביכם (10.25) or מסביב + כל־איביהם (21.44 × 2; 23.1), is another of the general categories for the occupants of the land.[2] In the DtrH כל־איבים (2 Sam. 3.18; 7.11; 22.1; 2 Kgs 17.39; 21.14) and מסביב + כל־איבים (Deut. 12.10; 25.19; Judg. 8.34; 1 Sam. 14.47; 2 Sam. 7.1), both phrases with their possessive pronouns are used to indicate the importance of a military victory and the subsequent peace. Therefore they often serve as an epoch marker.

The simple איבים plus the possessive pronoun has the sense of a general category (Deut. 20.1; Judg. 2.14, etc.). This is also true of איבים in Joshua (7.8, 12 × 2, 13; 10.19; 22.8), in which, even in the context of a battle against a particular city, it has a more general meaning.

The idea of the enemy as a threat to Israel is the basis for the theological explanation of the enemy of Israel as an enemy of YHWH. In particular the Psalms portray the enemy as the cause of sickness and hardship (cf. Pss. 6; 30; 38; 41; 102). This could generate the perception that the enemy is in association with a demonic power.[3] The expression 'all these nations' shares at least some of these ideological associations.

---

1. The narrative of the book concludes with two speeches made by Joshua in chs. 23 and 24. In the course of these speeches, which are reported in the perfect tense, the destruction of the combined force of the enemy is recorded as having already happened in the past.

2. Outside of Joshua 'the enemy round about' usually means those beyond Israel's territory who nevertheless constitute a serious threat to her continued existence.

3. Cf. H. Ringgren, איב, *ThWAT*, I, pp. 228-35 (234).

b. *'All These Nations'*

גוים is part of a king's title in 12.23. Apart from this occurrence, it appears in ch. 23. Here it plays a prominent role:

23.3	כל־הגוים האלה
23.4	הגוים הנשארים האלה
	כל־הגוים
23.7	בגוים האלה הנשארים האלה אתכם
23.9	¹גוים גדלים ועצמים
23.12	ביתר הגוים האלה הנשארים האלה אתכם
23.13	הגוים האלה

The nations which are destroyed are (כל־הגוים (האלה) (23.3, 4). Those remaining in the land are described as הנשארים האלה (23.4, 7, 12), or the parallel, יתר הגוים האלה (23.12) or simply הגוים האלה (23.13).[2] The distinction reinforces the point that the former situation of a united mass of opposition is over.[3] A set of formulas unique to Joshua are employed to achieve this distinction.

The formula כל־הגוים האלה is found only in Joshua and in Deut. 11.23.[4] One part of the formula, כל־הגוים, occurs elsewhere but its application to the pre-Israelite nations is an almost unique feature of the book of Joshua. In the DtrH it usually appears in the general sense of 'all nations' (Deut. 17.14; 26.19; 28.1; 30.1; 1 Sam. 8.5, 20;

---

1. The formula, גוים גדל ועצום is found elsewhere in Deut. 4.38; 9.1 (cf. also in 9.1, ערים גדלת ובצרת בשמם; and in 9.2, עם גדול ורם בני עקים); and Deut. 11.23. The singular גוי גדול ועצום appears in Gen. 18.18; Num. 14.12. Further variations are, עם . . . רב ועצום in Exod. 1.9; גוי גדול in Exod. 32.10; גוים־רבים in Deut. 7.1; and גוי גדול עצום ורב in Deut. 26.5. In Gen. 18.18; Num. 14.12; Exod. 1.9; 32.10; Deut. 26.5 the formulas are used of Israel, but in Deut. 4.38; 7.1; 9.1; 11.23; and in Josh. 23.9, they are applied to the *nations* in the land, and always, in the *plural*. Therefore, it would seem that this second usage is characteristic of Deuteronomy and Joshua.

2. The function of 'the remnant of these nations' will be discussed in the next chapter.

3. It is because he has overlooked the careful and deliberate language distinctions that R.G. Boling, 'Some Conflate Readings in Joshua–Judges', *VT* 16 (1966), pp. 293-98 (296-97), can speak of a 'bewildering array of variation' in regard to the 'nations' in MT as well as in the versions of Josh. 23, and maintain that the differences 'may be traced to scribal caution on the one hand, scribal fallibility on the other'.

4. The usage in Deut. 11.23 can be explained by the interest in the number and strength of the enemy; the land they occupy being the exaggerated 'Euphratic' territory.

1 Kgs 5.11), or of a particular group under discussion (2 Sam. 8.11).
The exceptions are Exod. 34.10 and Deut. 11.23. Here 'all the nations'
designates the pre-Israelites.

The other part of the formula הגוים האלה is used in a very specific
sense. The rare parallels outside Joshua 23 are:

Deut.	7.17		הגוים האלה
	7.22		הגוים האל[^1]
	9.4		הגוים האלה
	9.5		הגוים האלה
	11.23	גוים גדלים ועצמים . . . כל־הגוים האלה	
	12.30		הגוים האלה
	18.9		הגוים הדם
	18.14		הגוים הלה
	20.15		הגוים־האלה
	20.16		העמים האלה
	31.3		הגוים האלה
Judg.	2.23		הגוים האלה
	3.1		אלה הגוים

On one occasion in the DtrH the formula is used of nations other than
the primaeval occupants of the land (2 Kgs 17.41), but this appears to
be a deliberate way of maligning the occupants of Samaria who are
worshipping other gods.[2] Its rare, but specific, usage show that הגוים
האלה is a technical term to describe the doomed pre-Israelite
occupants of the land.[3] The precise meaning is clarified by Deut.
20.15 in which הערים הרחקת ממך מאד are distinguished from
ערי הגוים־האלה. It is 'the cities of these nations' that are destined for
חרם.

Therefore in Joshua the formula 'all these nations' functions as a
comprehensive category for the pre-Israelite nations.

1. The abbreviated demonstrative pronoun is also found in Deut. 4.42 and
19.11 where the formula, rather significantly, is הערים האל.
2. The usage is possibly similar to the expression העם הזה, a term of abuse
which is opposed to עמי, 'my people', a feature of the rhetoric of Isaiah (cf. Isa. 9.15
as opposed to 3.12) and Jeremiah (Jer. 6.19, 21, etc.). Cf. S. Japhet, 'People and
Land in the Restoration Period', in G. Strecker (ed.), *Das Land Israel in biblischer
Zeit* (Göttinger Theologische Arbeiten, 25; Göttingen: Vandenhoeck & Ruprecht,
1983), pp. 103-25 (121).
3. The formula is recognized as typically 'deuteronomic' by M. Weinfeld,
Deuteronomy and the Deuteronomic School (Oxford: Clarendon Press, 1972),
p. 343.

c. 'All Peoples'

Although עם is usually used of Israel, it can also be employed of the subjects of a particular king (8.1; 10.33), or of the pre-Israelite nations. In 24.18 כל־העמים, and the phrase in apposition, האמרי ישב הארץ, are identified as the collective nations that have been driven out of the land by the Lord.[1] A similar expression occurs in 4.24, כל־עמי הארץ, but it is not certain that it refers to the pre-Israelite nations because it is part of a set phrase that occurs elsewhere in relation to foreign nations in general. A brief comparison will illustrate this:

Josh. 4.24	למען דעת כל־עמי הארץ את־יד יהוה כי חזקה היא
1 Kgs 8.43	למען ידעון כל־עמי הארץ את־שמך ליראה
1 Kgs 8.60	למען דעת כל־עמי הארץ כי יהוה הוא האלהים אין עוד
2 Chron. 6.33	למען ידעו כל־עמי הארץ את־שמך וליראה אתך

There are similar formulations elsewhere (2 Kgs 19.19; Isa. 37.20), but instead of כל־עמי הארץ, they read כל־מלכות הארץ, and thus retain an interest in universality. There is, therefore, a strong case for viewing the instance in Josh. 4.24 in the sense of 'all the peoples of the whole world'. However, its presence in the narrative of Joshua presents the possibility that it is one of the comprehensive expressions for the inhabitants of the land. There can be no doubt, however, that כל־העמים in 24.18, which is parallel to האמרי ישב הארץ, is one of the terms expressing the unity of opposition to YHWH and the completeness of their subsequent ruin.

5. Conclusion

The nations are portrayed in the narrative as those who occupy the land that Israel has been promised. Thus, the Philistines who play such a prominent role later in Israel's story, are only once mentioned in passing because they never possessed the land.[2] The narrative of conquest in chs. 1–12 presents the nations as those who are to be eradicated. In order to magnify the significance of the conflict, and to demonstrate the thoroughness of destruction, the nations appear in comprehensive categories. They are called 'all the inhabitants of the land', 'Canaanites' or 'Amorites'. They appear as lists of nations or as

---

1. Cf. Deut. 20.16 where 'the cities of these peoples' are to be destroyed.

2. R. North, 'The Hivites', *Bib* 54 (1973), pp. 43-62 (46). Philistines are only part of the expanded territorial vision in Josh. 13.2-6.

lists of kings. The particular interest in presenting the nations as a totality is evident not only in the number of comprehensive expressions, but in the fact that formulas like כל־ישבי הארץ are unique to Joshua. A survey of the use of the various terms in the DtrH reveals that they are used of a particular category of nations—the pre-Israelite occupants of the land. They are remembered as the opponents of YHWH who serve as symbols of all that Israel is to avoid. F. Stolz's description of the lists of pre-Israelite nations as 'eine theoretische-summierende Bezeichnung der Feinde',[1] can also be applied to all the other titles.

The nations are presented as a shattered remnant of the once-mighty owners of the land in the narrative of settlement in chs. 13–22. They cling to little parcels of land. Their loss of power and glory is illustrated by the fact that they are no longer mentioned in association with their kings.

The two speeches in chs. 23 and 24 revert to the theme of the comprehensive destruction of the nations. While ch. 23 recognizes the continuing presence of a remnant, ch. 24 makes no mention of survivors. The latter presents Israel occupying cities that once belonged to the former inhabitants. The destruction of the nations is something which has *already* taken place in the past in both speeches.

Therefore, the presentation of the nations is a carefully constituted feature in the overall narrative. Each major shift is matched by a complementary change in the formulas which relate to the nations.

The nations are given dramatic impact both by being included in the construction, 'king(s) of...', and because they have heard about the previous mighty act of the Lord. This is a striking feature of the narrative in chs. 1–12.

---

1. Stolz, *Jahwes und Israels Kriege*, p. 23.

Chapter 7

'WHEN ALL THE KINGS HEARD. . . '

1. *Hearing as a Compositional Structure*

The notion of 'hearing' appears in a number of the references to the nations:

> I know that the Lord has given you the land, and that the fear of you has fallen upon us, and that all the inhabitants of the land melt away before you. For we have *heard* how the Lord dried up the water of the Red Sea before you when you came out of Egypt, and what you did to the two kings of the Amorites that were beyond the Jordan, to Sihon and Og, whom you utterly destroyed. And as soon as we *heard* it, our hearts melted, and there was no courage left in any man, because of you; for the Lord your God is he who is God in heaven above and on earth beneath (2.9-11).

> When all the kings of the Amorites that were beyond the Jordan to the west, and all the Canaanites that were by the sea, *heard* that the Lord had dried up the waters of the Jordan for the people of Israel until they had crossed over, their heart melted, and there was no longer any spirit in them, because of the people of Israel (5.1).

> For the Canaanites and all the inhabitants of the land will *hear* of it, and will surround us, and cut off our name from the earth; and what wilt thou do for thy great name? (7.9)

> When all the kings who were beyond the Jordan in the hill country and in the lowland all along the coast of the Great Sea toward Lebanon, the Hittites, the Amorites, the Canaanites, the Perizzites, the Hivites, and the Jebusites, *heard* of this, they gathered together with one accord to fight Joshua and Israel (9.1-2).

> But when the inhabitants of Gibeon *heard* what Joshua had done to Jericho and Ai, they on their part acted with cunning. . . (cf. 9.24 where they describe their response to the conquest as being 'we feared greatly for our lives') (9.3-4).

From a very far country your servants have come, because of the name of the Lord your God; for we have *heard* a report of him, and all that he did in Egypt, and all that he did to the two kings of the Amorites who were beyond the Jordan, Sihon the king of Heshbon, and Og king of Bashan, who dwelt in the Ashtaroth (9.9-10).

At the end of three days after they had made a covenant with them, they *heard* that they were neighbours, and that they dwelt among them. And the people of Israel set out and reached their cities on the third day (9.16-17).

When Adonizedek king of Jerusalem *heard* how Joshua had taken Ai, and utterly destroyed it, doing for Ai and its king as he had done to Jericho and its king, and how the inhabitants of Gibeon had made peace with Israel and were among them, he feared greatly... So Adonizedek king of Jerusalem sent to... (10.1-3).

When Jabin king of Hazor *heard* of this, he sent to... And all these kings joined their forces, and came and encamped together at the waters of Merom, to fight with Israel (11.1-5).

And the people of Israel *heard* say, 'Behold, the Reubenites and the Gadites and the half-tribe of Manasseh have built an altar at the frontier of the land of Canaan, in the region about the Jordan, on the side that belongs to the people of Israel.' And when the people of Israel heard of it, the whole assembly of the people of Israel gathered at Shiloh, to make war against them (22.11-12).

When Phinehas the priest and the chiefs of the congregation, the heads of the families, *heard* the words that the Reubenites and the Gadites and the Manassites spoke, it pleased them well. And Phinehas the son of Eleazar the priest said... (22.30-31).

The above references demonstrate how the nations are incorporated into the narrative by the regular use of שמע. In fact, שמע creates a narrative structure that connects the stories. It recalls an earlier stage in the narrative and, simultaneously, introduces the next stage, which serves to keep up pace.[1] The introductory formulas are, ויהי כשמע (5.1; 9.1;10.1; 11.1), כי שמענו (2.10; 9.9), וישמעו (7.9; 9.16; 22.11, 12), ונשמע (2.11), and שמעו (9.3). Of particular interest is the function of 'hearing' as a means of connecting the battle reports of Joshua 1–12.

---

1. The narrative device is not unique to Joshua, and is used to great effect in the book of Jeremiah, with the opposition repeatedly hearing what Jeremiah has done and then responding (e.g. Jer. 26.7, 10, 11, 12, 21). In contrast, Jeremiah repeatedly calls Israel to hear the word of the Lord (e.g. 26.3, 4, 5).

The act of hearing introduces the kings of the nations into the narrative. In spite of its importance in the development of the narrative,
little attention has been given to 'hearing' as a compositional element.

M. Noth views 5.1; 9.3; 11.1, 2 as part of the work of 'der
Sammler'. However, *hearing* does not appear to be regarded as a
significant element in this redaction. No reference is made to all the
remaining instances of שמע, and for example, 10.2 is included but not
10.1, which is the part of the text that refers to hearing.[1] Noth's
deuteronomistic framework excludes 'hearing' even when it includes
the surrounding texts (2.[9b], 10b, 11b; 9.9bß; 10.[1aßb], [2b]).[2] The
reference in 9.1 f. is viewed as post-deuteronomistic.

E. Noort's study of ch. 10 is a partial correction of the failure to
recognize the importance of שמע as a compositional element in the
text. He focuses on the function of ויהי כשמע in 5.1, 9.1, 10.1 and
11.1.[3] Although he describes the formulas as redactional, he views
them as integral to their literary contexts, and as a means of
connecting the stories they introduce.

The references to 'hearing' in the confessions of 2.9-11 and 9.9 f.
do not introduce the stories. They serve as a link with the previous
mighty acts of YHWH in Egypt and Transjordan. Thus, they may be
placed in the same category as those which connect the battle reports.
However, the references to 'hearing' in 9.16-17; 22.11-12; 22.30-31,
simply are part of the narrative technique.

'Hearing' serves as part of one of the most significant compositional
and theological structures in Joshua. It is always followed by a
response on the part of those who receive the information. Most often,
it is the nations who hear and fear.

2. *The Relationship between* ירא *and* ידע

a. *The Nations Hear and Fear*
Hearing is one of the few things the nations do apart from trembling
and fighting. The response of fear is described in a variety of ways:

1. Noth, *Josua*, p. 12. In the first edition of his commentary 9.1, 2 are listed,
but not 9.3.
2. Noth, *Josua*, p. 9. In the first edition of his commentary 10.1, 2 are not
included, and the way they are listed in the second edition suggests a very tentative
proposal.
3. Noort, *Mythos und Rationalität*, pp. 149-61.

2.9	וכי־נפלה אימתכם עלינו וכי נמגו
2.11	וימס לבבנו ולא־קמה עוד רוח באיש
2.24	ונם־נמגו
5.1	וימס לבבם ולא־היה בם עוד רוח
9.24	ונירא מאד לנפשתנו
10.2	וייראו מאד

The significance of the repeated references to the fear of the enemy kings could be dismissed as being nothing more than a typical feature of the vocabulary of holy war. It is true that it occurs often in these contexts, but reference to fear is frequently absent from accounts of war. For example, the idea hardly appears at all in the book of Judges.[1] It is significant that most of the examples of enemy fear cited by G. von Rad in his form-critical study of warfare texts are from Joshua.[2] The table above on the use of שמע demonstrates that the motif of the enemy *hearing* and *fearing* is part of the compositional structure of the work.

There is also a sense in which the fear on the part of the nations is characteristic of the period of the conquest. The transition from the epoch of unholy war to holy war is signalled by the simultaneous arrival at the borders of the promised land and the death of the wilderness generation in Deut. 2.14-25. This text concludes:

This day I will begin to put the dread and fear of you upon all the peoples that are under the whole heaven, who shall hear the report of you and shall tremble and be in anguish because of you.

Thus, according to Deut. 2.25, hearing and fearing are features of the conquest period.[3] In Joshua, once the conquest is over, the remaining nations are recorded as simply existing, neither hearing nor fearing. However, the activity of their kings, and the graphic and varied language employed to describe their fear, places the nations in the forefront during the conquest.

The table at the beginning of the chapter illustrates the causal relationship between hearing and fearing on the part of the nations. The only reference to the nations' fear outside of this structure is in 10.10 where it refers to the enemy's panic during a battle.

---

1.   Richter, *Untersuchungen*, p. 204.
2.   Von Rad, *Heilige Krieg*, pp. 10-11.
3.   Cf. Deut. 11.25 which also views the conquest as a period when 'all these nations' will fear.

The nations are afraid because of the mighty deeds of YHWH in the events of the exodus and the Jordan crossing. They fear Israel because of the victories over Sihon and Og in Transjordan, and the steady succession of victories in Cisjordan. All the events which precede the arrival in the land are combined in the confessions of Rahab (2.9-11) and the Gibeonites (9.9-10).

In contrast to the idea of the nations being afraid Israel is exhorted not to fear. This precedes a battle on many occasions:

8.1	אל־תירא ואל־תחת
10.8	אל־תירא
10.25	אל־תיראו ואל־תחתו חזקו ואמצו
11.6	אל־תירא

These exhortations are followed by a statement of the reason for not fearing, namely, the Lord's absolute power over the enemy. This statement is usually introduced by כי (10.8, 25; 11.6). Similar exhortations are to be found in speeches in which more general encouragement is given to the Israelites:

1.6	חזק ואמץ
1.7	רק חזק ואמץ מאד לשמר . . . התורה
1.9	חזק ואמץ אל־תערץ ואל־תחת
1.18	רק חזק ואמץ
23.6	וחזקתם מאד לשמר . . . תורה

The dramatic reversal at Ai, recorded in ch. 7, portrays for a moment Israel as the enemy. Here she is filled with fear and soundly defeated. However, the usual pattern is very different. While the kings of the nations hear of the mighty acts of YHWH and respond in fear, Israel responds in another way: she 'sees' and 'knows'.

b. *Israel Sees and Knows*

Israel's relationship to the activity of YHWH is in terms of seeing, ראה:

- 5.13 Joshua *saw* the Commander of the Army of the Lord
- 6.2 the Lord said to Joshua '*See* I have given into your hand Jericho'
- 8.1 '*See*, I have given into your hand the king of Ai'
- 8.8 'When you have taken the city...*see*, I have commanded you'
- 23.3 'And you have *seen* all that the Lord your God has done to

all these nations for your sake, for it is the Lord your God
who has fought for you'.

24.7 'And your eyes *saw* what I did in Egypt'.

Perhaps 6.2, 8.1 and 8.8 are no more than exclamatory. However,
there is an emphasis on seeing the deeds of YHWH in the events of
exodus and conquest in the other references.

On occasions, the Hebrew Bible distinguishes between hearing and
the more trustworthy experience of seeing,[1] and seeing is normally
linked to knowing.[2] An initial reading of Joshua supports this general-
ization.

Knowing is the response to the mighty acts of the Lord during the
river crossing (3.4, 7, 10). In 3.10 a statement about victory over the
nations in the land, made within the context of the miraculous river
crossing, is introduced, בזאת תדעון כי אל חי בקרבכם. Further, ידע is
Israel's typical reaction to the deeds of YHWH (14.6; 22.22, 31; 23.13,
14; 24.31).[3]

The passage in 24.31 is significant particularly if it is considered to
be an epoch marker for the period of the conquest:[4]

> And Israel served the Lord all the days of Joshua, and all the days of the
> elders who outlived Joshua and who had known (ידע) all the work which
> the Lord did for Israel.

There is an almost identical passage in Judg. 2.7:[5]

> And the people served the Lord all the days of Joshua, and all the days of
> the elders who outlived Joshua, who had seen (ראו) all the great work
> which the Lord did for Israel.

While illustrating the intrinsic connection between ראה and ידע, these

---

1. Cf. Num. 14.14-15; 1 Kgs 10.6-7.

2. E.g. Exod. 16.6. W. Zimmerli, *Erkenntnis Gottes nach dem Buche Ezechiel*
(Zürich: Zwingli, 1954) p. 21 n. 31, writes of a 'shöne Parallelität von ראה und ידע'.
However, this is no absolute rule, and for example in Deut. 31.12-13, knowing and
fearing the Lord is preceded by hearing. In Deuteronomy, this act of hearing is
usually related to התורה, where the knowledge of the Lord's deeds carries responsibility; cf. Deut. 4.3, 34; 6.22; 10.21; 11.4, 6; etc.

3. Other instances of ידע are in a mundane sense, 2.4, 5; 8.14.

4. It should also be noted how ידע functions as an epoch marker in Exod. 1.6,
8: 'Then Joseph died, and all that generation... And there arose a new king over
Egypt, who did not know Joseph.'

5. The record of Joshua's death and burial is in both contexts noticeably similar.

parallel passages also demonstrate that the period of Joshua is a time when Israel *saw* the Lord in action.[1] Israel is later rebuked for failure to *hear* the commands (Judg. 2.2, 7, 20, etc.). This is consistent with the new epoch in Judges. Although Josh. 24.31 and Judg. 2.5 are probably best considered as subsequent compositional elements linking Joshua to Judges,[2] they accurately sum up the emphasis in the body of the text in Joshua where Israel's relationship to YHWH is characterized by seeing as well as knowing. There are convincing reasons for recognizing the following pattern in Joshua: (a) Israel sees and knows, and (b) the nations hear and fear. While the two elements 'hearing' and 'fearing' stand in a causal relationship to each other, Israel's 'seeing' and 'knowing' tend to be parallel and never appear together in a causal relationship. Nevertheless, Israel's 'seeing' and 'knowing' serve as a contrast to the behaviour of the nations. Therefore, although it is a structural element of the narrative, the pattern is contradicted at several significant points.

c. *The Nations Know*

There are two more instances of ידע to consider, and both contradict the established pattern:[3]

> 2.9-11   Rahab not only hears and fears, but knows
> 4.24   all peoples of the earth will know. . . you (Israel) will fear
>   the Lord.

The following chapter contains a detailed discussion of Rahab's confession. At this stage it is sufficient to note that, while the acts of hearing and fearing identify Rahab with the occupants of the land, the fact that she *knows* as well makes her exceptional by placing her for a moment in the same category as Israel.

Two consequences follow the miracle at the Jordan in 4.24:

---

1.   I.L. Seeligmann, 'Erkenntnis Gottes und historisches Bewusstsein im alten Israel', in H. Donner and R. Hanhart (eds.), *Beiträge zur Alttestamentlichen Theologie: Festschrift für Walther Zimmerli* (Göttingen: Vandenhoeck & Ruprecht, 1977), pp. 414-45.

2.   Cf. Blum, *Studien zur Komposition des Pentateuch*, pp. 291ff. for discussion and bibliography.

3.   J. van Seters, *In Search of History: Historiography in the Ancient World and the Origins of Biblical History* (New Haven: Yale University Press, 1983), p. 325, solves the problem by allocating these verses to a post-deuteronomistic and post-priestly Pentateuchal redaction.

1. ‏למען דעת‏
2. ‏למען יראום‏

The river miracle will cause all peoples of the earth to know that the Lord is mighty. The connection between the mighty acts of the Lord and knowing is not surprising. However, that outsiders *know* and Israel *fears* is a direct reversal of the established pattern.

In the Hebrew Bible, foreigners are the subject of ‏ידע‏ either in a negative sense of being the victims of his power,[1] or in personal theological confessions by foreigners, ‏ידעתי כי‏ (Exod. 18.1ff.; Josh. 2.9-11; 1 Kgs 17.8-24; 2 Kgs 5.21; Isa. 45.3, ‏חדע כי‏).[2] When introduced by ‏למען‏, *knowing* is the response of 'all the peoples/kings of the earth' to YHWH's activity in answer to their prayers (1 Kgs 8.43, 60; 2 Chron. 6.33), or to his deliverance of Israel (2 Kgs 19.19; Isa. 37.20).[3] These texts are remarkably similar to Josh. 4.24. A missionary emphasis is evident in 1 Kgs 8.43 and the parallel account in 2 Chron. 6.33:

> in order that all peoples of the earth may know thy name and fear thee, as do thy people Israel, and that they may know that this house which I have built is called by thy name.

Thus, it is possible that the knowledge attained by 'all the peoples of the earth' in Josh. 4.24 has a confessional sense as well. Nevertheless, it is important to recognize the differences between the stylized presentations of the individual foreigner's confession, or that of 'all peoples', and the way in which Israelite confessions are usually presented. On most occasions, Israel is exhorted to know the Lord. Often, this activity is parallel to fearing the Lord.

d. *Israel Fears*

Opinion on the identity of the subject of the second verb in 4.24, ‏יראום‏, is divided between those who say that it is Israel[4] and those who

---

1. Therefore, through experiencing the plagues, Pharaoh will know that there is none like the Lord in all the earth (Exod. 9.14; cf. 7.5).

2. For this observation, I am indebted to participants in a seminar 'Israel und die Völker' conducted by Professor Rolf Rendtorff in Heidelberg during the Winter semester 1987/88.

3. Cf. the discussion of these texts in the previous chapter under 'all the peoples'.

4. For example, K. Arayaprateep, 'A Note on *YR'* in Jos. IV 24', *VT* 22 (1972), pp. 240-42 (240-41).

say it is 'all the peoples of the earth'.[1] There is no convincing reason to emend the text to read third person plural, and Israel should remain subject of the second person plural verb. The argument that the deuteronomistic conception of ירא 'never has anything to do with the nations, but speaks of Israel in the covenant relationship with Yahweh',[2] is exaggerated. There are texts in which the nations not only know YHWH but *fear* him as well.

It seems that there is a subtle juxtaposition of ideas in Josh. 4.24. The characteristic language of the book of Joshua is inverted to read:

a.   The nations know that the Lord is mighty.
b.   Israel fears the Lord their God forever.

The reversal of roles commands attention by the text's juxtaposition with the very next verse, 5.1. This reverts to the pattern of the nations hearing and fearing.

e. *Israel Hears and Fears*

On a few occasions, שמע is used of obedience to Moses, Joshua or the Lord (cf. 1.17-18; 5.6; 10.14; 22.2; 24.24).[3] It is a feature of Israel's covenant relationship to YHWH.[4] The contrast is noticeable between this feature, and the fact that almost all the other 'hearing' in Joshua is done by the nations.

Apart from the use of ירא to describe the fear of the nations and to

---

1.   For example, Noth, *Josua*, p. 32.

2.   Arayaprateep, 'A Note on *YR*'', p. 241. On the 'fear of God' as a feature of Deuteronomy and the DtrH, cf. S. Plath, *Furcht Gottes: Der Begriff* ירא *im Alten Testament* (AzTh, 2; Stuttgart: Calwer, 1963), pp. 32-54. Israelites are constantly exhorted to 'fear the Lord' (Deut. 4.10; 5.29; 6.2, 13, 24; 8.6; 10.12, 20; 13.5; 14.23; 17.19; 28.58; 31.12, 13; Josh. 4.24; 24.14; 1 Sam. 12.14, 24; 1 Kgs 8.40, 43). The nations are known as those who do not fear him (cf. esp. Deut. 25.18 in which the Amalekites are so characterized). In Josh. 24.14 את־יהוה ירא is parallel to עבד את־יהוה; cf. also Deut. 6.13; 10.20; 13.5; 1 Sam. 12.14, 24. Further on the relationship between the two concepts, cf. Floss, *Jahweh Dienen*, pp. 85-89.

3.   The formula, שמע בקול יהוה (5.6; 24.24; cf. 22.2; and conversely, 10.14), is characteristic of the deuteronomistic vocabulary, often serving as a compositional element; cf. particularly the conditional formulas in Deuteronomy, כי תשמע בקול יהוה אלהיך (e.g. 13.19), and the use of the formula as a theological characterization of a period in Israel's history, ולא שמעו לקולי (e.g. Judg. 2.20).

4.   A.K. Fenz, *Auf Jahwes Stimme Hören: Eine Biblische Begriffsuntersuchung* (WBTh, 6; Vienna: Herder, 1964), esp. pp. 81-94.

exhort Israel to be courageous, ירא is used in confessions of the Israelites to speak of reverence in response to the mighty deeds of the Lord (22.25; 24.14), and of the response to the deeds of Joshua (4.14).

On occasions Israel hears, and on occasions Israel fears. The two activities are never brought together in a single text.

3. Conclusion

The usual pattern in Joshua is that the nations hear and fear, while Israel sees and knows. Nevertheless, there are also occasions when the nations know, and Israel can hear and fear. The ambiguity created by the use of the same words, but with contrasting connotations to describe, on the one hand the nations and on the other Israel, is nowhere more apparent than in the stories of those who remain 'in the midst of Israel unto this day'.

Chapter 8

'AND THEY DWELT IN THE MIDST OF ISRAEL UNTO THIS DAY'

The impression gained from reading the narrative is that all the nations are eradicated from the land. However, there are persistent references to remaining nations, and it soon becomes obvious that the language employed in recording their presence is uniformly structured:

1. *Notes Recording the Continued Presence of the Nations*

The continuing presence of the nations in Israel's midst is recorded by variations of the formula וישב בקרב ישראל עד היום הזה:

Rahab
6.25   ותשב בקרב ישראל עד היום הזה
Gibeonites
9.7   בקרבי אתה יושב
9.16   קרבים הם אליו ובקרבו הם ישב ים
9.22   ואתם בקרבנו ישבים
9.27   (חטבי עצים ושאבי מים לעדה ולמזבח יהוה) עד־היום הזה
10.1   ויהיו בקרבם
Geshurites and Maacathites
13.13   וישב גשור ומעכה בקרב ישראל עד היום הזה
Jebusites
15.63   וישב היבוסי את־בני יהודה בירושלם עד היום הזה
Canaanites of Gezer
16.10   וישב הכנעני בקרב אפרים עד־היום הזה

For the most part, scholars have ignored the manner in which these notes provide a connecting framework between the accounts of the nations that remain in the land, particularly with reference to the Rahab and Gibeonite stories. Although M. Noth notices the continuity between 15.63, 16.10 and 17.12-13, calling them a 'negatives Besitzverzeichnis', he regards them as post-deuteronomistic and in a

different category to the formulas in the Rahab stories. These he
regards as aetiological indicators from the pre-deuteronomistic stage.[1]
Similarly, A.G. Auld connects together 13.13, 15.53, 16.10, 17.11-13
and 19.47 LXX, as part of a DtrN redaction, but pays no attention to
the formulas in the Rahab and Gibeonite stories.[2] In contrast, Karl
Budde notices the manner in which the formula בקרבי אחה ישב in Josh.
9.7, 16, 23 provides a link between the Gibeonite story and the later
notes in Joshua, and also those in Judges 1.[3]

The notes in Joshua have close parallels to those in Judges 1 as the
following table illustrates:[4]

Josh. 13.13

ולא הורישו בני ישראל
את־הגשורי ואת־המעכתי
וישב גשור ומעכה בקרב ישראל
עד היום הזה

Josh. 15.63	Judg. 1.21
ואת־היבוסי יושבי ירושלם	ואת־היבוסי ישב ירושלם
לא־יכלו בני־יהודה להורישם	לא הורישו בני בנימן
וישב היבוסי את־בני יהודה בירושלם	וישב היבוסי את־בני בנימן בירושלם
עד היום הזה	עד היום הזה

Josh. 16.10	Judg. 1.29
ולא הורישו	ואפרים לא הוריש
את־הכנעני היושב בגזר	את־הכנעני היושב בגזר
וישב הכנעני בקרב אפרים	וישב הכנעני בקרבו בגזר
עד־היום הזה	
ויהי למס־עבד	

Josh. 17.12-13	Judg. 1.27-28
ולא יכלו בני מנשה להוריש	ולא־הוריש מנשה
את־הערים האלה	את־בית־שאן
ויואל הכנעני לשבת בארץ הזאת	ויואל הכנעני לשבת בארץ הזאת
ויהי כי חזק בני ישראל	ויהי כי־חזק ישראל
ויתנו את־הכנעני למס	וישם את־הכנעני למס
והורש לא הורישו	והוריש לא הורישו

1. Noth, *Josua*, p. 11.
2. Auld, *Joshua, Moses and the Land*, pp. 64-65, 67.
3. K. Budde, 'Richter und Josua', *ZAW* 7 (1887), pp. 93-166 (139).
4. The concern of this comparison is confined to the notes which record the
continuing presence of foreign nations. For a thorough comparison between Judg. 1
and the book of Joshua, cf. A.G. Auld, 'Judges 1 and History: A Reconsideration',
VT 25 (1975), pp. 261-85.

Judg. 1.30

זבולן לא הוריש
את־יושבי קטרון ואת־יושבי נהלל
וישב הכנעני בקרבו
ויהיו למס

Judg. 1.31-32

אשר לא הוריש
את־ישבי עכו ...
וישב האשרי בקרב הכנעני ישבי הארץ

Judg. 1.33

נפתלי לא־הוריש
את־ישבי בית־שמש ואת־ישבי בית־ענה
וישב בקרב הכנעני ישבי הארץ
וישבי בית־שמש ובית ענת היו להם למס

Josh. 19.47   Judg. 1.35

...   ויואל האמרי לשבת בהר־חרס באילון ובשעלבים
ותכבד יד בית־יוסף ויהיו למס

The above table demonstrates that the statement 'and they dwelt in the midst of Israel unto this day' is related to a comprehensive formula which records the failure to conquer certain nations. Therefore, Josh. 17.12-13 is included in the discussion, even though the concluding formula, 'and they dwelt in their midst unto this day', is substituted by ויואל הכנעני לשבת בארץ הזאת.[1]

A further possibility is presented by 19.47. Like the parallel in Judg. 1.34-35, it is introduced by referring to an initial Danite defeat. There are several differences between the two passages and one relates to the Danites' resounding victory in Joshua, while in Judges the enemy is reduced to slavery, a mark of failure to conquer. The reduction to slavery formula, along with the fact that Judg. 1.34-35 is part of a list of similar notes, suggests that the Judges passage should be considered with the other notes in its context. However, Josh. 19.47 has none of the characteristic language of the notes in Joshua. It describes the destruction of the enemy, and not their continuing presence in Israel's midst. Therefore, it need not detain us any further.

---

1. The parallel text in Judg. 1.27-28 utilizes the same formulas.

The notes in the table above share some or all of the following features:

a. 'they did not conquer'
b. the name of the unconquered city or cities
c. 'and they dwelt in the midst of...'
d. 'unto this day'
e. 'and they reduced them to slavery'.

The continuation of the notes into Judges establishes that the formulas are relatively stereotyped. The similarities in both form and content suggest a common literary heritage for the notes.[1] In both Joshua and Judges 1 they serve to correct and supplement the emphasis of the text. However some differences between the two books are noticeable and will be discussed in an analysis of the various elements in the notes.

a. *'They Did Not Conquer'*

With the exception of the Rahab and Gibeonite stories, the formula 'and they dwelt in the midst of' is always part of a more comprehensive formula which begins by recording Israel's failure to conquer a particular group of occupants. This is expressed simply as ולא הורישו (Josh. 13.13; 16.10) or as לא־יכלו להורישם (15.63; cf. 17.12-13).[2]

The failure to conquer certain cities is explained by the formula לא־יכלו להורישם in the case of the Jebusites and Canaanites (Josh. 15.63 and 17.12).[3] However, the same failure to conquer these cities is described in Judges 1 as a simple negation, ולא הוריש (Judg. 1.21 and

---

1. Auld, 'Judges I and History', pp. 261-85. He distinguishes carefully the differences between the emphases of the two contexts. His conclusion is that the notes in both Joshua and Judges are part of a subsequent redaction, DtrN. H.N. Rösel, 'Das "Negative Besitzverzeichnis"—Traditionsgeschichtliche und historische Überlegungen', in M. Augustin and K.-D. Schunk (eds.), *'Wünschet Jerusalem Frieden': IOSOT Congress Jerusalem 1986* (Beiträge zur Erforschung des Alten Testaments und des Antiken Judentums, 13; Frankfurt: Peter Lang, 1988), pp. 121-35, argues differently. He suggests that the notes are based on a single literary work which was produced in the early monarchic period.

2. For a thorough study of these formulas, cf. Budde, 'Richter und Josua', pp. 99-100.

3. Cf. 1 Kgs 9.21, לא־יכלו לחרימם.

1.27).[1] Therefore, Joshua speaks of an inability to conquer, while Judges suggests an unwillingness to do so, and in this way emphasizes Israel's sin.[2]

b. *The Identity of the Nations*

The precise identity of the unconquered nation is given by means of an 'ethnological' designation. This is usually followed by a city name in a genitive construction, for example, 'the Canaanites occupying Gezer'. On one occasion the nations are listed without elaboration as 'the Geshurites and Maacathites' (Josh. 13.13). The groups mentioned in the notes are all pre-Israelite nations who escape their fate and continue in the land.

c. *'And They Dwelt in the Midst of'*

Every time the negative sense of הוריש appears in Joshua it is associated with the continued occupation of the nations, which is characterized by the verb ישב.[3] Similarly, conquest and settlement are inseparable for Israel. The conquest (chs. 1–12) needs to be completed before settlement can begin (chs. 13–21). Conquest gives the right to settle. Conversely, the implication is that the inhabitants who are not conquered have a right to remain.[4] These nations are said to live 'in the midst of' Israel.

Elsewhere in Joshua, בקרב can be employed in the mundane sense of 'in the midst of the people or the camp' (1.11; 3.2, 5; 4.6). It is also used of the Lord in the midst of his people (3.10; cf. 24.5), of forbidden objects or foreign gods in their midst (7.12, 13; 24.23), of the time during the exodus when Israel passes through the midst of

---

1.　The notes in Judges are usually introduced by simple negation, לא הוריש (Judg. 1.21, 27, 29, 30, 31, 33). The exception is 1.34-35, which varies the formula by saying that the Amorites pressed the Danites back into the hill country, and did not allow them down to the plain.

2.　M. Weinfeld, 'The Period of the Conquest and of the Judges as Seen by the Earlier and the Later Sources', *VT* 17 (1967), pp. 93-113. The one possible exception, Judg. 1.19, 'but he could not conquer (כי לא להורש) the inhabitants of the plain, because they had chariots of iron', Weinfeld explains as indicative of a tendency to minimize Judah's failures (p. 94 n. 1).

3.　Cf. above, Chapter 4 on the theological significance of ישב as the climax of the conquest.

4.　Cf. Deut. 2.9-12, 17-23, in which the Lord recognizes, by the right of conquest, the territory of Moab and Ammon.

nations (24.17), or of the Levites who do not have an inheritance but live in Israel's midst (18.7). However, it is in the context of the statements about nations that continue to dwell in Israel's midst that it emerges as an almost fixed formula, וישב בקרב. In 15.63, instead of בקרב, the preposition את is used, which suggests a parallel function.[1] Similarly, the 'remnant of the nations' is said to live אתכם, 'with' Israel (23.7, 17).

The Gerim also live in the midst of Israel, as הגר ההלך בקרבם (8.35), or as הגר בתוכם (20.9). However, these formulas are different to the notes under discussion. The theologically significant word, ישב, is reserved for the nations that remain unconquered in Israel's midst.

The relationship characterized by בקרבם is more than geographical in Joshua. The covenant between Israel and the Gibeonites is included in the grounds for the southern kings' fear in ch. 10. The act, which is reported as השלימו with Israel (10.1, 4),[2] is parallel to ויהיו בקרבם. A further illustration that בקרב means more than physical location is evident when the Gibeonites appeal for help while in Gibeon, and the Israelites leave their camp at Gilgal to come to their assistance.

The playful use of language, which is such a feature of the story of the Gibeonites, is also evident in the shift of meaning in the use of בקרב. In ch. 9, the distinction between the nations 'far away' and those in the land utilizes בקרב. Thus, in 9.22, the distinction is between ואתם בקרבנו ישבים and רחוקים אנחנו מכם מאד, and in this way associates בקרב with the doomed occupants of the land. However, in ch. 10, ויהיו בקרבם is parallel to בשלימו. Thus, in the space of two chapters the meaning of בקרב in relation to the Gibeonites has shifted from a state of impending destruction to a covenant relationship with Israel. It is possible that the same subtle ambiguity is also utilized in the other notes about the status of nations remaining in Israel's midst.

While these groups live in the midst of Israel, they are distinguished from Israel, for example, Rahab and her family are set outside the camp of Israel (6.23). The camp of Israel, מחנה ישראל, is more than a geographical location. It is a religious and national entity and, according to this text, Rahab and her people are excluded. The distinctive

---

1. The parallel text in Judg. 1.21 also employs this formulation. In Judg. 1.16 the descendants of the Kenites travel *with* the people of Judah (את־בני יהודה) and settle *with* the people (וישב את־העם).

2. The relationship in these chapters of שלם to 'covenant' will be discussed shortly.

function of וישב בקרב in Joshua is illustrated by a brief survey of the formula elsewhere in the DtrH.

No idea of foreign nations remaining in the land is present in Deuteronomy. The nearest references are to the Gerim 'in your midst' or 'inside your gates' (16.11; 26.11; 28.43; 29.10), the escaped slave 'living in your midst' (23.17), the poor in the land, the Levites and the prophets. The description of Israel in Egypt also arises (4.34; cf. 29.15).

After Joshua, the formula 'and they dwelt in the midst of Israel' appears again in Judges. The Canaanites living in Gezer, Kitron and Nahol continue to live in the midst of the Israelites (1.29, 30). Then the formula is reversed. The Israelite tribes are described as living in the midst of the Canaanites (1.32, 33; 3.5)! There is no other reference to the formula in the DtrH. Another formula that is distinctive for the notes in Joshua is 'unto this day'.

d. *'Unto This Day'*

The debate which relates to the formula עד היום הזה has focused on the question of aetiology. For example, M. Noth maintains that the story of Rahab is intended to explain the presence of the house of Rahab in the midst of Israel. Support for this interpretation is found in the words 'and she dwelt in the midst of Israel unto this day'.[1]

B.S. Childs and B.O. Long have contested the aetiological analysis of the formula.[2] After studying the various functions of the formula, they conclude that it has an aetiological function on few occasions. In most instances it is added as a redactional commentary on existing traditions, and usually serves as a personal testimony to authenticate the story. The associated verb ותשב supports this conclusion. It refers to the past and the formula does not modify it. This observation is noticeable particularly in 6.25 where the subject of the verb is feminine.[3] The evidence suggests to B.S. Childs that the Rahab story is not aetiological because its conclusion in 6.17, 22-23, 25 is a redactional addition. An evaluation of this analysis is postponed until

1.   Noth, *Josua*, pp. 22-23.
2.   B.S. Childs, 'A Study of the Formula "Until This Day"', *JBL* 82 (1963), pp. 279-92; B.O. Long, *The Problem of Etiological Narrative in the Old Testament* (BZAW, 108; Berlin: Töpelmann, 1968); *idem*, 'Etymological Etiology and the DT Historian', *CBQ* 31 (1969), pp. 35-41.
3.   Childs, 'The Formula "Until this Day"', p. 284 n. 16.

later. Nevertheless, it is possible to agree that the formula cannot be used mechanically as a sign of the aetiological origin of a story.[1] The literary function of the formula 'unto this day' in the notes, and in the book of Joshua generally, is a more interesting avenue to explore.

The formula 'unto this day' is commonplace in Joshua. It refers to heaps of stones which remain, and serves to emphasize the extent and permanence of the destruction.[2] Heaps of stones are also reminders of the river crossing (4.9), or of circumcision (5.9). The permanence of the gift of land to Caleb is indicated in this way (14.14). The formula is found in speeches in which it indicates and emphasizes a condition: faithfulness in the case of the Transjordanian tribes (22.3), Israel's continuing guilt (22.17) or Israel's faithfulness (23.8) and invincibility (23.9). Therefore, 'unto this day' is a means of emphasizing something by showing its lasting character on most occasions.

The only time the formula appears in the notes in Judges is in Judg. 1.21. This indicates that the formula in Joshua is utilized in a deliberate and precise manner. In Josh. 6.25, the formula establishes a parallel to the idea of the permanent destruction of the city. Indeed, in all the notes it serves as a counterpoint to the possible destruction of a city. A formula concerning the enslavement of the nations in Israel's midst appears on occasions.

e. 'And They Reduced Them to Slavery'

The Israelites cannot drive out the Canaanites in Gezer (16.10). As a consequence, they dwell in the midst of Israel 'unto this day'. However, they reduce them to slavery, למס־עבד. Similarly, in 17.12-13, the Canaanites in several cities which Israel is unable to conquer are reduced למס. The connection with the formula 'and they dwelt in the midst of Israel' is even more obvious in the notes encountered in Judges. מס is there, employed in a similar manner and describes the enslavement of an undefeated populace (Judg. 1.27-8, 30, 33, 35).

All the inhabitants of a conquered town are reduced למס in Deut. 20.11. There are a few incidental references to מס in the remainder of the DtrH, but the identity of those subjected to this form of

---

1. F. Golka, 'The Aetiologies in the Old Testament, Part I', *VT* 26 (1976), pp. 410-28; F. Golka, 'The Aetiologies in the Old Testament, Part II', *VT* 27 (1977), pp. 36-47.
2. Cf. above, Chapter 2.

enslavement is not specified.[1] Israelites are enslaved by Solomon according to 1 Kgs 5.27. Finally, in 1 Kgs 9.20-21, the pre-Israelite nations as a whole are reduced למס־עבד:

> All the remnant of the Amorites, the Hittites, the Perizzites, the Hivites, and the Jebusites, who were not of the people of Israel—their descendants who were left after them in the land, whom the people of Israel were unable to destroy (לא־יכלו להחרימם)—these Solomon made a forced levy of slaves (למס־עבד), and so they are to this day.

The next verse presents a contrast. It is stated that no Israelite is made עבד. A few verses later, in 1 Kgs 9.27, there is a reference to עבדי שלמה. I. Mendelsohn comes to the conclusion that they are three technical terms for the various categories of forced labour in Israel on the basis of these terminological differences in 1 Kings 9.[2] However, there is insufficient textual support for such a claim, and it is more likely that the terms are parallel.[3] מס־עבד in Josh 16.10 performs no different function to מס in the rest of Joshua and Judges. Therefore, R. North rightly describes them as identical descriptions of 'das ziemlich theoretische Schicksal der Stämme deren Gebiete erobert wurden, die aber nicht ausgerottet wurden'.[4] It is significant that, apart from one other instance in Gen. 49.15, the expression מס־עבד occurs only in the two passages under discussion, Josh. 16.10 and 1 Kgs 9.20. This connection is one of several between 1 Kgs 9.20-21 and the notes in Joshua and Judges.

The perplexing feature of all these references is that the enslavement of the enemy is connected with Israel's *failure* to conquer. Enslavement is an activity associated with victory in most battle reports. מס is often used in this sense (Isa. 31.8; Lam. 1.1; and Deut. 20.11 where מס and עבד are parallel). The reason for the departure from the norm is that *all* were meant to be killed. Survival, even as slaves, marks a major departure from the original plan.

---

1. 2 Sam. 20.24; 1 Kgs 4.6; 5.28; 9.15; 12.18.

2. I. Mendelsohn, *Slavery in the Ancient Near East: A Comparative Study of Slavery in Babylonia, Assyria and Palestine from the Middle of the Third Millenium to the End of the First Millenium* (London: Oxford University Press, 1949), pp. 95-99.

3. J.A. Soggin, 'Compulsory Labor under David and Solomon', in T. Ishida (ed.), *Studies in the Period of David and Solomon and Other Essays* (Winona Lake, IN: Eisenbrauns, 1982), pp. 259-67 (262).

4. R. North, 'מס', *ThWAT*, IV, pp. 1006-1009 (1007).

However, in the context of an incomplete conquest, the enslavement formula lessens the sting of failure.

The explanations of the Gibeonites' servile status usually overlook any possible relationship to other references to enslavement in Joshua. The enslavement formula in the notes appears as a way of compensating for the failure to conquer, and the enslavement of the Gibeonites is presented as a sensible compromise. Therefore, enslavement is the peculiar destiny of the surviving nations.

f. Preliminary Conclusions

The enslavement formula draws attention to 1 Kgs 9.20-21. In the DtrH, lists of pre-Israelite nations are mentioned for the last time in a statement which refers to their destiny. The reference to חרם as the fate of the occupants of the land also appears for the last time. The language of destruction is in a negative construction, לא־יכלו להחרימם, as is the case in the notes. The enslavement formula appears together with the now familiar 'unto this day' formula.[1] It is evident that the formulas in 1 Kgs 9.20-21 are specialized constructions which are found in the notes from the period of the conquest. Thus, the text serves as the conclusion to a carefully conceived presentation of the nations that remain in Israel's midst.[2]

The notes in Joshua–Judges, and their conclusion in 1 Kings 9, utilize a special set of formulas to designate the role of the nations that remain in Israel's midst. The appearance of these formulas in the Rahab and Gibeonite stories establishes the connection of these stories to each other and to the other notes.

2. Rahab

The formula וחשב בקרב ישראל עד היום הזה, at the conclusion to the Rahab story summarizes a central theme of the story, namely, that she survives in the midst of destruction. Indeed almost everything she does comes as a surprise to the reader.

---

1. עד־היום הזה is scattered throughout the DtrH. It appears usually in connection with the naming of a place, or the establishment of a permanent institution. However, it is particularly prominent in texts dealing with the period of conquest.

2. Cf. Richter, *Bearbeitungen*, p. 43. He maintains that the lists of pre-Israelite nations form part of deuteronomistic theological schema consisting of land promise and fulfilment.

a. *Confession*

The story of Rahab facilitates the smooth flow in the narrative of
conquest. In fact, the conquest itself does not begin until the will of
the Lord has been determined.[1] Thus, Rahab's confession is the focal
point of the story in the wider context, and emphasizes the themes of
holy war and the gift of land:

> I know that the Lord has given you the land, and that the fear of you has
> fallen upon us, and that all the inhabitants of the land melt away before
> you. For we have heard how the Lord dried up the water of the Red Sea
> before you when you came out of Egypt, and what you did to the two
> kings of the Amorites that were beyond the Jordan, whom you utterly
> destroyed (החרמתם אותם). And as soon as we heard it, our hearts melted,
> and there was no courage left in any man, because of you; for the Lord
> your God is he who is God in heaven above and on earth below.

In her confession she refers to the great fear of the inhabitants caused
by:

a.   The knowledge that the Lord has given the land to Israel.
b.   The events surrounding the exodus.
c.   The destruction of Sihon and Og in Transjordan.

Her confession is introduced by ידעתי כי. This is a feature of
confessions by foreigners (Jethro, Exod. 18.11; Widow of Zarephath,
1 Kgs 17.24; Naaman, 2 Kgs 5.15; and Cyrus, Isa. 45.3, תדע כי).[2] The
cross-references do not reduce the paradox of a foreigner making
such a confession in the context of the book of Joshua in which ידע
characterizes Israel's relationship to YHWH. Elsewhere, ידע can refer
to Israel's recognition of the Lord as sovereign (e.g. Hos. 13.4), as
well as to a change of heart and a new covenant (Jer. 24.7). In treaty-
making texts, it can be a technical term for the recognition that treaty
stipulations are binding.[3] The covenantal significance in Rahab's use of
ידע is supported by the agreement into which she and the spies enter.

---

1.   Tucker, *Use of the Old Testament*, pp. 66-86.
2.   H. Schult, 'Naemans Übertritt zum Yahwismus (2 Könige 5, 1-19a) und die
biblischen Bekehrungsgeschichten', *DBAT* 9 (1975), pp. 2-20, insists that these
texts are best understood as post-exilic legitimation of a liberal missionary practice.
However, it seems more likely that the primary function of these confessions by
foreigners is to emphasize the truth of a theological statement (for this observation the
writer is indebted to E. Noort).
3.   Cf. H.B. Huffmon, 'The Treaty Background of Hebrew *YADA*', *BASOR*
181 (1966), pp. 31-37.

b. *Covenant*

It is intriguing that the first foreigner encountered in the book is remarkably resourceful, and for a time has the representatives of Israel completely dependent on her. She makes a pious, theologically exact confession, and then proposes a covenant of mutual protection (2.12).[1] Her initiative is made unambiguous by the words of the spies, 'this oath of yours which you have made us swear' (2.17, 20). The relationship is characterized by חסד,[2] and bound by a set of conditional clauses, אם לא (2.14, 20) which, unmistakably, is juridical language.[3]

Directly after her confession, she says ועתה השבעו־נא לי ביהוה. Whether the spies promise because of her confession, or because she promises to help them, is unclear in ch. 2. In 6.25, it is said that she is saved because she hides the spies. Some ambiguity also arises concerning her status. In 6.25 she is in the midst of Israel, and in 6.23 she and her people are *outside* the camp of Israel. There is no sense in which her group is a threat: the danger to Israel's existence lies *within* the camp. This is illustrated by the manner in which the narrative proceeds in ch. 7. The ambiguity surrounding the status of Rahab in Israel is brought to the fore by her role as a 'foreign woman'.

c. *A Foreign Woman*

The position of this story about the covenant with Rahab at the outset of a book about conquest is remarkable. A reader familiar with the deuteronomic חרם texts, in which the danger of syncretism is the justification for exterminating the inhabitants of the land, will be surprised that ch. 23 presents the first such warning in Joshua. Here, in ch. 2, it is only hinted at. As a foreign woman Rahab is a potential snare. And then she is called זרנה, which can mean 'a prostitute'![4] This

1. K.M. Campbell, 'Rahab's Covenant. A Short Note on Joshua ii 9-21', *VT* 22 (1972), pp. 243-44.

2. The covenant relationship is also characterized by חסד in Gen. 21.22 f. and 1 Sam. 20.8.

3. M. Ottosson, 'Rahab and the Spies', in H. Behrens (ed.), *Studies in Honor of Åke W. Sjöberg* (Philadelphia: University Museum, 1989), pp. 419-27 (422-24). He also draws attention to the fact that '*two* men' usually occurs in juridical situations where witnesses are required (e.g. Deut. 17.6).

4. D.J. Wiseman, 'Rahab of Jericho', *TynBul* 14 (1964), pp. 8-11, argues that it does not always mean an immoral person, and that 'barmaid' is a more likely translation. However, it is difficult to remove all sexual connotations from the story.

is not the same as being a cult prostitute. Therefore, some of the
religious connotations are lacking. Nevertheless, a sexual relationship
with the spies is hinted at, and the words seem deliberately ambiva-
lent.[1] In 2.1, 8 שכב is usually translated as 'spent the night'. However,
the word can also have a sexual meaning.[2]

A similar ambiguity is evident in the use of בוא. In Joshua the term
is associated with the entrance into the land, and always employed in
direct speech (1.11; 2.3, 18; 18.3; 24.8). It refers to conquering a city
or a people (8.11, 19; 9.17; 10.9; 11.5, 7, 21; 24.8, 11)[3] and appears
in the mundane sense of movement toward something (e.g. 2.22, 23).
Finally, it is used in a veiled sexual sense of coming to the woman
Rahab in 2.1, 2, 3 × 2. This is less likely in 6.22, 23, although it is
more obvious in 15.18, which refers to the consummation of a
marriage, and in 23.7, 12, which warns against Israel mixing with the
nations by intermarriage and religious contact.[4]

According to M. Ottosson, זונה suggests not only 'to whore' but 'to
prostitute oneself to other gods', and the connection to Shittim (2.1)
serves as a reminder of the apostasy at Peor (Num. 25.1ff.). He
concludes, 'as the Peor episode is described as an educational warning
just on the arrival in the land (Deut. 4.1ff.; Josh. 22.17) Rahab's
actions can also be understood in a didactic way'.[5] Ottosson argues
that foreign women have a significant role in the deuteronomistic
version of the past which offers an explanation for the loss of the
land. Thus, in 1 Kgs 11.1ff., King Solomon's association with foreign
women is the ground for the eventual division of the kingdom into
north and south. Likewise, in encouraging Israel to make a covenant
with her and spare her life, Rahab has caused Israel to begin its

---

H.M. Barstad, 'The Old Testament Feminine Personal Name *rāḥab̲*. An Onomastic
Note', *SEÅ* 54 (1989), pp. 43-49, points out that the name רחב is used of the female
genital organ in Ugaritic and Arabic texts; and furthermore, הרחבת is parallel to זכרון
in Isa. 57.8. He concludes that the name 'Rahab' in our story is a ' "nickname",
harshly indicating the woman's métier'.

1.   Butler, *Joshua*, p. 31, remarks that the story is dominated by an ironic
humour, going to bed being exactly what is expected in such a setting.

2.   Langlamet, 'Gilgal et les récits', p. 174.

3.   It usually appears in the indirect speech of a battle report.

4.   בוא serves to describe Solomon's marriages to foreign women in 1 Kgs 11.2,
in which it is parallel to דבק.

5.   Ottosson, *Studies in Honor of Åke W. Sjöberg*, pp. 420-21.

history of apostasy at the moment of arriving in the land.[1] However, it must be recognized that the story in Joshua 2 does not present Rahab as a temptress. She appears not as a threat, but as a supporter of Israel. It seems that the reader is invited to appreciate the ambiguity rather than opt for one or other of the interpretations of Rahab's role.

While her role as a foreign woman and as a prostitute does introduce an element of *risque* into the story, there could also be an additional dimension to the emphasis on sleep in Joshua 2. It suggests a wondrous element, of 'security, even rest, in the midst of perils'.[2] The Israelites are passive, and the Lord protects them in a most remarkable way. Their lives are made to depend on the courage and initiative of a Canaanite woman.[3] The real enemies of Israel are represented by the king and his messengers, and Rahab, a model of resourcefulness, tricks them. The reader is treated to the humour of them hurrying off in the wrong direction.

The two main themes of the chapter are the mission of the spies and the story of Rahab. In fact, she is prominent, and almost all the dialogue is initiated by her. Her confession focuses the theology of the chapter and, indeed, of the book as a whole. The report of the spies (2.24) sounds like a prophetic oracle, but is a quotation from a speech by a Canaanite prostitute!

Rahab's survival contradicts the חרם legislation, and the expectations of apostasy created by the reference to her profession are contradicted by her piety. The way in which her person serves as a focus of contrast remains evident in ch. 6. At each stage in the story her survival is presented as being parallel to the destruction of Jericho.

d. *The Rahab Story and the Structure of Joshua 6*
The account utilizes a series of emphatic contrasts. They are signalled by the use of רק, a word which serves as a means of emphasizing a command, as is illustrated by the following table:

---

1. Ottosson, *Erövring och fördelning av Land.*

2. W.L. Moran, 'The Repose of Rahab's Israelite Guests', in G. Buccellati (ed.), *Studi sull 'Oriente e la Bibbia, offerti a p Giovanni Rinaldi* (Genoa: Editrice Studia e Vita, 1967), pp. 273-84.

3. N. Steinberg, 'Israelite Tricksters, Their Analogues and Cross-Cultural Study', *Semeia* 42 (1988), pp. 1-13 (10), writes: 'Through trickery, by both women and men, the underdog plays the part of a power broker and the one expected to wield authority is under the thumb of the weak.'

6.15	only on the seventh day
6.17	only Rahab and her family are to be spared
6.18	only keep away from the חרם
6.24	only the precious metals are not to be destroyed but are to go into the Temple
8.2	only the spoil is to be kept
8.27	only the spoil is to be kept
11.13	only Hazor is burned
11.14	only all the people are destroyed
11.22	only a remnant is not destroyed.

The contrast in the treatment of Rahab on the one hand, and the doomed city on the other hand, is noticeable in Joshua's command concerning the destruction of the city (6.16-19), and in the account of the fulfilment of the command (6.20-26). The city and 'all that is in it' (כל־אשר־בה, 6.17, 24)[1] is contrasted to Rahab and 'all that is with her' (כל־אשר־אתה, 6.17; cf. כל־אשר־לה,[2] 6.22, 23, 25). Just as the men, women and children of Jericho are destroyed, so Rahab and her family are spared. A subsequent contrast is created with the destruction of the family of Achan and all that belongs to him (כל־אשר־לו, 7.24).[3] The story of the destruction of Jericho concludes with a statement about the permanence of that state of affairs: a curse against the rebuilding of the city (6.26). This is matched by the comment that 'Rahab dwelt in the midst of Israel unto this day' (6.25). The two stories are inextricably intertwined from the collapse of the walls until the end.

It has been suggested that the Rahab account is a later addition to the text as means of integrating chs. 2 and 6.[4] The two appear to be from different hands. They use different words to describe the spies, the act of hiding and the act of spying.[5] There is also the problem of Rahab's house in the city walls in ch. 2. This location is not recognized in ch. 6

---

1. The same formula is used in connection with the doomed city in Deut. 13.16.

2. This formula is used of all of a person's material possessions (BDB, pp. 82-83), cf. Gen. 14.23; 31.1.

3. M.A. Beek, 'Josua und Retterideal', in H. Goedicke (ed.), *Near Eastern Studies in Honour of William Foxwell Albright* (London: Johns Hopkins, 1971), pp. 35-42 (39), draws attention to the contrast between Rahab the Canaanite and Achan the Israelite.

4. Cf. for example, Soggin, *Joshua*, pp. 37-40.

5. McCarthy, 'The Theology of Leadership', pp. 169-70.

in which it is recorded that her house still remains after the collapse of the walls.

However, the story in ch. 2 requires a sequel, and the details about Rahab in ch. 6. are much more than a simple attempt at tidying up the narrative. She is mentioned three times, and provides a contrast to the doomed city. The story of the conquest of Jericho is a carefully conceived account which utilizes a series of contrasts and, even if the end product is the result of the combination of various traditions, the result is a well-integrated unit.

While considering the question of the redactional process that combined the story of Rahab and the destruction of Jericho, it is necessary to ask how the most prominent account of destruction is combined with the story of the most famous 'survivor'? It is interesting to observe how the survival of the Kenites in 1 Samuel 15 also serves as a contrast to the doomed Amalekites, and the symmetry between Jethro and Amalek in Exodus 17–18 is even more evident.[1] Another text that holds intriguing possibilities is Judg. 1.16, 'the descendants of the Kenite, Moses' father-in-law, went with the people of Judah from the city of palms into the wilderness and settled with the people (וישב את־העם)'.[2] The next verse describes Judah destroying the city of the Canaanites of Zephath, ויחרימו אותה, which, consequently, is renamed Ḥormah.[3] Yet even these cross-references do not match the stark contrast in Joshua 6: in order to express the same, a tale of destruction would need to contain an account of legitimate *Amalekite* or *Canaanite* survivors. Many of the ambiguities surrounding Rahab's position are also evident in the story of the Gibeonites.

3. The Gibeonites

As with the Rahab story, the central ambiguity surrounding the role of the Gibeonites is their survival in spite of the legislation concerning

1. The symmetries in Exod. 17–18 are discussed in B.P. Robinson, 'Israel and Amalek. The Context of Exodus 17.8-16', *JSOT* 32 (1985), pp. 15-22.

2. The association with Jericho is established by the reference to 'the city of palms', cf. Deut. 34.3.

3. Judges uses the word חרם very sparingly, and this is the only instance of its application to the nations. On the name change as a reminder of the act of חרם, cf. Num. 21.3.

the complete destruction of all the occupants of the land. This ambiguity is developed in very subtle ways.

a. *Deception*

The account of the kings hearing and gathering together to fight (9.1-2) is paralleled in the next verse (9.3) by the inhabitants of Gibeon hearing and responding with cunning. The word ערם, which is translated as 'cunning', can be used in a positive or in a negative sense. It can also have a double meaning as in 1 Sam. 23.27. Here, Saul uses it of David: from Saul's perspective it is a bad characteristic but from the narrator's perspective it is admirable.[1]

In this chapter, it is evident that the Israelites in the story regarded the deception as despicable (cf. 9.22). However, the narrator is not nearly as negative. The previous battle called upon the audience to revel in the cleverness of the Israelites. There is an element of comedy in the unfolding of the story of the Gibeonites. The Israelites are duped by the unlikely tale that the Gibeonites have been on a long journey. This is followed by the ironical account of people who have been assured the fruit of the land sharing a meal of mouldy bread with those whose land they are meant to capture. Rahab is applauded for tricking the king's men in ch. 2, and here again outsiders use craftiness. This time the victim is Israel.

The point of the deception is to impress upon the Israelites that they have come from 'far away' (9.6, 9, 22; cf. ch. 13), and are, therefore, not subject to the חרם legislation. Simultaneously, the Gibeonites introduce the legislation with a new clarity. In this respect they are similar to Rahab who is the first to mention the word חרם. These notable exceptions to the legislation remind the reader of its existence.

b. *Confession*

Another remarkable similarity arises between the confession of Rahab (2.8-9) and the confession of the Gibeonites (9.9-10, 24). In spite of some difference in formulation, they are included in the 'hearing' structure by means of the same formula, כי שמענו.[2] In both, there is a statement about the exodus, the gift of land,[3] the destruction of Sihon

---

1. Butler, *Joshua*, p. 101.

2. The observation has added significance because the first person plural formula for 'hearing' does not appear elsewhere in Joshua.

3. The formula, לתת לכם את־כל־הארץ, is relatively rare. It occurs only in these

and Og,[1] and the fear on the part of the inhabitants. This surpasses the language of diplomacy. Furthermore, whenever the themes of exodus and land gift occur together, they are part of confessions which usually are part of the prologue to the divine covenant. They have the force of establishing the Lord's right over his people.[2]

The language of the confession is typically deuteronomistic. Therefore, it has been understood as a later insertion and part of the deuteronomistic redaction. Most scholars have not paused to examine the way in which the presence of these confessions in chs. 2 and 9 amount to a direct contradiction of what is usually understood as the theology of the DtrH. O. Bächli recognizes the problem and proposes that the confessions of Rahab and the Gibeonites have as their original background a ceremony for bringing strangers into the cult community.[3] This is an interesting solution if only as a reminder of the exceptional nature of the confessions.

Unlike the other occupants of the land, Rahab and the Gibeonites 'hear' and confess. Their confessions form part of the overall compositional structure of the work. Arguably, the references in their confessions to the victories in Transjordan can also be related to the composition of Joshua.[4] One explanation why the victories over Sihon

two confessions, 2.9, 14; 9.24. Cf. Gen. 15.7; Exod. 6.4; Lev. 25.38; Num. 36.2; Deut. 4.38; 6.23; Neh. 9.8.

1. When Sihon and Og appear in the Hebrew Bible they are usually described as 'the kings of the Amorites'. It is only in Josh. 2.10 and 9.10 that the formula 'the two kings of the Amorites' appears. The way in which they are introduced by אשר עשה is also unique to these passages:

2.10	ואשר עשיתם לשני מלכי האמרי אשר העבר הירדן לסיחן ולעת
9.10	ואת כל־אשר עשה לשני מלכי האמרי אשר בעבר הירדן
	לסיחן . . . ולעת . . .

2. J.N.M. Wijngaards, *The Formulas of the Deuteronomic Creed* (Tilburg: Reijnen, 1963).

3. O. Bächli, 'Zur Aufnahme von Fremden in die altisraelitische Kultgemeinde', in H.J. Stoebe (ed.), *Wort—Gebot—Glaube. Beiträge zur Theologie des Alten Testaments. W. Eichrodt zum 80. Geburtstag* (Zürich: Zwingli, 1970), pp. 21-26. Van Seters, 'Joshua's Campaign', pp. 1-12, regards the story of Rahab as 'a late tale added to the earlier Dtr History in order to modify the Deuteronomic principle of the *herem*...and to allow for conversion to Israel's faith'. He does not find it necessary to explain the Gibeonite story in the same way.

4. Cf. above, Chapter 1, the excursus on the symmetry between Transjordan and Cisjordan.

and Og are mentioned by the Gibeonites, and not the immediately preceding victories in Cisjordan, is that this is part of the deception. They give the impression of being a far country and, therefore, unaware of the most recent events.[1] However, this is not the only reason for the interest in Transjordan. It can be demonstrated that the summarized generalizations of the conquest in Cisjordan, notably in chs. 12 and 13, are preceded by an account of the destruction of Sihon and Og in Transjordan.

The preliminaries disposed with—an introduction and an opportune confession—the Gibeonites can proceed to the real reason for coming, namely, to establish a covenant.

c. *Covenant*

The Gibeonites single-mindedly pursue a covenant with Israel in ch. 9. They say that they have come in order to establish a covenant with Israel, and the formula is כרת ברית (9.6, 7, 11, 15, 16). The repetition of עבד (9.8, 9, 11, 23, 24 × 2;10.6) confirms this undertaking. This is a word associated with the vassal status in a covenant. Furthermore, there is the ritual of a covenant meal,[2] the reference to שלום (9.15), the oath which Israel swears (9.15, 18, 19, 20),[3] the threat of divine wrath on those who break the covenant (9.20), and the fact that the famine in 2 Sam. 21.1-14 is understood as a covenant curse.

The narrator underlines that all this was done without consulting the Lord (9.14), a point which is ironically emphasized by the oath being sworn in his name. When the Israelites discover that they have been tricked, they set out to attack and kill the Gibeonites. At this point the narrative is confusing and there are two versions of what happens. In the first, the Israelites are stopped by their leaders who remind them of their oath, and the Gibeonites subsequently become hewers of wood and drawers of water for all the congregation (9.20-21). In the second account (9.22-27), Joshua takes the lead decisively for the first time. He reprimands the Gibeonites and reminds Israel of the oath, thereby rescuing them out of the hand of the Israelites. Finally, he solemnly curses them to a future of servitude as hewers of wood and drawers of water for the temple. However, both accounts combine in 9.27 in which the Gibeonites are reduced to being servants of the people as

1. J. Bright, 'Joshua', *IB*, II, pp. 541-673 (599).
2. A covenant meal normally finalizes the relationship (Gen. 26.30; 31.54).
3. The Israelites also swear an oath to Rahab in 2.12.

well as in the temple. An explanation of the different versions of the story will be discussed in due course.

In the two cases of covenants with outsiders, Joshua is not involved in the negotiations. Nevertheless, it is he who is directly responsible for rescuing the covenant partners from death. While his initial inconspicuousness helps to express disapproval, his subsequent involvement serves as a way of expressing the ambiguity in the relationship of the Gibeonites to Israel.

Joshua not only rescues them, but also utters a curse on the Gibeonites for their deception. The curse is viewed as commensurate with the crime, and not contrary to the covenant.[1] Guilt has been established through questioning, and the verdict pronounced in the form of a curse (cf. Gen. 4.9-16).[2] The irony is that in their earlier description of themselves, for purposes of diplomacy, as Israel's servants, and in their pretended pitiable condition, at the beginning of the story, the Gibeonites unknowingly take on their own punishment.[3] Nevertheless, they are no ordinary slaves.

d. Temple Slaves

The Gibeonites are cursed to a servile status. The language is reminiscent of the cursing of Canaan in Gen. 9.25-27, but at the same time, they are consigned to service in 'the house of my God' (9.23) or 'for the altar of the Lord. . . in the place that he will choose' (9.27).[4]

Their status as temple servants, even though menial, could be religiously controversial. On the one hand, it was common in the ancient Near East for some of the captured enemy to be presented to the temple as the victorious deity's share of the booty.[5] There is some evidence for this idea in Israelite literature; for example, included in the booty given to the Lord by Moses are prisoners of war (Num.

---

1. Cf. S. Gervitz, 'West-Semitic Curses and the Problem of the Origins of Hebrew Law', *VT* 11 (1961), pp. 137-58.

2. Butler, *Joshua*, p. 100.

3. H.N. Rösel, 'Anmerkungen zur Erzählung vom Bundesschluss mit den Gibeoniten', *BN* 28 (1985), pp. 30-35 (31).

4. Cf. B. Halpern, 'The Centralization Formula in Deuteronomy', *VT* 31 (1981), pp. 20-38.

5. Temple slaves were usually former prisoners of war, but could also be slaves dedicated by individuals to temple service as a gift to the gods. The actual duties of the slave could be stipulated in the dedication (Mendelsohn, *Slavery in the Ancient Near East*, pp. 99-106).

31.25-47). On the other hand, Ezekiel expresses grave concern at the presence of foreigners in temple service (Ezek. 44.7-9).

It is possible that the references to 'Nethinim' and 'sons of Solomon's servants' in Ezra 2.55-58; Neh. 7.57-60; 11.3 are to the same group of temple servants as the Gibeonites. Thus the story of the cursing of the Gibeonites is understood as an aetiology, not simply of the enslavement of part of the population,[1] but of the presence of foreign cult personnel.[2] However, even enthusiastic proponents of this theory have to admit that there is no clear relationship between the 'Nethinim' or 'sons of Solomon's servants' and *foreign* temple slaves.

According to A.D.H. Mayes, the phenomenon and the tradition of foreigners in the temple presents a theological problem for some parties in Israelite society.[3] This would be the reason, he argues, for the insertion of 9.17-21, in which the leaders reduce the Gibeonites to hewers of wood and drawers of water for all the *congregation* and not for the temple as in 9.23. Similarly, Deut. 29.10, which is viewed as a deliberate interpretation of Joshua 9,[4] identifies the Gibeonites as גרך אשר בקרב מחניך, who are also 'hewers of wood and drawers of water'. It goes a step further and makes them an integral part of the covenant community but, at the same time, it breaks the connection with the sanctuary. According to Mayes, this serves to undermine the tradition that rejects all foreigners while simultaneously ensuring that there are no foreigners in temple service. The point well illustrated by Mayes' hypothesis is that the role of the Gibeonites in the temple is no less of a problem than their confession of faith.

Although the story of the enslavement of the Gibeonites in Joshua 9

1. Cf. the cursing of Canaan to a status of hewer of wood and drawer of water in Gen. 9.

2. M. Haran, 'The Gibeonites, the Nethinim and the Sons of Solomon's Servants', *VT* 11 (1961), pp. 159-69.

3. A.D.H. Mayes, 'Deuteronomy 29, Joshua 9, and the place of the Gibeonites in Israel', in N. Lohfink (ed.), *Das Deuteronomium: Entstehung, Gestalt und Botschaft* (BETL, 68; Leuven: University Press/Peeters, 1985), pp. 321-25.

4. Several earlier studies have sought to demonstrate the traditio-historical relationship between the two texts, cf. J. Blenkinsopp, 'Are there Traces of the Gibeonite Covenant in Deuteronomy?', *CBQ* 28 (1966), pp. 207-19; P.J. Kearney, 'The Role of the Gibeonites in the Deuteronomic History', *CBQ* 35 (1973), pp. 1-19; J. Halbe, 'Gibeon und Israel. Art, Veranlassung und Ort der Deutung ihres Verhältnisses in Jos IX', *VT* 25 (1975), pp. 613-41.

is far more graphic than the terse formulas of the notes, it is also a record of the failure to conquer. In ch. 9, the Gibeonites are humble beggars who are reduced to slavery, but in the next chapter they have no insignificant status.

e. *Valuable Covenant Partners*
Usually, the kings of the nations are afraid because they hear about the awesome activity of the Lord and his people. In 10.1-2, an additional reason is forthcoming. They fear because of the covenant between Israel and the Gibeonites, reported as, 'they made peace (השלימו) with Israel' (10.1, 4),[1] and parallel to this ויהיו בקרבם, 'they were in the midst of Israel'. In this context בקרב also functions to make explicit the connection with the previous chapter. While בקרב is a technical term used in relation to the doomed occupants in the land in ch. 9, here it is used of the special status the Gibeonites enjoy in their relationship to Israel.

No longer portrayed as humble beggars, the king of Jerusalem fears greatly because 'Gibeon was a great city, like one of the royal cities,[2] and because it was greater than Ai, and all its men were mighty.' So fearsome are they that he calls on all the kings of the hill country to help him smite Gibeon.

This includes the covenant with the Gibeonites in the series of mighty acts performed by YHWH. The comparison with Ai is not incidental because Ai is the previous battle which is recalled in 10.1, and further serves to emphasize the great significance of the covenant. In other words, Gibeon is an even bigger coup than Ai!

Joshua and the Israelites respond with alacrity. A journey which takes three days in 9.17 is now achieved in a night's march. Now, for the first time in the story, Joshua and Israel take the initiative. The reader has been lead to expect a steady repetition of Israel attacking

---

1.　D.J. Wiseman, 'Is it Peace?—Covenant and Diplomacy', *VT* 32 (1982), pp. 311-26, cautions against the conclusion that שלם automatically signals a covenant. Nevertheless, chs. 9 and 10 make it abundantly clear that covenant is intended. Were it not so, the Gibeonites' appeal for help would not be understandable. Furthermore, in their appeal they describe themselves as Israel's servants (10.6). The parallel between שלום and ברית puts the question beyond doubt in 9.15.

2.　ערי הממלכה can mean a city in which a king lives (1 Sam. 27.5; cf. Deut. 3.10), and serves primarily as an expression of the kingly attributes of authority, dignity and power.

and destroying in obedience to the Lord. Here the attack is initiated by
the enemy and Israel enters the fray not so much as an act of conquest
but in response to the appeal of a covenant partner. It becomes a clash
between two coalitions. The story serves primarily as an illustration
of Israel's covenant loyalty.[1]

The noble image of the Gibeonites in ch. 10 is certainly in marked
contrast to the way they are presented in ch. 9. The difference could
be explained in terms of a variety in the source material. However, in
keeping with what is evidently a story-telling device in the Gibeonite
story is the recognition that this is another example of the use of
contrast and ambiguity.

A closer look at the structure of 10.1 reveals two statements introduced by כי:

כי־לכד . . .ויחרימה

וכי השלימו . . .ויהיו בקרבם

In a careful study which draws attention to the composition of ch. 10,
E. Noort describes the two statements as 'die (Schein-) Wahl zwischen
Leben und Tod', and notes how this formulation is part of the
structure of 'hearing' introduced by ויהי כשמע.[2] Indeed, hearing has
served earlier as a means of contrasting the reaction of the Gibeonites
to that of the nations. In 9.1-2, when all the kings of the nations hear
of the mighty acts of YHWH, they gather together to fight. In 9.3, the
Gibeonites, for their part, hear and respond with cunning. The
contrast between life and death appears again in the conclusion to the
campaign in the north.

f. A City That Makes Peace (11.19)

The next reference to the Gibeonites is also in connection with their
covenant relationship to Israel. While all the other nations have their
hearts hardened so that they attack Israel and are destroyed, and not a
single city makes peace with Israel, the Gibeonites are the only exceptions. Although שלם, which describes the Gibeonites' relationship to
Israel (9.15; 10.1, 4; 11.19), can be understood as a covenant term,

---

1. Gibeon's role in the story would be particularly remarkable if the present
account is based on an earlier tradition about a Gibeonite attack on the Israelites (cf.
Weimar, 'Die Jahwekriegerzählungen', pp. 51-62).

2. Noort, *Mythos und Rationalität*, pp. 149-61.

there is another dimension to it. In 11.19-20, as in 10.1, חרם and שלם are polar opposites.

The text appears to offer two options to the inhabitants of the land: שלם or שמד/חרם. The situation is clearly another 'Schein-Wahl'. It is noted that YHWH has already hardened their hearts making it impossible for the nations to escape their fate. Inexplicably, the Gibeonites are an exception: they make peace, and are placed on the fortunate side of the cleft between life and death.

At first glance, the situation is reminiscent of the account of the conquest of Sihon's kingdom. Hostilities commence with דברי שלום in Deut. 2.26, even though the Lord hardens their heart (2.30). It has been decided that Israel will take the land, and no serious allowance is made for the occupants of the land making peace.

The reason for the exception of the Gibeonites remains a mystery. Whenever they are mentioned it is in connection with their enigmatic survival. Their lives are spared; nevertheless, it is evident that they are one of the 'nations'.

g. *Hivites*

The ethnic identity of the Gibeonites has been the subject of some debate. The reference in 9.7 associates them with Hivites in MT and Horites in the LXX. E.A. Speiser says that the MT reading is the result of a confusion between ר and ו, as in Gen. 36.2. He identifies the Horites with the Hurrians who are known from extra-Biblical sources.[1] The problem with this is that Horites are said to have lived in regions where no evidence suggests that Hurrians have lived.[2] O. Margalith suggests that the original Hebrew name was 'Ahivi'. Because it always appears with the definite article the initial *A* is assimilated. This opens the way for an identification with the *Ahhijawa* of Hittite texts, the *Akaiwasha* of the Egyptian, and the Αχαιοι of the Greek.[3] Intriguing as this discussion may be, it should be appreciated that the association between the Gibeonites and the 'Hivites' is much more than an incidental item of historical or ethnological information.

The Hivites appear in 19 of the lists of pre-Israelite nations, which identifies them with the distant past. The Gibeonites are also called

1. E.A. Speiser, 'Hurrians', *IDB* II, pp. 664-66.
2. De Vaux, 'Les Hurrites', pp. 481-503.
3. Margalith, 'The Hivites', pp. 60-70.

Amorites (10.5; 2 Sam. 21.2), a further identification with the doomed early inhabitants. Therefore, their ethnic designation serves as an ideological statement which, in turn, compounds the paradox of their survival.[1]

The story concerning the Hivites in Genesis 34 is a particularly interesting cross-reference. It raises the problem of the paradoxical relationship between Israel and the nations by including an account of the circumcision of the menfolk, a mark of incorporation into the covenant community, prior to their slaughter.[2] The identification of the Gibeonites as Hivites in Josh. 9.7 and 11.19 focuses their unusual status in Israel as those who are set apart for extinction yet who survive.

The Rahab and Gibeonite stories are not the only ones to 'contradict' their contexts.[3] The same is true of the remaining notes about the nations which remain in the land. These are positioned strategically in the settlement narrative.

4. *The Geshurites and Maacathites (13.13)*

a. *The Relationship of 13.13 to the Territorial Descriptions of Chapter 13*
The conquest of Transjordan and Cisjordan is accomplished in ch. 12. Therefore, the detailed account of the unconquered land in 13.2-6 comes as a complete surprise. However, 13.2-6 does not contradict the earlier narrative as much as supplement it, and the territory is described as being in Philistia and Phonecia. In other words, an expanded territorial vision is presented.[4] The failure to conquer is reinforced by means of the contrast to the successful conquest of Transjordan (13.8-12). This contrast is given additional thrust by the fact that included amongst the vanquished in Transjordan are the Geshurites and Maacathites. Directly after this description comes the note about Israel's failure to conquer these very people in Cisjordan who continue to live in their midst (13.13; cf. 13.2). The position of

1. North, 'The Hivites', pp. 43-62.
2. Cf. Rose, *Deuteronomist und Jahwist*, pp. 171-213.
3. 'Contradiction' describes the relationship between two opposing pieces of information which deal with the same issue. This does not imply that one is true and the other false.
4. Cf. Noort, *Studies in the History and Archaeology of Jordan III*, p.125.

13.13 in a context of success heightens the sense of failure. The 'Geshurites and Maacathites' play a key role in the contrast, first as a sign of success, and then as a sign of failure.

It is interesting to observe the manner in which this nation pair is utilized in ch. 13. They are listed amongst the conquered in Transjordan (13.11), which is unusual because elsewhere the 'Geshurites and Maacathites' are mentioned with regard to the fact that the conquered territory in Transjordan extends to their borders (Deut. 3.14; Josh. 12.5).[1] Then, on this one occasion, the same nations are placed within the expanded territorial description of Cisjordan so as to serve as the focal point in the contrast with Transjordan. Therefore, there can be little doubt that they serve an ideological function in ch. 13.

b. The Identity of the Geshurites and Maacathites

The Geshurites and Maacathites are usually listed together. They are situated on the borders of Transjordan (Deut. 3.14; Josh. 12.5), as the nations conquered in Transjordan (Josh. 13.11), and as those who remain unconquered in the land (Josh. 13.3). Geshurites are mentioned on their own in the description of the unconquered land (Josh. 13.2).

Later in the DtrH, Geshurites are, along with the Girzites and Amalekites, described as 'the inhabitants of the land from of old' (1 Sam. 27.8). Geshur comes into prominence through association with Absalom (2 Sam. 3.3; 13.37, 38; 14.23, 32; 15.8), and is located in Syria (2 Sam. 15.8). The link with Israel's archaic enemies heightens the sense of an ideological conflict between David and Absalom.

The subsequent information about the Maacathites is limited to individuals described as בן־המעכתי (2 Sam. 23.34; 2 Kgs 25.23; cf.

---

1. In Deut. 3.14 and Josh. 12.5 the construction is עד־גבול, and in 13.11 it is simply וגבול, which is part of a sentence beginning, 'And Gilead and the territory of the Geshurites and the Maacathites'. The distinction between עד־גבול, 'to the border of . . . ', and גבול, 'the territory of. . . ' is established in the contexts discussed here. Therefore, in 12.4-5, it is possible to describe the גבול עג which extends עד־גבול הגשורי והמעכתי. The distinction is even more noticeable in ch. 13. Here, עד גבול is employed in describing the borders of the unconquered territory (13.3, 4, 10), while גבול is applied to the territory itself. The formulation ויהי גבול introduces the territories of the Transjordanian tribes (13.16, 23, 25, 30).

Jer. 40.8).[1] The king of Maacah is part of the confederacy ranged against King David (2 Sam. 10.6; cf. 1 Chron. 19.7).

Attempts at writing a history of the Geshurites and Maacathites by employing these scattered biblical references and general archaeological information, remain unconvincing.[2] The ideological use of these names in the DtrH to portray the enemies of Israel is detected more easily.

While Josh. 13.13 makes the whole of Israel responsible for the failure to conquer, the remainder of the notes blame individual tribes.

5. The Jebusites (15.63)

a. *The Relationship of 15.63 to Judah's Territorial Description in 15.1-62*

Elsewhere in Joshua, Jerusalem is part of the inheritance of Benjamin (18.16, 28; cf. 15.8),[3] and its king is conquered (10.23 and 12.10). The variety of source material and redactional interest provides a ready explanation for the manner in which this material is contradicted by 15.63. However, the way in which 15.63 purposefully contradicts its immediate context requires further explanation.

The territory of Judah is outlined at great length in 15.1-62. Then, in 15.63, there is a brief note about a significant failure on the part of the people of Judah, namely that Jebusites dwell with the people of Judah in Jerusalem! Such a contradiction to an otherwise glowing account of Judahite settlement can hardly remain unnoticed.

b. *The Identity of the Jebusites*

The Jebusites are identified with the pre-Israelite occupants of the land by being included in 22 of the 28 lists, and are positioned at the end in most of the lists. Their association with the future capital accentuates their prominence (cf. 2 Sam. 5.6-7; 1 Chron. 11.4-6). Therefore,

---

1. In Gen. 22.20-24 Maacah is one of the sons of Nahor's concubine Reumah.

2. For example, B. Mazar, 'Geshur and Maacah', *JBL* 80 (1961), pp. 16-28, who identifies the Geshurites as the *Garu*' of the Amarna letters. Cf. M. Kochavi, 'The Land of Geshur Project', *IEJ* 39 (1989), pp. 1-17.

3. In Judg. 1.8, the conquest of Jerusalem is ascribed to Judah, but in Judg. 1.21, Benjamin is blamed for the failure to conquer. The issue of the conquest of Jerusalem or lack of it is clearly a controversial one in Israelite tradition.

there is no sense in which they are a neutral ethnological designation. A similar ideological function is also evident in the title, 'the Canaanites of Gezer'.

6. *The Canaanites of Gezer (16.10)*

a. *The Relationship of 16.10 to Ephraim's Territorial Description in 16.5-9*
The king of Gezer is destroyed (10.33; 12.12), and the city is allocated to the Levites (21.21). Although 16.10 is in tension with these statements, the reader's attention is not drawn to this fact. However, the note in 16.10 is in direct contradiction to its immediate context. The demarcation of Ephraim's territory (16.5-9) concludes with a note about the failure to possess Gezer (16.10).

b. *The Identity of the Canaanites of Gezer*
After the note about their continuing occupation of Gezer in Josh. 16.10 (and Judg. 1.29), the 'Canaanites of Gezer' are referred to again in 1 Kgs 9.16. This portrays Gezer as Canaanite until the Egyptian invasion during the period of Solomon. There is probably some irony in the fact that the Egyptians defeat these people and present them as a gift to Solomon. This reference occurs shortly before the note about the enslavement of the pre-Israelite nations in 1 Kgs 9.20, which settles the matter of the unconquered nations. The identification of the occupants of Gezer as Canaanites, and their carefully calculated appearance in the DtrH, suggests that they perform an ideological function. The same may be said of the Canaanites occupying cities in Manasseh's territory.

7. *The Canaanites of Bethshean, Ibleam, Dor, Endor, Taanach, Megiddo and All Their Villages (17.12-13)*

a. *The Relationship of 17.12-13 to Manasseh's Territorial Description in 17.1-11*
The territorial description of the tribe of Manasseh in 17.1-11 is concluded in an unexpected way by the list of cities in 17.11,

Bethshean, Ibleam, Dor, Endor, Taanach and Megiddo.[1] For a moment there is some doubt as to which tribe these cities belong. This is created by the remark in 17.10 concerning the land of Ephraim in the north and Asher in the south. In the first part of 17.11, these tribes are mentioned again. However, this text insists that the cities are part of Manasseh.[2] These cities are listed as part of a structure, 'the occupants of. . . ', יושבי.[3] The shift in interest from the geographical to the human prepares the way for 17.11-12 which focuses on these people.

The wording of 17.12-13 is typical of the notes which begin by recording a failure to conquer: ולא יכלו בני מנשה להוריש את־הערים האלה. The connection with the city list in the previous verse is established by הערים האלה.[4] The occupants of these cities are then identified as Canaanites in a parallel statement. Therefore, it seems that the text labours the point that these cities are part of Manasseh's territory and yet, at the same time, demonstrates Manasseh's failure to conquer them, with the consequence of continued occupation by the Canaanites. The paradox is made more apparent by the fact that the note is

---

1. The list appears to be a set formulation for Manasseh's cities and is paralleled elsewhere:

Josh. 17.11	Judg. 1.27	1 Chron. 7.29
Bethshean	Bethshean	Bethshean
Ibleam	Taanach	Taanach
Dor	Dor	Megiddo
Endor	Ibleam	Dor
Taanach	Megiddo	
Megiddo		

The city names are coupled with ובנתיה, 'and their villages'. This is evidence that the lists are stereotyped. The conclusion to the list in Joshua is a puzzling construction which is possibly another city name, שלשת הנפת. *BHS* suggests reading דאר; cf. דאר נפת 11.2; 12.23; 1 Kgs 4.11.

2. It has been suggested that the somewhat confusing account is the result of an attempt to harmonize lists of boundary points with town and district lists (Soggin, *Joshua*, p. 182).

3. Bethshean and Ibleam are exceptions as they appear simply as city names. The parallel city list in Judg. 1.27 also has the cities as part of the structure, but this time the exceptions are Bethshean and Taanach. It is the first two cities in both lists that are the exceptions.

4. The parallel text in Judg. 1.27 includes the city list in the failure to conquer formula. By prefacing each city with the sign of the definite object, את, it is established that they are in the predicate.

preceded by the detailed territorial description of Manasseh in 17.1-11.[1] In other words, the territory of Manasseh is outlined in 17.1-11, and a specific list of towns is included (17.11); the passage then concludes with a note about their failure to conquer the Canaanite occupants of these very same cities (17.12-13)!

The note about the failure to conquer is strengthened by an account of the difficulties the tribe of Joseph has in routing the Canaanites from the valley (17.14-18).[2] The Canaanites have 'chariots of iron' (17.16, 18) and great numbers. These Canaanites are 'those who dwell in Bethshean and its villages and those in the towns of the Valley of Jezreel'. The reference to Bethshean and its villages, as well as to towns in the Valley of Jezreel, establishes a link to the list in 17.12-13.[3] The account concludes with an exhortation that repeats the reason for the failure to conquer, 'you shall destroy (תוריש) the Canaanites, though they have chariots of iron, and though they are strong'.

b. The Identity of the Canaanites of 'These Cities'

The long list of cities and their villages offers more than geographical information. They are identified as Canaanite cities. Their large numbers, and their chariots of iron, further establish their ominous character. Their association with the archaic occupants of the land is supported by the parallel in 17.15. Here, the unconquered land is 'the land of the Perizzites and the Rephaim'.

The presence of the note in 17.12-13 is particularly striking when considered in relation to the dominant themes of chs. 13–21.

1.   Elsewhere in Joshua the kings of Dor, Taanach and Megiddo are said to have been destroyed (12.21-23), and in 21.25 Taanach is allocated to the Levites. However, it is the immediate context of the note that is most severely contradicted by 17.12-13.

2.   This text appears to consist of two parallel narratives, 17.14-15 and 17.16-18 (Soggin, *Joshua*, pp. 182-83).

3.   Bethshean heads the list in 17.11, as well as in Judg. 1.27 and 1 Chron. 7.29. The use of בנותיה) to designate dependent villages is uncommon. It appears almost exclusively in accounts of conquest and settlement where the concern is to magnify the importance of the activity by the employment of high numbers (Num. 21.25, 32; 32.42; Josh. 15.45, 47; 17.11, 16; Judg. 1.27; 11.26; Neh. 11.25, 27, 28, 30, 31; 1 Chron. 2.23; 7.28, 29; 8.12; 18.1; 2 Chron. 13.19; 28.18).

8. *The Notes in Relation to the Settlement Narrative*

The territorial description of the three tribes, Judah, Ephraim and Manasseh, is followed by a stinging rebuke to the remaining tribes for failing to occupy their allotted territory (18.1-3). Nevertheless, the settlement of the three tribes is itself disrupted by the notes at the conclusion to each of the three territorial descriptions.

The notes in both Joshua and Judges serve as contradictions. However, in Joshua they stand in a particularly contradictory relationship to their immediate contexts. The ideological connotations associated with the names of the remaining nations emphasizes the disharmony. Therefore, the effect of the notes is to introduce an uncertainty, or perhaps ambiguity into the narrative by undermining its prevailing themes.

The notes are an expression of the polarity between the notion of the land as *tabula rasa*, and the continuing presence of the nations. The formula לא הוריש explains why they still occupy the land, and thus expresses a relationship of polarity between ישב בקרב and הוריש. A similar polarity occurs in ch. 23 between 'the remnant of these nations' and the *promise* of הוריש.

9. *The Remnant of These Nations (23.1-16)*

The demonstrative pronoun האלה features in the formula הנשארים האלה (23.4, 7, 12), as well as in the parallel formulas for the remnant of the nations, יתר הגוים האלה (23.12) and הגוים האלה (23.13). This places the remnant in the same class as the doomed nations.[1] The relationship of this remnant to Israel is said to be אתכם (23.7, 12).[2]

The notion of a remnant usually implies a severe military defeat or natural catastrophe. It provides a fitting sequel to the conquest account in the first twelve chapters. Nevertheless, reference to 'the remnant of these nations' contradicts the claim that the nations have been completely destroyed. In the context of ch. 23, the problem is partially solved by the statement that YHWH *will* conquer them (23.5, 13). Although the idea of a remnant of the nations 'living with' Israel

1.   כל־הגוים האלה is a technical term for the pre-Israelite occupants of the land. Cf. above under Chapter 6.

2.   Cf. 15.63 and Judg. 1.21.

is not technically contradictory to הוריש understood as a future possibility, the two do represent polarities.

In the battle reports in chs. 6–12, the complete destruction of the enemy is strengthened by including the destruction of the remnant.[1] However, the language of remnant can be associated with the pre-Israelite nations which survive in a specific sense.[2] Apart from the nations that remain in ch. 23, there is the idea of the remnant of the land, הארץ) ה(נשארה, in 13.1, 2. YHWH says, אנכי אורישם מפני בני ישראל of the occupants of this territory in 13.6. Therefore it appears that the two expressions 'remnant of the land' and 'remnant of the nations' belong to the same set of ideas, and both stand in a polar relationship to הוריש.

In the DtrH, the Gibeonites are 'the remnant of the Amorites' (2 Sam. 21.2), and Solomon enslaves 'the remnant of the Amorites, the Hittites, the Perizzites...' (1 Kgs 9.20-21). In these texts the formula is made explicit by adding that they are 'not of the people of Israel'. In 1 Kgs 9.20-21, the existence of a remnant is due to a failure to carry out the חרם. In 2 Samuel 21, the issue concerns the life or death of the Gibeonites. It is thus possible to conclude that not only does 'remnant' serve as a reminder of a failure to wipe out the occupants of the land, but the concept functions as a paradigm of life and death.

The attitude to these survivors is not always negative. In the post-exilic literature the idea of remnant comes to have a profound meaning of hope for a shattered Israel.[3] There emerges a relatively positive attitude to the survival of non-Israelites, as is the case with the Philistines in Zech. 9.7.[4] However, this is not at all obvious in Joshua 23, in which the remnant of the nations is viewed as a serious threat to Israel. This is not because of any military prowess on their part, but

1. Josh. 8.22; 10.28, 30, 33, 37, 39, 40; 11.8, 11, 14, 22.
2. Og as a remnant of the Rephaim appears in 12.4; 13.12 × 2.
3. J. Hausmann, *Israels Rest: Studien zum Selbstverständnis der nachexilischer Gemeinde* (BWANT, 124; Stuttgart: Kohlhammer, 1987), locates the theology of a remnant in the self-understanding of the post-exilic community. Earlier studies, W.E. Müller, *Die Vorstellung vom Rest im Alten Testament*, and Hasel, *The Remnant*, offer other explanations. Müller finds the origin of the idea in the accounts of total destruction in battle reports, and Hasel appeals to religious parallels in the ancient Near Eastern environment.
4. Hausmann, *Israels Rest*, esp. pp. 49-50, 203-204.

because their religion is a source of temptation.

The continued survival of a remnant of the pre-Israelite nations is viewed in a most serious light but YHWH promises to conquer them.

10. *Conclusion*

The contrast between the nations' dwelling in Israel's midst and their complete destruction is a feature of all the references to the nations which remain. This is illustrated by the simplified schematization of the following table:

6.1ff.	ותשב בקרב ישראל	and	ויחרימו את־כל־אשר בעיר
10.1	השלימו . . . ויהיו בקרבם	and	לכד . . . ויחרימה
11.19-20	השלימה	and	החרימם . . . השמידם
13.1ff.	הארץ הנשארה	and	אורישם
13.13	וישב בקרב ישראל	and	הורישו
15.63	וישב את־בני יהודה	and	להורישם
16.10	וישב בקרב אפרים	and	הוריש
17.12-13	ויואל לשבת בארץ הזאת	and	להוריש
23.1ff.	הנשארים האלה אתכם	and	והוריש

The two elements are in close proximity on most occasions, and always constitute a relationship of contrast. The juxtaposition of the two ideas is not merely an integral feature of some of the key stories (6.1ff.; 9.1ff.) and theologically reflective passages (13.1ff.; 23.1ff.), but is found in single texts where they are grammatically related (10.1; 11.19-20), and in the notes of chs. 13–19 which persistently recall the tension.

This reading of Joshua has focused on the role of the nations. In the flow of the narrative they are prominent, both in the compositional structures and in the stories themselves. The survival of some of the nations is in tension with the prevailing emphasis on their complete annihilation, and further serves to focus attention on the nations. The way in which their fate provides an object lesson for Israel, places them in the theological mainstream of the book.

1. *The Contrast between Israel and the Nations*

Two important themes in the narrative, the gift of land and the necessity for obedience, are developed in relation to each other by means of a series of contrasts between Israel and the nations:

a. Israel is given the land.
b. The nations are eradicated from the land.
c. Israel is threatened with a loss of the land.

a. *Israel is Given the Land*
Israel receives the land as a divine gift. In the course of the conquest and settlement accounts, topographical detail is prominent. The land is at issue. It is given to Israel and is designated a 'good land'. However, if Israel is to take possession of this land then the former occupants must be eradicated.

Set in the dramatic pause between promise and fulfilment, a lengthy account of the river crossing marks a transition in the story of Israel's destiny. It also serves to distinguish Israel from the nations. At the outset of the narrative, Israel is on one side of the river and the nations on the other. Even after the crossing, the sense of separation between them is retained by means of an immediate celebration of distinctively Israelite ceremonies. The walls of Jericho, which receive considerable attention in the story, separate Israel from the occupants of the city. When the walls come tumbling down the residents of the

city are obliterated. The city is not occupied by Israelites. Furthermore, throughout the campaign described in chs. 6–12, the Israelites
return to their camp after each battle. This narrative device both
distinguishes the period of conquest from the period of settlement, and
draws attention to Israel's separateness. The emphasis on spatial
distance is most prominent in the notion that all its inhabitants must be
destroyed before Israel can settle in the land.

b. *The Nations are Eradicated from the Land*

Israel is the instrument of YHWH when she conquers the land. The
nations resist but their resistance is futile because it contradicts the
divine will. They are prominent in the narrative and a distinct vocabulary is developed to describe them. They appear in lists of pre-
Israelite nations, or described as 'all the occupants of the land', 'all
these nations', 'Canaanites' and 'Amorites'. There is an interest in
representing them in comprehensive categories. This is evident in the
titles 'the occupants of the land' and 'these nations'. Although the
nations appear in other conquest narratives, only in Joshua are they
qualified by 'all'. In this manner their implacable opposition and
comprehensive destruction are effectively portrayed.

Another feature of the narrative is that the nations are incorporated
into the activity of the narrative by means of the formula 'the king(s)
of. . . ' These kings serve as part of a compositional structure in which
the nations hear, and either respond in fear or decide to resist.
Additional definition is conveyed by contrasting their response to
Israel's response. Israel sees and knows!

No matter how impressive the coalition of resisting kings may be,
their destruction follows. The major concern of the battle reports is to
record the total destruction of the nations in which the fate of the
kings is highlighted. While the destruction of nations and their kings is
a feature of the individual stories, it is also to be found in the compositional structures. An important connecting element between the
stories is the formula 'and he did to B and its king as he had done to A
and its king'. After the long list of defeated kings in ch. 12, city names
and surviving nations are listed without any reference to their kings.
This illustrates that the once menacing power of the mighty has been
shattered. It is noteworthy that the Rahab and Gibeonite stories
demonstrate that they are the only foreigners in chs. 1–12 not

represented by a king, and have this feature in common with the notes in chs. 13–19.

The main reason for mentioning the nations or their kings is to record their end. Yet they are not the only ones who can suffer this fate!

c. *Israel is Threatened with Loss of the Land*

On occasions, the contrast between Israel and the nations is inverted, and a disobedient Israel becomes the enemy of YHWH. The reversal in roles is noticeable when the two accounts of destruction are located side by side. This establishes that Israel is receiving precisely the same treatment as that given to the nations.

The story of the Israelite defeat at Ai follows the defeat and destruction of Jericho. The language of holy war is reversed: now Israel is defeated and filled with terror. The systematic and thorough destruction of Achan that ensues is reminiscent of the fate of Jericho. There is some irony in the fact that it is Rahab the Canaanite who survives and Achan the Israelite who is destroyed.

In ch. 22, the Transjordan tribes appear in a drama of apostasy. The crime of which they are accused is associated with Achan, and the threat against them is a war that will destroy their land. Even though they prove blameless, the possibility of what might have happened to them provides a salutary lesson. The threat of destruction is repeated in ch. 23. Once again, there is an association with the Achan incident. This is achieved by the covenant breaking and divine anger formulas which are reminiscent of those in ch. 7.

The vision of the land which has been emptied of foreigners and unworthy Israelites is contradicted by references to nations that remain.

2. *Nations That Remain*

The Rahab and the Gibeonites stories present a relatively positive image of foreigners. They demonstrate daring initiative, utter theologically profound confessions, and establish binding covenants with Israel. Their role is nevertheless fraught with ambiguities. Rahab is a Canaanite woman and a prostitute, and yet, rather than being a source of religious temptation, she makes a remarkable confession of faith and acts to further YHWH's plans. For their part, the Gibeonites also record a comprehensive confession of faith and, even though condemned to slavery, they serve in the temple. They too act to further YHWH's plans, emerging as valuable covenant partners.

Can this view of foreigners be reconciled with that which sees the nations as symbols of all that is to be eradicated from Israel's midst? Before attempting to answer this question, it should be observed that a key formula in the two stories just discussed, 'and they dwelt in the midst of Israel unto this day' (6.25; 9.7, 16, 22, 27; 10.1) is also a feature of the notes in 13.13; 15.63; 16.10, which describe the nations that remain. These notes are also in noticeable contradiction to their context which describes a final Israelite settlement. The easiest explanation for these contradictions is that of separate sources or redactional levels. Plausible as this might be in the case of the brief notes in chs. 13–19, the Rahab and Gibeonite stories cannot be explained in this way.

חרם is an integral element of both stories. It is Rahab who is the first to introduce the word into the narrative, and in ch. 6 each turn in the story of the destruction of Jericho is paralleled by statements about the survival of Rahab. For its part, the Gibeonite story is built on the notion that חרם is the fate of all the occupants of the land. These stories are thoroughly integrated into the wider context of conquest and settlement. Now, if this point is granted, then the status of the notes in chs. 13–19 needs to be raised again. These notes are in *no greater contradiction* to their context than the Rahab and Gibeonite stories. Furthermore, they are all linked by common formulas and share the same relation to their immediate contexts. Therefore, even though the notes contradict the prevailing themes of the narrative, they must be understood in relationship to their context.

The study of the narrative technique in Joshua shows that the juxtaposition of contrasting ideas is a feature of the compositional arrangement. Contrast and contradiction repeatedly surprise the reader when it is least expected.[1] However, what is achieved by the juxtaposition of the idea of the survival of some of the nations with that of complete destruction?

---

1. Sternberg, *The Poetics of Biblical Narrative*, p. 243, insists that the juxtaposition of opposing points of view 'pinpoints the incongruity', and their close proximity highlights 'their semantic distance'.

3. *Opposing Points of View*

The technique of juxtaposition is most evident in the issue of booty taking in chs. 6–8. Licence to take booty is preceded by the most horrific punishment for the very crime of booty taking. Here, the idea of חרם is undermined and, significantly, in its most extreme form. The destruction of the property, along with the owners, is a striking way of expressing rejection and abhorrence of them. The undermining of this by means of contradiction possibly indicates a modification to the point of view that prohibits all forms of contact with foreigners.

The problem with such a reading of the narrative is that the 'implied audience' is nowhere encouraged to understand חרם as a powerful literary device for promoting a social distance from foreigners and their religion. Nowhere is a religious threat offered as the reason for destroying the occupants of the land, and it is only in ch. 23 that they are first mentioned as a religious danger, but here Israel is exhorted to avoid them, not to kill them. There is, however, an internal structural connection between the Achan story and chs. 22–23: religious apostasy and intermarriage result in divine anger in the same way as a breach of the חרם legislation. Nevertheless, the meaning of חרם in the narrative cannot be restricted to a particular pedagogical function. The overriding concern of the narrative is to stress the need to empty the land of foreigners, not to learn how to live with them.

If חרם is a way of warning against a foreign cult, then it is possible to argue that references to nations existing after the conquest are not necessarily inconsistent. However, one still has to account for the *prominence* of the Rahab and Gibeonite stories. They are so much more than an attempt to provide the notion of חרם with a logical consistency by introducing foreigners as a real live source of temptation.

The ambiguities evident in the Rahab and Gibeonite stories become a feature of the conquest as a *whole* when the stories are considered in relation to the overall narrative. The two stories are by no means inconspicuous. Each occupies at least as much space in the narrative as any of the major battles. Furthermore, the issue is introduced unavoidably by the location of the Rahab story at the outset of the narrative. The notes in chs. 13–19 also introduce an element of ambiguity into the settlement narrative.

The notion of 'ambiguity' is sufficiently flexible to include the various ways in which opposing points of view may be held together in unresolved tension. However, it is important to recognize that the exact character of the tension differs from context to context. At one end of the spectrum, the function of the booty report in chs. 6–8 demonstrates that it is appropriate to speak of 'undermining'; and at the other end of the spectrum, 13.2-6 presents an expanded territorial vision in which 'supplementing' is the more appropriate way to describe its relationship to the context. The subtle play on expectations and their reversal in the Rahab and Gibeonite stories are fine examples of ambiguity. These two stories serve as an interpretative key in the narrative. They express with unsurpassed clarity both the command to destroy the nations, as well as the fact of their partial survival.

4. *Dream and Reality*

There is a desire for a land free of foreigners, and a vivid dream which brings death and destruction to the nations and results in the one, holy nation alone occupying the land. However, even within this world created by the narrator, there is the recognition that foreigners remain. The narrative moves to and fro between 'dream' and 'reality'. The implied author lives with this unresolved tension, while the implied audience enters the dreamworld only to find that the dawn presents the reality.

The world of post-exilic Judaism is one of disillusionment and hope. The narrative is an attempt to reconcile the challenge of living together with others in the promised land, and the hope of their effective removal. The opinion of the implied author in Joshua is that it would be best if there were no foreigners. However, there is a grudging acceptance of a certain class of foreigner which is represented by exceptional outsiders like Rahab and the Gibeonites. It is the powerful kings with whom it is impossible to live. For a people living under colonial rule, tales set in a distant age before they have been alienated from their land, and which describe the death of the kings, offer a vision of the future which makes the present bearable. A powerless people is able to find consolation.

Appendix

THE LISTS OF PRE-ISRAELITE NATIONS

In the table below the following six nations are referred to by their initials: the Canaanites, Amorites, Hittites, Perizzites, Jebusites and Girgashites, and the Hivites by the letter V.[1]

Gen.	10.15-18	Canaan, Sidon, Heth, J A G V, Arkites, Sinites, Arvadites, Zemarites, Hamathites
	13.7	C P
	15.19-21	Kenites, Kenizites, Kadmonites, H P, Rephaim, A C G J
	34.30	C P
Exod.	3.8	C H A P V J
	3.17	C H A P V J
	13.5	C H A V J
	23.23	A H P C V J
	23.28	V C H
	33.2	C A H P V J
	34.11	A C H P V J
Num.	13.29	Amalek, H J A C
Deut.	7.1	H G A C P V J
	20.17	H A C P V J
Josh.	3.10	C H V P G A J
	5.1	A C
	9.1	H A C P V J
	11.3	C A H P J V
	12.8	H A C P V J
	24.11	A P C H G V J
Judg.	1.4, 5	C P
	3.5	C H A P V J
1 Sam.	27.8	Geshurites, Girzites, Amalekites[2]

---

1. The abbreviations are the same as those in Ishida, 'The Lists of Pre-Israelite Nations', pp. 461-90.

2. This text is normally not treated in discussions of the pre-Israelite nation lists. However, the explanatory phrase, כי דנה ישבות הארץ מעולם, makes it evident that they are in the same category. Arguably, the 'Geshurites and Maacathites' (Deut. 3.14; Josh. 12.5; 13.11; 13.13) should also be

1 Kgs	9.20	A H P V J
Ezra	9.1	C H P J, Ammonites, Moabites, Egyptians, A
Neh.	9.8	C H A P J G
1 Chron.	1.13-16	Canaan, Sidon, Heth, J A G V, Arkites, Sinites, Arvadites, Zemarites, Hamathites
2 Chron.	8.7	H A P V J

considered. However, their status as pre-Israelite nations in the land is not unambiguous, cf. above, Chapter 8.

BIBLIOGRAPHY

Alfrink, B.J., *Het 'Stil Staan' van Zon en Maan in Jos. 10, 12-15* (StC, 24; Nijmegen, 1949).

—'Die Achan-Erzählung (Jos. 7)', in *Miscellanea Biblica et Orientalia. R.P. Athanasio Miller O.S.B. Completis LXX Annis Oblata* (ed. A. Metzinger; StAns; Rome, 1951), pp. 114-29.

Alt, A., 'Erwägungen über die Landnahme der Israeliten', *PJ* 35 (1939), pp. 8-63 (= A. Alt, *Kleine Schriften zur Geschichte des Volkes Israel I* [Munich: C.H. Beck, 1953], pp. 126-75).

Altmann, A. (ed.), *Biblical Motifs: Origins and Transformations* (Cambridge, MA: Harvard University Press, 1966).

Arayaprateep, K., 'A Note on *YR*', in Jos. IV 24', *VT* 22 (1972), pp. 240-42.

Astour, M.C., 'Political and Cosmic Symbolism in Genesis 14 and in its Babylonian Sources', in *Biblical Motifs: Origins and Transformations* (ed. A. Altmann; Cambridge, MA: Harvard University Press, 1966), pp. 65-112.

Auld, A.G., 'Judges I and History: A Reconsideration', *VT* 25 (1975), pp. 261-85.

—*Joshua, Moses and the Land: Tetrateuch–Pentateuch–Hexateuch in a Generation since 1938* (Edinburgh: T. & T. Clark, 1980).

Bächli, O., *Israel und die Völker: Eine Studie zum Deuteronomium* (ATANT, 41; Zürich/Stuttgart: Zwingli, 1962).

—'Zur Aufnahme von Fremden in die altisraelitische Kultgemeinde', in *Wort–Gebot– Glaube. Beitrage zur Theologie des Alten Testaments. W. Eichrodt zum 80. Geburtstag* (ed. H.J. Stoebe; Zürich: Zwingli, 1970), pp. 21-26.

—'Von der Liste zur Beschreibung. Beobachtungen und Erwägungen zu Jos. 13–19', *ZDPV* 89 (1973), pp. 1-14.

Barstad, H.M., 'The Old Testament Feminine Personal Name rāhāb. An Onomastic Note', *SEÅ* 54 (1989), pp. 43-49.

Beek, M.A., 'Josua und Retterideal', in *Near Eastern Studies in Honour of William Foxwell Albright* (ed. H. Goedicke; London: Johns Hopkins, 1971), pp. 35-42.

Begg, C.T., 'The Destruction of the Calf (Exod. 32, 20/Deut. 9, 21)', in *Das Deuteronomium: Entstehung, Gestalt und Botschaft* (ed. N. Lohfink; BETL, 68; Leuven: University Press/Peeters, 1985), pp. 208-51.

Bertholet, A., *Die Stellung der Israeliten und der Juden zu den Fremden* (Freiburg: Mohr, 1896).

Blenkinsopp, J., 'Are there Traces of the Gibeonite Covenant in Deuteronomy?', *CBQ* 28 (1966), pp. 207-19.

—*Gibeon and Israel* (Cambridge: Cambridge University Press, 1972).

—'The Structure of P', *CBQ* 38 (1976), pp. 275-92.

Blum, E., *Die Komposition der Vätergeschichte* (WMANT, 57; Neukirchen–Vluyn: Neukirchener, 1984).

—*Studien zur Komposition des Pentateuch* (dissertation, published privately, Heidelberg, 1988).

Boling, R.G., 'Some Conflate Readings in Joshua–Judges', *VT* 16 (1966), pp. 293-98.

Borger, R., *Einleitung in die Assyrischen Königsinschriften I (Das zweite Jahrtausend V.CHR.)* (HO, 1; Leiden: Brill, 1961).

Braulik, G., 'Zur deuteronomistischen Konzeption von Freiheit und Frieden', *Congress Volume Salamanca 1983* (ed. J.A. Emerton; VTS, 36; Leiden: Brill, 1985), pp. 28-39.

Brekelmans, C.H.W., *De Herem in het Oude Testament* (Nijmegen: Centrale Drukkerij NV, 1959).

Brichto, H.C., 'Taking-off of the Shoe(s) in the Bible', *Proceedings of the Fifth World Congress of Jewish Studies Vol. I* (ed. P. Peli; Jerusalem: World Union of Jewish Studies, 1969), pp. 225-26.

Bright, J., 'Joshua', *IB*, II, pp. 541-673.

Brueggemann, W., 'Kingship and Chaos (A Study in Tenth Century Theology)', *CBQ* 33 (1971), pp. 317-32.

—'Weariness, Exile and Chaos', *CBQ* 34 (1972), pp. 19-38.

—*The Land: Place as Gift, Promise, and Challenge in Biblical Faith* (Philadelphia: Fortress, 1977).

Buccellati, G., *Cities and Nations of Ancient Syria: An Essay on Political Institutions with Special Reference to the Israelite Kingdoms* (Rome: Istitutio di Studi del Vicino Oriente, 1967).

Budde, K., 'Richter und Josua', *ZAW* 7 (1887), pp. 93-166.

Butler, T.C., *Joshua* (Word Biblical Commentary, 7; Waco, TX: Word Books, 1982).

Campbell, K.M., 'Rahab's Covenant. A Short Note on Joshua ii 9-21', *VT* 22 (1972), pp. 243-44.

Childs, B.S., 'A Study of the Formula "Until This Day" ', *JBL* 82 (1963), pp. 279-92.

Coats, G.W., *Rebellion in the Wilderness: The Murmuring Motif in the Wilderness Traditions of the Old Testament* (Nashville: Abingdon, 1968).

—'An Exposition for the Conquest Theme', *CBQ* 47 (1985), pp. 47-54.

Cody, A., 'When Is the Chosen People Called a Gôy?', *VT* 14 (1964), pp. 1-6.

Cross, F.M., and G.E. Wright, 'The Divine Warrior in Israel's Early Cult', in *Biblical Motifs: Origins and Transformations* (ed. A. Altmann; Cambridge, MA: Harvard University Press, 1966), pp. 11-30.

Curtis, A.H.W., 'The "Subjugation of the Waters" Motif in the Psalms; Imagery or Polemic?', *JSS* 23 (1978), pp. 245-56.

Dekkers, A., 'Der Kriegsherem und das Naturrecht mit einem Religionswissenschaftlichen Vergleich' (unpublished dissertation, Vienna, 1964).

Deurloo, K.A., 'Om Pesach te Kunnen Vieren in het Land (Joz. 5.2-9)', in *Verkenningen in een Stroomgebied. Proeven van Oudtestamentisch Onderzoek. Ter gelegenheid van het afschied von Prof. Dr. M.A. Beek van de Universiteit van Amsterdam* (ed. M. Boertien; Amsterdam, 1974), pp. 41-50.

Diepold, P., *Israels Land* (BWANT, 95; Stuttgart: Kohlhammer, 1972).

Dion, P.-E., 'The "Fear Not" Formula and Holy War', *CBQ* 32, (1970), pp. 565-70.

Donner, H., and R. Hanhart (eds.), *Beiträge zur Alttestamentlichen Theologie: Festschrift für Walther Zimmerli* (Göttingen: Vandenhoeck & Ruprecht, 1977).

Driver, G.R., 'Affirmation by Exclamatory Negation', *Journal of the Ancient Near Eastern Society of Columbia University* 5 (1973), pp. 107-13.

Elat, M., *Economic Relations in the Lands of the Bible (c. 1000–539 BC)* (Jerusalem, 1977).

—'The Impact of Tribute and Booty on Countries and People within the Assyrian Empire', *28. Recontre Assyriologique Internationale, Wien 6–10 Juli 1981* (Horn, Austria, 1982), pp. 244-51.

Fast, T., 'Verkehrswege zwischen dem südlichen West- und Ostjordanland', *ZDPV* 72 (1956), pp. 149-51.

Fenz, A.K., *Auf Jahwehs Stimme Hören: Eine Biblische Begriffsuntersuchung* (WBTh, 6; Vienna: Herder, 1964).

Fish, T., 'War and Religion in Ancient Mesopotamia', *BJRL* 23 (1939), pp. 387-402.

Floss, J.P., *Jahwe Dienen—Göttern Dienen: Terminologische, literarische und semantische Untersuchung einer theologischen Aussage zum Gottesverhältnis im Alten Testament* (BBB, 45; Köln/Bonn: Peter Hanstein, 1975).

Fritz, V., 'Die sogenannte Liste der besiegten Könige in Josua 12', *ZDPV* 85 (1969), pp. 136-61.

—Das Ende der spätbronzezeitlichen Stadt Hazor Stratum XIII und die Biblische Überlieferung in Josua 11 und Richter 4', *UF* 5 (1973), pp. 123-39.

Gerleman, G., 'Nutzrecht und Wohnrecht. Zur Bedeutung von hzja und hljn', *ZAW* 89 (1977), pp. 21-325.

Gervitz, S., 'West-Semitic Curses and the Problem of the Origins of Hebrew Law', *VT* 11 (1961), pp. 137-58.

—'Jericho and Shechem: A Religio-Literary Aspect of City Destruction', *VT* 13 (1963), pp. 52-62.

Goetze, A., 'Warfare in Asia Minor', *Iraq* 25 (1963), pp. 124-30.

Golka, F., 'The Aetiologies in the Old Testament, Part I', *VT* 26 (1976), pp. 410-28.

—'The Aetiologies in the Old Testament, Part II', *VT* 27 (1977), pp. 36-47.

Good, R.M., 'The Just War in Ancient Israel', *JBL* 104 (1985), pp. 385-400.

Gordis, R., 'Quotations as a Literary Usage in Biblical, Rabbinic and Oriental Literature', *HUCA* 22 (1949), pp. 157-219.

Gottwald, N.K., *The Tribes of Yahweh: A Sociology of the Religion of Liberated Israel 1250–1050 BCE* (London: SCM Press, 1980).

Grayson, A.K., 'Assyria and Babylonia', *Or* 49 (1980), pp. 140-94.

Greenberg, M., 'ḤEREM', *EncJud* 8 (Jerusalem, 1971), pp. 344-50.

Grønbaek, J., 'Juda und Amalek: Überlieferungsgeschichtliche Erwägungen zu Exodus 17, 8-16', *ST* 18 (1964), pp. 26-45.

Gunn, D.M., 'Narrative Patterns and Oral Tradition in Judges and Samuel', *VT* 24 (1974), pp. 286-317.

—'The "Battle Report": Oral or Scribal Convention?', *JBL* 93 (1974), pp. 513-18.

—'On Oral Tradition: A Response to John van Seters', *Semeia* 5 (1976), pp. 155-63.

—*The Fate of King Saul: An Interpretation of a Biblical Story* (JSOTSup, 14; Sheffield: JSOT Press, 1980).

Halbe, J., *Das Privilegrecht Jahwes: Ex 34:10-26. Gestalt und Wesen, Herkunft und Wirken in vordeuteronomistischer Zeit* (FRLANT, 114; Göttingen: Vandenhoeck & Ruprecht, 1975).

—'Gibeon und Israel. Art, Veranlassung und Ort der Deutung ihres Verhältnisses in Jos IX', *VT* 25 (1975), pp. 613-41.

Haldar, A., 'Canaanites', *IDB*, I, pp. 494-98.

Halpern, B., 'The Centralization Formula in Deuteronomy', *VT* 31 (1981), pp. 20-38.

Haran, M., 'The Gibeonites, the Nethinim and the Sons of Solomon's Servants', *VT* 11 (1961), pp. 159-69.

Hasel, G.F., *The Remnant: The History and Theology of the Remnant Idea from Genesis to Isaiah* (Berrien Springs: Andrews University Press, 2nd edn, 1974).

Hausmann, J., *Israels Rest: Studien zum Selbstverständnis der nachexilischer Gemeinde* (BWANT, 124; Stuttgart: Kohlhammer, 1987).

Hermisson, H.-J., *Sprache und Ritus im Altisraelitischen Kult zur 'Spiritualisierung' der Kultbegriffe im Alten Testament* (WMANT, 19; Neukirchen–Vluyn: Neukirchener, 1965).

Hesse, F., *Das Verstockungsproblem im Alten Testament* (Berlin: Töpelmann, 1955).

Hoffmann, H.-D., *Reform und Reformen: Untersuchungen zu einem Grundthema der deuteronomistischer Geschichtsschreibung* (ATANT, 66; Zürich: Theologischer Verlag Zürich, 1980).

Hoffner, H.A., 'The Hittites and Hurrians', in *Peoples of Old Testament Times* (ed. D.J. Wiseman; Oxford: Clarendon, 1975), pp. 197-228.

Huffmon, H.B., 'The Treaty Background of Hebrew *YADA*', *BASOR* 181 (1966), pp. 31-37.

Ishida, T., 'The Structure and Historical Implications of the Lists of Pre-Israelite Nations', *Bib* 60 (1979), pp. 461-90.

Japhet, S., 'People and Land in the Restoration Period', in *Das Land Israel in biblischer Zeit* (ed. G. Strecker; Göttinger Theologische Arbeiten, 25; Göttingen: Vandenhoeck & Ruprecht, 1983), pp. 103-25.

Jobling, D., 'The Jordan a Boundary: Transjordan in Israel's Ideological Geography', in *idem* (ed.), *The Sense of Biblical Narrative: Structural Analyses in the Hebrew Bible II* (JSOTSup, 39; Sheffield: JSOT Press, 1986).

Kaiser, O., *Die Mythische Bedeutung Des Meeres in Ägypten, Ugarit und Israel* (BZAW, 78; Berlin: Töpelmann, 1959).

Kallai, Z., *Historical Geography of the Bible: The Tribal Territories of Israel* (Jerusalem: Magnes Press, 1986).

Kaufmann, Y., *The Biblical Account of the Conquest of Palestine* (Jerusalem, 1953).

Kearney, P.J., 'The Role of the Gibeonites in the Deuteronomic History', *CBQ* 35 (1973), pp. 1-19.

Kochavi, M., 'The Land of Geshur Project', *IEJ* 39 (1989), pp. 1-17.

Köppel, U., *Das deuteronomistische Geschichtswerk und seine Quellen: Die Absicht der deuteronomistischen Geschichtsdarstellung aufgrund des Vergleichs zwischen Nu 21, 21-35 und Dtn 2, 26-3, 3* (EHS.T, 122; Bern, 1970).

Kraus, H.-J., 'Vom Kampf des Glaubens', in *Beiträge zur Alttestamentlichen Theologie: Festschrift für Walther Zimmerli* (ed. H. Donner and R. Hanhart; Göttingen: Vandenhoeck & Ruprecht, 1977), pp. 239-56.

Kühnhert, G., *Das Gilgalpassah: Literarische, überlieferungsgeschtliche und geschichtliche Untersuchungen zu Josua 3–6* (Steinen–Endenburg, 1982).

Langlamet, F., *Gilgal et les récits de la traversée du Jourdain* (CRB, 11; Paris: Gabalda, 1969).

—'Josué, II, et les traditions de l'Hexateuch', *RB* 78 (1971), pp. 5-12, 161-83, 321-54.

Liverani, M., 'The Amorites', in *Peoples of Old Testament Times* (ed. D.J. Wiseman; Oxford: Clarendon, 1975), pp. 100-33.

Lohfink, N., 'Darstellungskunst und Theologie in Dtn 1.6–3.29', *Bib* 41 (1960), pp. 105-34.

—'Die deuteronomistische Darstellung des Übergangs der Führung Israels von Moses auf Josue', *Schol* 37 (1962), pp. 32-44.

—'Bilanz nach der Katastrophe. Das deuteronomistische Geschichtswerk', in *Wort und Botschaft: Eine theologische und kritische Einführung in die Probleme des Alten Testaments* (ed. J. Schreiner; Würzburg: Echter, 1967).

—*Die Landverheissung als Eid: Eine Studie zu Gn 15* (SBS, 28; Stuttgart: Verlag Katholisches Bibelwerk Stuttgart, 1967).

—'Die Bedeutungen von hebr. jrš *qal* und *hif*', *BZ NF* 27 (1983), pp. 14-33.

—'Die Schichten des Pentateuch und der Krieg', *Gewalt und Gewaltlosigkeit im Alten Testament* (Questiones disputatae, 96; Freiburg: Herder, 1983).

—ɥrh, *ThWAT*, III, pp. 191-213.

—çry, *ThWAT*, III, pp. 953-85.

—'Die *ḥuqqîm ûmišpāṭîm* im Buch Deuteronomium und ihre Neubegrenzung durch Dtn 12, 1', *Bib* 70 (1989), pp. 1-30.

Long, B.O., *The Problem of Etiological Narrative in the Old Testament* (BZAW, 108; Berlin: Töpelmann, 1968).

—'Etymological Etiology and the DT Historian', *CBQ* 31 (1969), pp. 35-41.

Luckenbill, D.D., *Ancient Records of Assyria and Babylonia* (2 vols; Chicago: University of Chicago Press, 1926–27).

McCarthy, D.J., ' "Creation" Motifs in Ancient Hebrew Poetry', *CBQ* 29 (1967), pp. 393-406

—'An Installation Genre?', *JBL* 90 (1971), pp. 31-41.

—'Some Holy War Vocabulary in Joshua 2', *CBQ* 33 (1971), pp. 228-30.

—'The Theology of Leadership in Joshua 1–9', *Bib* 52 (1971), pp. 165-75.

—'The Wrath of Yahweh and the Structural Unity of the Deuteronomistic History', in *Essays in Old Testament Ethics. J. Philip Hyatt, In Memorium* (eds. J.L. Crenshaw and J.J. Willis; New York: KTAV Publishing House, 1974), pp. 99-110.

Macholz, G.Ch., 'Gerichtsdoxologie und israelitisches Rechtsverfahren', *DBAT* 9 (1975), pp. 52-69.

Malamat, A., 'The Danite Migration and the Pan-Israelite Exodus-Conquest: A Biblical Narrative Pattern', *Bib* 51 (1970), pp. 1-16.

—'The Ban in Mari and in the Bible', *Mari and the Bible: A Collection of Studies* (Jerusalem: Hebrew University Press, 1975), pp. 52-61.

—'Israelite Conduct of War in the Conquest of Canaan According to the Biblical Tradition', in *Symposia Celebrating the Seventy-Fifth Anniversary of the Founding of the American Schools of Oriental Research (1900–1975)* (ed. F.M. Cross; Cambridge, MA: American Schools of Oriental Research, 1979), pp. 35-55.

Malina, B.J., *The Palestinian Manna Tradition: The Manna Tradition in the Palestinian Targums and its Relationship to the New Testament Writings* (AGSU, 7; Leiden: Brill, 1968).

Margalith, O., 'The Hivites', *ZAW* 100 (1988), pp. 60-70.

Martin, W.J., *Tribut und Tributleistungen bei den Assyrern* (StudOr, 8, 1; Helsinki: Finnish Literary Society, 1936).

Mayes, A.D.H., 'Deuteronomy 29, Joshua 9, and the Place of the Gibeonites in Israel', in *Das Deuteronomium: Entstehung, Gestalt und Botschaft* (ed. N. Lohfink; BETL, 68; Leuven: University Press/Peeters, 1985), pp. 321-25.

Mazar, B., 'Geshur and Maacah', *JBL* 80 (1961), pp. 16-28.

Mendelsohn, I., *Slavery in the Ancient Near East: A Comparative Study of Slavery in Babylonia, Assyria, Syria and Palestine from the Middle of the Third Millenium to the End of the First Millenium* (London: Oxford University Press, 1949).

Mendenhall, G.E., 'The "Vengeance" of Yahweh', in *idem* (ed.), *The Tenth Generation: The Origins of the Biblical Tradition* (Baltimore/London: Johns Hopkins University Press, 1973), pp. 60-95.

Millard, A.R., 'The Canaanites', in *Peoples of Old Testament Times* (ed. D.J. Wiseman; Oxford: Clarendon, 1975), pp. 29-52.

Miller, P.D., 'Fire in the Mythology of Canaan and Israel', *CBQ* 27 (1965), pp. 256-61.

—*The Divine Warrior in Early Israel* (Cambridge, MA: Harvard University Press, 1975).

Möhlenbrink, K., 'Josua im Pentateuch. Die Josuaüberlieferungen ausserhalb des Josuabuchs', *ZAW* 59 (1942–43), pp. 14-58.

Moran, W.L., 'The End of the Unholy War and the Anti-Exodus', *Bib* 44 (1963), pp. 333-42.

—'The Repose of Rahab's Israelite Guests', in *Studi sull 'Oriente e la Bibbia, offerti al P. Giovanni Rinaldi* (ed. G. Buccellati; Genoa: Editrice Studio e Vita, 1967), pp. 273-84.

Müller, H.-P., 'Die Kultische Darstellung der Theophanie', *VT* 14 (1964), pp. 183-91.

—çdq, *THAT*, II, pp. 590-610.

Müller, W.E., *Die Vorstellung vom Rest im Alten Israel* (Borsdorf–Leipzig: Wilhelm Hoppl, 1939).

Nelson, R.D., 'Josiah in the Book of Joshua', *JBL* 100 (1981), pp. 531-40.

—'The Anatomy of the Book of Kings', *JSOT* 40 (1988), pp. 39-48.

Nielson, E., *Shechem: A Traditio-Historical Investigation* (Copenhagen: Gad, 1959).

Noort, E., 'Transjordan in Joshua 13: Some Aspects', in *idem* (ed.), *Studies in the History and Archaeology of Jordan III* (Amman/London: Department of Antiquities, 1988), pp. 125-29.

—'Zwischen Mythos und Rationalität. Das Kriegshandeln Yhwhs in Josua 10, 1-11', in *Mythos und Rationalität* (ed. H.H. Schmid; Gütersloh, 1988), pp. 149-61.

North, R., 'The Hivites', *Bib* 54 (1973), pp. 43-62.

—sm, *ThWAT*, IV, pp. 1006-1009.

Noth, M., 'Bethel und Ai', *PJ* 31 (1935), pp. 7-29 (= M. Noth, *Aufsätze zur biblischen Landes- und Altertumskunde* [ed. H.W. Wolff; Neukirchen–Vluyn: Neukirchener, 1971], I, pp. 210-28).

—Studien zu den historisch-geographischen Dokumenten des Josua-Buches', *ZDPV* 58 (1935), pp. 185-255 (= M. Noth, *Aufsätze zur biblischen Landes- und Altertumskunde* [ed. H.W. Wolff; Neukirchen–Vluyn: Neukirchener, 1971], I, pp. 229-80).

—'Die fünf Könige in der Höhle von Makkeda', *PJ* 33 (1937), pp. 22-36 (= M. Noth, *Aufsätze zur biblischen Landes- und Altertumskunde* [ed. H.W. Wolff; Neukirchen–Vluyn: Neukirchener, 1971], I, pp. 281-93).

—'Nu 21 als Glied der "Hexateuch"-Erzählung', *ZAW* 58 (1940–41), pp. 161-89 (= M. Noth, *Aufsätze zur biblischen Landes- und Altertumskunde* [ed. H.W. Wolff; Neukirchen–Vluyn: Neukirchener, 1971], I, pp. 75-101).

—Review of G. von Rad, *Deuteronomium-Studien*, *ThLZ* 73 (1948), pp. 536-37.

—*Josua* (HAT, 7; Tübingen: Mohr, 2nd edn, 1953).

—'Der Jordan in der alten Geschichte Palästinas', *ZDPV* 72 (1956), pp. 123-48.
—*Überlieferungsgeschichtliche Studien* (Tübingen: Max Niemeyer Verlag, 2nd edn, 1957).
Otto, E., *Das Bundes-Mazzotfest von Gilgal: Ein Beitrag zur Kultgeschichte Israels und Überlieferungsgeschichte des Hexateuch* (dissertation, Hamburg, 1973).
Ottosson, M., 'Tradition and History, with Emphasis on the Composition of the Book of Joshua', in *The Productions of Time: Tradition History in Old Testament Scholarship* (ed. K. Jeppesen and B. Otzen; Sheffield: Almond, 1984), pp. 81-143.
—'Rahab and the Spies', in *Studies in Honor of Åke W. Sjöberg* (ed. H. Behrens; Philadelphia: University Museum, 1989), pp. 419-27.
—*Erövring och fördelning av Land: Studier i Josuaboken* (to be published).
Peckham, B., 'The Composition of Joshua 3–4', *CBQ* 46 (1984), pp. 413-31.
Perlitt, L., *Bundestheologie im Alten Testament* (WMANT, 36; Neukirchen–Vluyn: Neukirchener, 1969).
Plath, S., *Furcht Gottes: Der Begriff ary im Alten Testament* (AzTh, 2; Stuttgart: Calwer, 1963).
Plöger, J.G., *Literarkritische, formgeschichtliche und stilkritische Untersuchungen zum Deuteronomium* (BBB, 26; Bonn: Peter Hanstein, 1967).
Polzin, R., *Moses and the Deuteronomist: A Literary Study of the Deuteronomic History* (New York: Seabury, 1980).
Porter, J.R., 'The Legal Aspects of the Concept of "Corporate Personality" in the Old Testament', *VT* 15 (1965), pp. 361-80.
—'The Succession of Joshua', in *Proclamation and Presence: Old Testament Essays in Honour of Gwynne Henton Davies* (eds. J.I. Durham and J.R. Porter; London: SCM Press, 1970), pp. 102-32.
—'The Background of Joshua II–V', *SEÅ* 36 (1971), pp. 5-23.
Rad, G. von, 'Es ist noch eine Ruhe vorhanden dem Volke Gottes', *ZZ* 11 (1933), pp. 104-11 (= *Gesammelte Studien zum Alten Testament I* [TBü, 8; Munich: Kaiser, 1958], pp. 101-108).
—'Verheissenes Land und Jahwes Land im Hexateuch', *ZDPV* 66 (1943), pp. 191-204 (= *Gesammelte Studien zum Alten Testament I* [TBü, 8; Munich: Kaiser, 1958], pp. 87-100).
—'The Origin of the Concept of the Day of Yahweh', *JSS* 4 (1959), pp. 97-108.
—*Der Heilige Krieg im alten Israel* (Göttingen: Vandenhoeck & Ruprecht, 5th edn, 1969).
Radjawane, A.N., 'Das deuteronomistische Geschichtswerk', *ThR* 38 (1974), pp. 177-216.
Rendtorff, R., 'Das Land Israel im Wandel der Alttestamentlichen Geschichte', in *Jüdisches Volk—gelobtes Land: Die biblischen Landverheissung als Problem des jüdischen Selbstverständnisses und die christlichen Theologie* (eds. W.P. Eckert and N.P. Levinson; Munich: Kaiser, 1970), pp. 153-68.
—*Das überlieferungsgeschichtliche Problem des Pentateuchs* (BZAW, 147; Berlin: de Gruyter, 1977).
—*Das Alte Testament: Eine Einführung* (Neukirchen–Vluyn: Neukirchener, 1983).
Richter, W., *Traditionsgeschichtliche Untersuchungen zum Richterbuch* (BBB, 18; Bonn: Peter Hanstein, 1963).

—*Die Bearbeitungen des 'Retterbuchs' in der deuteronomischen Epoche* (BBB, 21; Bonn: Peter Hanstein, 1964).

Ringgren, H., bya, *ThWAT*, I, pp. 228-35.

—zzb, *ThWAT*, I, pp. 585-88

Robinson, B.P., 'Israel and Amalek. The Context of Exodus 17.8-16', *JSOT* 32 (1985), pp. 15-22.

Robinson, H.W., *Corporate Personality in Ancient Israel* (Edinburgh: T. & T. Clark, rev. edn, 1981).

Rose, M., *Der Ausschliesslichkeitsanspruch Jahwes* (BWANT, 196; Stuttgart: Kohlhammer, 1975).

—*Deuteronomist und Jahwist: Untersuchungen zu den Berührungspunkten beider Literaturwerke* (ATANT, 67; Zürich: Theologischer Verlag Zürich, 1981).

Rösel, H.N., 'Anmerkungen zur Erzählung vom Bundesschluss mit den Gibeoniten', *BN* 28 (1985), pp. 30-35.

—'Das "Negative Besitzverzeichnis"—Traditionsgeschichtliche und historische Überlegungen', in *'Wünschet Jerusalem Frieden': IOSOT Congress Jerusalem 1986* (ed. M. Augustin and K.-D. Schunk; Beiträge zur Erforschung des Alten Testaments und des Antiken Judentums, 13; Frankfurt: Peter Lang, 1988), pp. 121-35.

Rudolf, W., *Der 'Elohist' von Exodus bis Josua* (BZAW, 68; Berlin: Töpelmann, 1938).

Saggs, H.W.F., 'Assyrian Warfare in the Sargonid Period', *Iraq* 25 (1963), pp. 145-54.

—'Assyrian Prisoners of War and the Right to Live', *28. Recontre Assyriologique Internationale, Wien 6–10 Juli 1981* (Horn, Austria, 1982), pp. 85-93.

Sawyer, J.F.A., 'The Meaning of *barzel* in the Biblical Expressions "chariots of iron", "yoke of iron", etc.', in *The History and Archaeology of Late Bronze and Iron Age Jordan and North-West Arabia* (ed. J.F.A. Sawyer and D.J.A. Clines; JSOTSup, 24; Sheffield: JSOT Press, 1983), pp. 129-34.

Schäfer-Lichtenberger, C., *Stadt und Eidgenossenschaft im Alten Testament: Eine Auseinandersetzung mit Max Webers Studie 'Das antike Judentum'* (BZAW, 156; Berlin: de Gruyter, 1983).

—'Das gibeonitische Bündnis im Lichte deuteronomischer Kriegsgebote. Zum Verhältnis von Tradition und Interpretation in Jos. 9', *BN* 34 (1986), pp. 58-81.

Scharbert, J., *Solidarität in Segen und Fluch im Alten Testament und in seiner Umwelt.* I. *Väterfluch und Vätersegen* (BBB, 14; Bonn: Peter Hanstein, 1958).

Schmitt, G., *Du sollst keinen Frieden schliessen mit den Bewohnern des Landes: Die Weisungen gegen die Kanaanäer in Israels Geschichte und Geschichtsschreibung* (BWANT, 91; Stuttgart: Kohlhammer, 1970).

Schmuttermayr, G., 'Psalm 18 und 2 Samuel 22: Studien zu einem Doppeltext' (StANT, 25; Munich: Kösel, 1971).

Schottroff, W., *Der altisraelitische Fluchspruch* (WMANT, 30; Neukirchen–Vluyn: Neukirchener, 1969).

Schramm, W., *Einleitung in die Assyrischen Königsinschriften II (934–722 V. Chr)* (HO, 1; Leiden: Brill, 1973).

Schult, H., 'Naemans Übertritt zum Yahwismus (2 Könige 5,1-19a) und die biblischen Bekehrungsgeschichten', *DBAT* 9 (1975), pp. 2-20.

Schwally, F., *Semitische Kriegsaltertümer* I. *Der heilige Krieg im alten Israel* (Leipzig: Dieterich'sche Verlagsbuch handlung, 1901).

Seebass, H., 'Gerizim und Ebal als Symbole von Segen und Fluch', *Bib* 63 (1982), pp. 22-31.

Seeligmann, I.L., 'Erkenntnis Gottes und historisches Bewusstsein im alten Israel', in *Beiträge zur Alttestamentlichen Theologie: Festschrift für Walther Zimmerli* (ed. H. Donner and R. Hanhart; Göttingen: Vandenhoeck & Ruprecht, 1977), pp. 414-45.

Seitz, G., *Redaktionsgeschichtliche Studien zum Deuteronomium* (BWANT, 93; Stuttgart: Kohlhammer, 1971).

Sheriffs, D.C.T., 'Empire and the Gods: Mesopotamian Treaty Theology and the Sword in the First Millenium BC' (dissertation, Stellenbosch, 1976).

Smend, R., 'Das Gesetz und die Völker. Ein Beitrag zur deuteronomistischen Redaktionsgeschichte', in *Probleme biblischer Theologie: G. von Rad zum 70. Geburtstag* (ed. H.W. Wolff; Munich: Kaiser, 1971), pp. 494-509.

—'Das uneroberte Land', in *Das Land Israel in biblischer Zeit* (ed. G. Strecker; Göttinger Theologische Arbeiten, 25; Göttingen: Vandenhoeck & Ruprecht, 1983), pp. 91-102.

Snaith, N.H., *Distinctive Ideas of the Old Testament* (London: Epworth, 1945).

—'The Altar at Gilgal: Joshua XXII 23-29', *VT* 28 (1978), pp. 330-35.

Soggin, J.A., *Joshua* (OTL; London: SCM Press, 1972).

—'The Negation in Joshua 5.14 (Emphatic *Lamed*)', in *idem* (ed.), in *Old Testament and Oriental Studies* (BibOr, 29; Rome: Biblical Institute Press, 1975), pp. 219-20.

—'The Prophets on Holy War as Judgment against Israel', in *Old Testament and Oriental Studies* (BibOr, 29; Rome: Biblical Institute Press, 1975), pp. 67-71.

—'Compulsory Labor under David and Solomon', in *Studies in the Period of David and Solomon and Other Essays* (ed. T. Ishida; Winona Lake, IN: Eisenbrauns, 1982), pp. 259-67.

Speiser, E.A., 'Hurrians', *IDB*, II, pp. 664-66.

Steinberg, N., 'Israelite Tricksters, Their Analogues and Cross-Cultural Study', *Semeia* 42 (1988), pp. 1-13.

Sternberg, M., *The Poetics of Biblical Narrative: Ideological Literature and the Drama of Reading* (Indiana Literary Biblical Series; Bloomington: Indiana University Press, 1985).

Stoebe, H.J., 'Raub und Beute', in *idem* (ed.), *Hebräische Wortforschung: Festschrift für Walter Baumgartner* (VTS, 16; Leiden: Brill, 1967), pp. 340-54.

Stolz, F., *Jahwes und Israels Kriege: Kriegstheorien und Kriegserfahrungen im Glauben des alten Israel* (ATANT, 60; Zürich: Theologischer Verlag Zürich, 1972).

Sumner, W.A., 'Israels' Encounters with Edom, Moab, Ammon, Sihon, and Og According to the Deuteronomist', *VT* 18 (1968), pp. 216-28.

Thompson, L.L., 'The Jordan Crossing: *SIDQOT YAHWEH* and World Building', *JBL* 100 (1981), pp. 343-58.

Tov, E., 'Midrash-Type Exegesis in the LXX of Joshua', *RB* 85 (1978), pp. 50-61.

Tucker, G.M., 'The Rahab Saga (Joshua 2): Some Form-Critical and Traditio-Critical Observations', in *The Use of the Old Testament in the New and Other Essays: Studies in Honour of William Franklin Stinespring* (ed. J.M. Efird; Durham: Duke University Press, 1972), pp. 66-86.

Tunyogi, A.C., 'The Book of the Conquest', *JBL* 84 (1965), pp. 374-80.

Van Seters, J., 'The Conquest of Sihon's Kingdom: A Literary Examination', *JBL* 91 (1972), pp. 182-97.

—'The Terms "Amorite" and "Hittite" in the Old Testament', *VT* 22 (1972), pp. 64-81.

—'Oral Patterns or Literary Conventions in Biblical Narrative?', *Semeia* 5 (1976), pp. 139-54.

—*In Search of History: Historiography in the Ancient World and the Origins of Biblical History* (New Haven: Yale University Press, 1983).

—'Joshua 24 and the Problem of Tradition in the Old Testament', in *In the Shelter of Elyon: Essays on Ancient Palestinian Life and Literature in Honor of G.W. Ahlström* (ed. W.B. Barrick and J.R. Spencer; JSOTSup, 31; Sheffield: JSOT Press, 1984), pp. 139-58.

—'Joshua's Campaign of Canaan and Near Eastern Historiography', *SJOT* 4 (1990), pp. 1-12.

Vaux, R. de, 'Les Hurrites de l'Historie et les Horites de la Bible', *RB* 74 (1967), pp. 481-503.

—*The Early History of Israel* (Philadelphia: Westminster, 1978).

Veijola, T., 'Das Klagegebet in Literatur und Leben der Exilsgeneration am Beispiel einiger Prosatexte', in *Congress Volume Salamanca 1983* (ed. J.A. Emerton; VTSup, 36; Leiden: Brill, 1985), pp. 286-307.

Vogt, E., 'Die Erzählung vom Jordanübergang. Josua 3–4', *Bib* 46 (1965), pp. 125-48.

—'Einige hebräische Wortbedeutungen', *Bib* 48 (1967), pp. 57-74.

Wagner, S., 'Die Kundschaftergeschichten im Alten Testament', *ZAW* 76 (1964), pp. 255-69.

Weimar, P., 'Die Jahwekriegerzählungen in Exodus 14, Josua 10, Richter 4 und 1 Samuel 7', *Bib* 57 (1976), pp. 38-73.

Weinfeld, M., 'The Period of the Conquest and of the Judges as Seen by the Earlier and the Later Sources', *VT* 17 (1967), pp. 93-113.

—*Deuteronomy and the Deuteronomic School* (Oxford: Clarendon Press, 1972).

—' "They fought from Heaven"—Divine Intervention in War in Ancient Israel and in the Ancient Near East', *ErIs* 47 (1978), pp. 23-30.

—'The Extent of the Promised Land—the Status of Transjordan', in *Das Land Israel in biblischer Zeit* (ed. G. Strecker; Göttinger Theologische Arbeiten, 25; Göttingen: Vandenhoeck & Ruprecht, 1983), pp. 59-75.

Weippert, H., 'Das deuteronomistische Geschichtswerk. Sein Ziel und Ende in der neueren Forschung', *ThR* 50 (1985), pp. 213-49.

Weippert, M., ' "Heiliger Krieg" in Israel und Assyrien. Kritische Anmerkungen zu Gerhard von Rads Konzept des "Heiligen Krieges im alten Israel" ', *ZAW* 84 (1972), pp. 460-93.

Weiss, M., *The Bible from Within* (Jerusalem: Magnes Press, 1984).

Welch, A.C., *The Code of Deuteronomy: A New Theory of Its Origin* (London: James Clark, 1924).

—*Deuteronomy: The Framework of the Code* (London: James Clark, 1932).

Wijngaards, J.N.M., *The Formulas of the Deuteronomic Creed* (Tilburg: Reijnen, 1963).

—*The Dramatization of Salvific History in the Deuteronomic Schools* (*OTS*, 16; Leiden: Brill, 1969).

Wilcoxen, J.A., 'Narrative Structure and Cult Legend: A Study of Joshua 1–6', in *Transitions in Biblical Scholarship* (ed. J.C. Rylaarsdam; Chicago/London: University of Chicago Press, 1968), pp. 43-70.

Wildberger, H., 'Israel und sein Land', *EvT* 16 (1956), pp. 404-22.

Wiseman, D.J., 'Rahab of Jericho', *TynBul* 14 (1964), pp. 8-11.

—(ed.) *Peoples of Old Testament Times* (Oxford: Clarendon Press, 1975).

—'Is it Peace?—Covenant and Diplomacy', *VT* 32 (1982), pp. 311-26.

Wolff, H.W., 'Das Kerygma des Deuteronomistischen Geschichtswerks', *ZAW* 73 (1961), pp. 171-86.

—(ed.), *Probleme biblischer Theologie: G. von Rad zum 70. Geburtstag* (Munich: Kaiser, 1971).

Wüst, M., *Untersuchungen zu den siedlungsgeographischen Texten des Alten Testaments. I. Ostjordanland* (Beihefte zum Tübinger Atlas des Vorderen Orients, 19; Wiesbaden: Reichert, 1975).

Zevit, Z., 'Archaeological and Literary Stratigraphy in Joshua 7–8', *BASOR* 251 (1983), pp. 23-35.

Zimmerli, W., *Erkenntnis Gottes nach dem Buche Ezechiel* (Zürich: Zwingli, 1954).

INDEXES

INDEX OF REFERENCES

JOURNAL FOR THE STUDY OF THE OLD TESTAMENT

Supplement Series